ResEdit™ Complete
Second Edition

ResEdit™ Complete
Second Edition

Peter Alley
Carolyn Strange

Addison-Wesley Publishing Company

Reading, Massachusetts • Menlo Park, California • New York
Don Mills, Ontario • Wokingham, England • Amsterdam
Bonn • Sydney • Singapore • Tokyo • Madrid • San Juan
Paris • Seoul • Milan • Mexico City • Taipei

Library of Congress Cataloging-in-Publication Data

Sponsoring Editor: David J. Clark
Project Editor: Joanne Clapp Fullagar
Production Coordinator: Gail McDonald Jordan
Technical Reviewer: Stephen Hart
Cover Design: Barbara T. Atkinson
Set in 11 point Palatino by S.T. Associates, Inc.

1 2 3 4 5 6 7 8 9 - MA - 9796959493
First printing, December 1993

Addison-Wesley books are available for bulk purchases by corporations, institutions, and other organizations. For more information please contact the Corporate, Government, and Special Sales Department at (617) 944-3700 x2915.

Acknowledgments

We thank the whole ResEdit team—especially Craig Carper—for their efforts on version 2.1.1. In addition, Craig and Alexander Falk made significant contributions to the first edition of this book that still influence the present edition. So, thanks again.

Stephen Hart deserves special recognition. He suggested nifty tips, provided moral support, and, most importantly, user-tested the manuscript for us. Drawing on his experience as a writer, editor and, well, somewhat of a Mac maniac, he improved the manuscript in numerous ways. Thanks for keeping us on our toes, Steve.

Last, but by no means least, we appreciate the advice and encouragement of numerous people at Addison-Wesley, especially Keith Wollman, David Clark, Joanne Clapp Fullagar, and Gail McDonald Jordan.

Contents

ResEdit Basics

Chapter 1

 Introduction

As friendly as the Mac is, and as much as you love it, there may very well be some things about it that have always bugged you. Go on, admit it. Maybe a confusing, perhaps grammatically incorrect, screen message has always set your teeth on edge. Perhaps you've always wished you had a keyboard equivalent for a certain command, or that you could change existing Command-key assignments. Why is a certain alert's default "Yes" when it should be "No"? Then there's that stupid-looking icon, and the menu that bewilders. Wouldn't it be nice if you could see more and longer file names in standard file directory dialogs? Come to think of it, sometimes you wish your mouse responded more quickly than the Control Panel's fastest setting. And aren't you tired of removing "alias" from the names of your aliases? Why can't you get rid of it once and for all?

You can.

You can change every one of these things and more. All these user interface components are stored in resources, and you can change them with ResEdit, the Resource Editor.

If you're a programmer, you're probably already familiar with ResEdit. But you might be wondering whether you're getting the most out of it as you develop the user interface for your applications. From creating and editing standard resources to designing your own templates, ResEdit is a powerful ally to help you in your work.

Introducing ResEdit 2.1.1

"What is ResEdit anyway?" some may ask. As its name implies, ResEdit is an application that allows you to create and edit resources, which are an important part of what makes the Macintosh the friendly, malleable machine it is. Just about everything you see on your screen can be (in fact *should* be) stored in resources. Figure 1-1 shows just some of the changes you can make to common graphic resources. But resources control more than just visual effects. Sounds are resources, too. By using ResEdit to change the appropriate resources, you can modify your keyboard's character layout and the default copy number and paper sizes you choose from the print dialog, just to name a few possibilities. In short, ResEdit can help you create a customized Macintosh environment that's a pleasure to work in.

Although ResEdit may once have deserved a reputation as somewhat of a doomsday program, those days are gone. Even though it has become much safer and friendlier, ResEdit remains a powerful program that you use on very valuable files—your

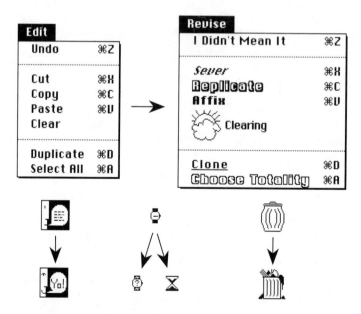

Figure 1-1. The changes you can make with ResEdit range from reasonable to radical.

applications. But there's no reason to fear ResEdit; like any powerful tool, it can be used safely and productively if treated with the proper respect.

Is This Book for You?

We've addressed this book to two general types of readers. If you're a Macintosh user who wants to customize your work environment for greater enjoyment and productivity, this book is for you. If you're a programmer interested in learning fast, efficient ways to create and edit resources for the applications you're developing, this book is for you. Of course, these audiences overlap—programmers customize their Macs for increased enjoyment and productivity, too!

The first part of the book is aimed at both audiences and focuses on editing resources for customization. We've included enough information to keep programmers interested, but not so much that everyone else drowns in technical details. The last part of the book is aimed at programmers and focuses on creating resources and programming with ResEdit.

To sum up, if you have any interest in creating or changing aspects of the Macintosh user interface, this book is for you.

System 7 Savvy Second Edition

This edition is completely revised and thoroughly System 7 savvy. We removed projects specific only to System 6 and updated the remainder for System 7. Even better, we added numerous new tips and tricks. For instance, you'll learn how to take better advantage of the Fonts Folder in System 7.1. And you'll be able to change Finder menus, which is annoyingly difficult under System 7—unless you have the ResEdit add-on we've included on the disk with this book.

How to Use This Book

This is a modular, task-oriented book and the chapters are organized functionally by grouping related resource types together. Generally, each chapter describes one or more related resource types and how they're used, explains how to edit them, and includes some projects you might want to try. We encourage you to browse and try whatever projects interest you—dip into chapters as you please—but bear in mind that the chapter topics and projects gradually increase in difficulty and complexity. If you've never used ResEdit, you should probably gain a little experience nearer the beginning of the book first rather than diving right into later chapters.

The section about color resource types assumes you're familiar with corresponding black-and-white resource types. If you have a color monitor (and therefore a color Mac), you'll have to read about black-and-white resource types in order to understand the corresponding color ones. If you have a black-and-white monitor, you may need to read some parts of the color section. We'll make it clear in the places where it matters.

By The Way   When it comes to thinking about color resources and ResEdit, there's a difference between color monitors and color Macs. Color Macs have Color QuickDraw in the ROM, which requires a 68020 (or higher) processor. So, whether you see a black-and-white resource, or the black-and-white version contained within a corresponding color resource, depends on your Mac, not your monitor. ResEdit automatically figures out what to show you. We'll discuss this further when we get to the pertinent resources.

First we need to get you oriented and set some ground rules. Following our advice will not only help you get more out of this book, more out of ResEdit, and ultimately more out of your Macintosh, but it will also help prevent unfortunate mistakes with important files.

What You Need to Know

This book contains five parts. Readers interested in customizing their Macintoshes will find Parts 2 through 4 most useful. Readers interested in programming with ResEdit will find Parts 3 and 5 most useful. *No matter who you are, you should read all of Part 1, ResEdit Basics.* All of the subsequent chapters assume you've read Part 1, which covers the basic information you need to understand how to use ResEdit effectively and safely. Besides, if you skip it, you'll miss out on several helpful hints for working with ResEdit. (Appendix A lists a collection of shortcuts and hints, but it's not a substitute for reading the chapters.)

Every book is built on at least a few assumptions. To help you use this book more effectively, we've summarized our most important assumptions about you.

- You didn't get your Macintosh yesterday. You're experienced and comfortable using it. You've probably used a paint or draw program, and navigating in the Mac user interface is second nature, or very nearly so. And this probably isn't the only Macintosh book on your bookshelf. Therefore, we won't waste your time rehashing basics described elsewhere.
- The section directed at programmers, Part 5, assumes you're already familiar with programming the Macintosh.
- Our discussions and examples assume you're using System 7.1, which seems like a safe bet. Many projects probably work just fine with earlier Systems—including later versions of System 6—but weren't tested that way so we can't vouch for them.

Warnings

Even though we've tested the projects and examples we present, we couldn't possibly test all of them on every possible hardware configuration with every possible assortment of software. Your system may very well be unique—in fact, that's one of the joys of the Macintosh and part of the purpose of this book. It's *your* Macintosh, and you can make it work the way you want it to. You spend a lot of time setting up your machine just the way you like it, so you should protect that investment by maintaining backups of all your important files. You should have copies of all your files backed up on floppy disks, a separate hard disk, or tape. It's up to you whether you use a backup program or your own scheme. We also recommend that you always have a "rescue disk" to restart your machine if disaster strikes. In Chapter 4 we discuss rescue disks in more detail.

We assume you already follow this sage advice, but we generally suggest that before you work on a file with ResEdit you make another copy anyway—especially in the beginning. Because this book is modular, we can't assume readers will try things in any particular order, so we've sprinkled reminders and warnings throughout the

book. Our intent with warnings is not to frighten, but to remind you
that you're using a powerful tool on valuable files. In any
undertaking, mistakes are notoriously easy to make, especially for
beginners, and accidents can always strike anyone, anytime. Be sure
you read and understand the following warning because it's the only
full-length version; the rest of them are abbreviated reminders.

**Warning Changing resources can cause unpredictable and
disastrous results. Never change resources in your only
copy of a file. Always work on an expendable copy.** ResEdit is
a programmer's utility; it actually changes application programs.
Altering most resources shouldn't affect how your program works.
However, some applications may rely on complex relationships
and interactions between various software components, so the
final results of your changes may not always be entirely
predictable. Although side effects are rare, they can be serious.
That's why you should work only on an extra copy of any
application.

Making a copy is analogous to using a seat belt when riding in an
automobile. It doesn't take much time or effort, and it just might save
your file.

Make a copy first.

Hint Before you use ResEdit to open a file, use the Finder's
Duplicate command to make a copy. Keep the original version
until you're sure your changes are working correctly and you want
to keep them.

Here's another good rule to follow: Avoid changing things you
don't understand. If you feel you must change things "just to see
what happens," make sure you're prepared to deal with the
consequences. (OK, we admit that changing things just to see what
happens can be educational and fun, but since we have no idea what
you're going to change, we have to be clear that if you do this you're
on your own.) To follow up with the automobile analogy, don't go

joy-riding with ResEdit. Try to be clear about where you're going and have a plan for getting there. You want to be wide-awake and sober when you take ResEdit out for a spin.

Approaches to Working on Files

There are three possible approaches to editing files with ResEdit; we recommend only the first two.

1. Safest: You have a backup of the file, but you make another copy before you work on it with ResEdit.

    The advantage of this approach is that if you don't like your changes, restoring the original is a snap. Even if some accident befalls you, you won't have to start over from the backup. This is definitely the best approach for inexperienced ResEdit users.

2. Safe: You have a backup, so you go ahead and work on the file with ResEdit.

    If you're absolutely positive you have a recent backup, then technically, the copy you work with is an expendable copy. But if you have an accident or need to switch back to the original, you'll have to start all over from the backup, which may be a nuisance. Once you become familiar with ResEdit and understand more about what you're doing, you'll be better able to gauge the seriousness of the tasks you undertake. For someone experienced with ResEdit who's performing only simple changes, this approach is usually adequate.

3. Dangerous: You don't have a backup, but you go ahead and work on your only copy of the file anyway.

    If you know people who do this, don't let them near your Mac.

Hint Why not consider keeping a log of all the changes you make using ResEdit? If your Mac or applications begin to behave strangely weeks or months later, such a log could prove valuable in helping you track down and eliminate problems.

Debunking a Myth

Before we conclude the warnings, we have to debunk a myth you may have run across. You may have read that you should only use ResEdit on files stored on floppy disks, suggesting that you can somehow "break" your hard disk.

Even if you suffer a tragic mental lapse and somehow manage to destroy data on your disk, all you lose is time as long as you have a rescue disk and backups. In any case, these gloomy scenarios just don't reflect reality. We routinely use ResEdit on files or copies of files right on our hard disks, and we've never—well, OK, rarely—had to resort to our backups or rescue disks.

The Disk with This Book

ResEdit 2.1.1 occupies most of the disk with this book, but a few other files of interest are also included. We've included some fun resources for you to browse through. The Finder Menu Template can be copied to ResEdit's Preferences file; Chapter 15 tells you what to do. For other details, see the appropriate chapters and the ReadMe files on the disk.

Summary

This chapter introduces ResEdit and briefly describes in general terms some of the things you can do with it. This modular, task-oriented book is aimed at two general audiences: all users interested in customizing their Macintoshes for enjoyment and productivity, and programmers interested in using ResEdit to create resources for applications they're developing. Topics are organized functionally by grouping related resource types together in chapters that generally increase in difficulty or complexity as you progress through the book. Because ResEdit is a powerful program, this chapter also warns you to make copies of files before editing them. Finally, we describe what's on the disk with this book.

Chapter 2

 # What Are Resources?

So far we've talked about resources in rather general terms. Now it's time to get a little more specific. To understand how your Macintosh applications work and, more important, how ResEdit works on those applications, you need to know something about resources.

Resources are one of the most powerful and innovative ideas in the Macintosh programming world. They're an essential key to the design of Macintosh software and form the foundation of every application. Properly written applications store as much as possible in resources, including all the familiar user interface components. The apt term *resource* can apply to anything of use to an application—including the program code itself. In fact, you could say that a Macintosh application is a collection of resources. Before the Macintosh, everything an application needed, including user interface components such as menus, was "hard-coded," or buried in bulky chunks of program code. Macintosh applications, on the other hand, are split into numerous building blocks, such as dialog and alert boxes and their messages, fonts, menus, icons, and patterns, as well as the program code. In other words, Macintosh applications are modular. Each of these resource modules is created, stored, and modified separately.

Advantages of Using Resources

Dealing with resources separately gives software much greater flexibility. This modular, resource-based approach to software design offers several advantages.

- Foreign language translation—Using resources for the user interface makes translation into foreign languages easier. All screen messages and menu items are separate from the program code, so nonprogrammers can translate the pertinent text. With the "hard-coded" approach used in the non-Macintosh community, you have to change the program itself, then recompile it after each translation—a time-consuming, laborious process.

- Shared resources—Standard data, such as mouse pointer shapes, fonts, or Open and Save dialogs can be made available to every application. Sharing resources promotes consistency between applications and saves disk space because standard building blocks are stored only once, usually in the System file. You may think of the System file as a space hog, but actually it saves space by functioning as a library, therefore allowing applications to be smaller.

- Responsive memory management—The Mac can manage memory more efficiently because it doesn't have to store whole applications; it can store just the bits and pieces required at a given time. Application developers can designate resources that aren't being used at the moment as purgeable, and if the Mac needs more memory for a specific task, it can clear those resources from memory.

- Customization—As a spin-off benefit, using resources enables Mac owners to personalize applications. "So much for shared resources promoting consistency between applications," you may be muttering to yourself. But wait a minute. Consistency and customization don't really conflict; they're just useful at different times. Consistency between applications is one of the reasons novices can sit down with a new Macintosh application and become productive in almost no time. But most people eventually settle into their own preferred ways of doing things. As you become more adept at using your computer and applications, you can harness more of your Macintosh's power by creating the individualized working environment that best suits you. You don't have to take things as they come—after all, it's *your* Macintosh.

Resource Basics

Chaos would inevitably result if you tossed the bazillion or so possible resources together in a big box labeled simply, "Resources," as Figure 2-1 illustrates. Rummaging through such a multitude of building blocks becomes easier for both you and your Mac when there's some basis for categorizing them. A Macintosh resource is identified by its *type* and *ID* number. Resources can also have names, but they're optional.

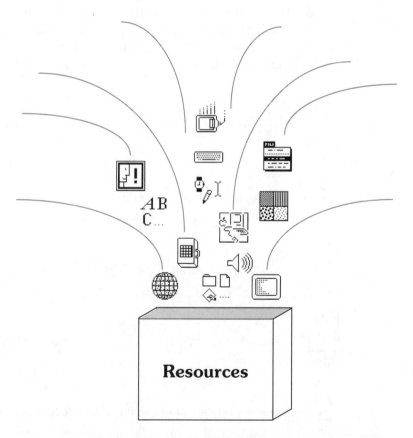

Figure 2-1. Simply throwing unidentified resources together would lead to chaos.

Resource Types

Resources are grouped logically into resource types. Each type performs a particular function and holds a particular kind of data. You're
probably already familiar with some of the resource types shown in
Figure 2-2. The only thing that all the various resource types have in
common is that they are chunks of specially formatted data and are
identified by four-character labels, or types. Some common resource
types may appear to have only three characters in their names, but the
fourth may be a nonprinting character, such as the space in the 'PAT '
(pattern) and 'snd ' (sound) resources. Nonprinting characters, which
can occur in any of the positions in the resource type, are just as
important as printing characters. Case (upper or lower) also matters.
For example, the Mac won't recognize 'font' or 'Font' as the 'FONT'
resource type. Appendix B lists the standard resource types, but you
may encounter others because software developers are free to define
new ones as necessary. By convention, resource types are written
enclosed in single quotation marks; the marks are not part of the type.

PATH

Pattern lists are stored in the 'PAT#' resource type.

FONT

Fonts are stored in the 'FONT' resource type.

CURS

Cursors are stored in the 'CURS' resource type.

MENU

Menus are stored in the 'MENU' resource type.

ICON

Some icons are stored in the 'ICON' resource type.

**Figure 2-2. Resources are grouped logically by their function
and identified by their type.**

> **By The Way** In the early days of the Macintosh, the resource types Apple created had all uppercase letters, such as 'MENU' and 'FONT'. Later, when the Mac II came out, Apple switched to using lowercase letters, such as 'cicn' (color icon) and 'ppat' (pixel pattern). Currently, Apple reserves for its use all resource types having only lowercase letters.

Sooner or later (and probably sooner) you will come across a resource type containing a pound sign (#). By frequently ignored convention, this symbol means that resources of that type contain a collection or *list* of similar elements. For instance, the 'PAT#' resource type stores pattern lists, and the 'STR#' resource type stores lists of strings. These lists can contain any number of elements.

> **By The Way** Although 'ICN#' was initially defined as a law-abiding icon list, this resource type doesn't follow the rules anymore. The 'ICN#' type is now defined for Finder icons and always contains exactly two elements, the icon and its mask.

For nearly every list resource type, there's a corresponding resource type that contains only one such element per resource. For instance, a 'PAT ' resource contains only one pattern, an 'STR ' contains only one string and an 'ICON' contains only one icon. Now you're probably scratching your head wondering why you need two types of resources to handle one kind of data. From a programmer's point of view, each approach has pluses and minuses. In a nutshell, list resource types come in handy because they allow you to group a large number of related elements together and to save space both in memory and on disk. For example, 20 patterns stored in separate 'PAT ' resources occupy more space than those same 20 patterns stored in a single 'PAT#'. On the other hand, a 20-pattern list resource takes up a good chunk of space if you only need one pattern at a time.

Resource IDs

Within each resource type, individual resources are identified by a resource ID number. IDs are unique within each resource type, but resources of different types can have the same ID. With just these two pieces of information, type and ID, an application can find any resource it needs. 'MENU' ID 2 refers to a unique menu resource within an application, just as 'DLOG' ID 2 refers to a unique dialog. An application doesn't say "OK, the user wants to see the Set Margins dialog," it says, "OK, the user wants to see 'DLOG' ID 15." The usual way the application knows which particular resource to display or use in any situation is by type and ID. (It's also possible to look for a resource by type and name instead of ID, but not many applications do that.) That's why you have to keep track of ID numbers carefully as you substitute resources to personalize your applications. We'll show you how to substitute your custom resources and change their resource IDs in later chapters.

We mentioned that one of the advantages of using resources is that applications can share the resources stored in the System file. But they don't have to. Just because there's a certain resource in the System file doesn't mean an application has to use it. Because of the way it searches for resources, the Macintosh gives you a way to override the System resource with a custom resource specific to your application. As illustrated in Figure 2-3, when an application needs a

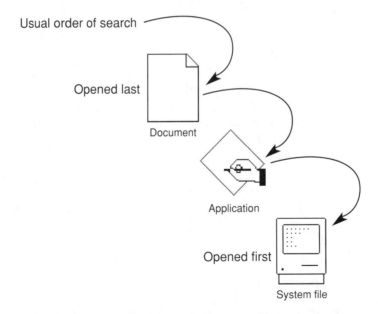

Usual order of search

Opened last

Document

Application

Opened first

System file

Figure 2-3. The Mac usually searches for resources starting with the file opened most recently.

resource, the Mac normally begins its search with the most recently opened file, and works backward to the System file, which opens at startup. (We said "normally" because an application can change where the search starts.) Therefore, if an application resource has the same type and ID number as a System file resource, the application resource is used; otherwise the System resource is used. Keep this search order in mind as you modify resources. If the change you made in the System file doesn't show up in your application, you may need to modify the corresponding resource in the application.

Numbering Conventions

Although resource IDs can fall between -32,768 and 32,767, resources don't acquire their ID numbers willy-nilly. Resource IDs follow certain rules, which are summarized in Table 2-1. Other restrictions may also apply; for instance, if you want to put an icon in a menu, the icon's ID has to be greater than 256 but less than 512.

Table 2-1. Guidelines for Allocating Resource IDs

Resource ID Range	Use
-32,768 to -16,385	Reserved by Apple
-16,384 to 127	Used for System resources
128 to 32,767	Available for applications

As you become familiar with ResEdit you'll notice that whenever you ask it to create or duplicate a resource, it seems to always hand out the same number for the new resource's ID. Well, it doesn't just seem to, it usually does. When it has to assign a new resource ID, ResEdit starts with 128, the lowest number available for use, and increases by one until it finds a number that isn't already taken by a resource of that type in that file.

Forked File Structure

Now you know a bit about how resources are identified, but you may be wondering where and how they're stored. Macintosh files are unique in that every one can have two parts, or *forks:* the *data fork* and the *resource fork*.

Either fork of a file can be empty. The resource fork of an application file, for instance, normally contains all the resources the application uses, including the program code. The data fork can contain anything the application puts there, but often it's empty. (For example, ResEdit has no data fork.) Many of the documents that applications create have no resource fork. For instance, the text you type into a word processing document is stored in the data fork. Some applications may use their documents' resource forks to store customized settings that pertain only to that document.

By The Way The System file's resource fork contains the standard resources shared by all applications and by the Macintosh Toolbox, which is the built-in software that makes the Macintosh user interface available to programmers and their applications. Some resources that are too big to fit in ROM (Read-Only Memory) have to be stored in the System file instead. Other resources may also exist in the various ROMs but are duplicated in System software releases for the sake of compatibility with machines that don't have the newer ROMs. If you want to be sure you only copy resources you need when updating to a new System, use Apple's Installer.

A file's two forks handle their assigned data differently. The data fork contains one big chunk of unstructured data. The resource fork, on the other hand, is divided into two parts, as illustrated in Figure 2-4. The *resource map* is the table of contents or index your Mac uses to find the individual resources that are stored in the *resource data* part of the resource fork.

By The Way The resource map is part of the reason that list resources take up less memory. Each entry in the map requires a 12-byte parcel of memory. So 20 'PAT ' resources take up 240 bytes in the resource map, plus the space needed for the pattern resources themselves. Those same 20 patterns stored in a 'PAT#' resource require the same amount of space for the patterns, but take up only one 12-byte parcel in the resource map.

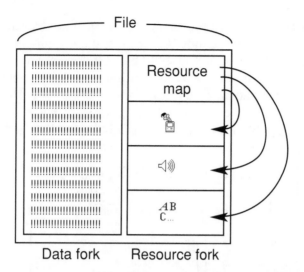

Figure 2-4. **The resource map tells the Mac where to find individual resources within the resource data part of the resource fork.**

This forked file structure may sound a little schizophrenic. To confuse matters, people sometimes refer to the forks as files (the "data file" or the "resource file"). You can relax, though, because you never have to worry about keeping tabs on the two parts of your files. Your Mac takes care of that for you.

What ResEdit Does

ResEdit is a general-purpose resource editor that provides understandable representations of resources so you can edit them and, in the case of graphic resources, immediately see how they'll look. ResEdit lets you browse through a file's resource fork, open any resource present, and change it. Because changing a file's resources can have unpredictable and disastrous results, you should always edit an expendable copy. Like any powerful tool, ResEdit can be dangerous if used carelessly.

By The Way Although ResEdit opens only a file's resource fork, for convenience people generally say that it opens the file.

The resources in a file are specially formatted chunks of data that your Mac can understand, but they're incomprehensible to most people, and at best unwieldy to the rest. ResEdit makes those chunks of data understandable by presenting usable representations of them. For instance, the data that describe an icon can be displayed several ways, two of which are shown in Figure 2-5. They can be displayed literally (as a series of hexadecimal characters), or graphically. Most

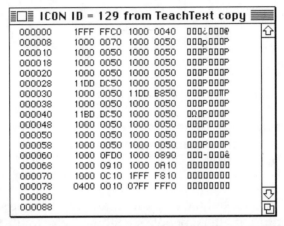

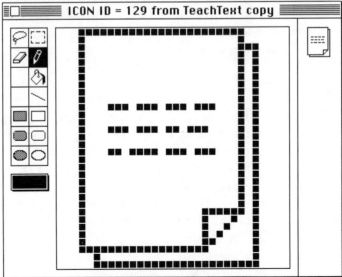

Figure 2-5. ResEdit's hexadecimal editor (top) and 'ICON' editor (bottom) display two very different representations of the same icon. Which one would you rather edit?

people would choose to work with the more understandable graphic representation.

ResEdit can show you a resource in three general ways. First, it has numerous resource-specific special editors, and it automatically opens a resource in the appropriate special editor if one exists. For example, a 'MENU' resource opens in the 'MENU' editor, which provides all the tools you need for editing menus, but no others. While you're editing a menu, you won't trip over the tools required for editing icons, dialogs, patterns, or other resources. ResEdit also presents resources in templates—windows that resemble big dialog boxes. A template is like a blueprint; it lists parameters used to build a particular resource, but it's not the resource itself. You can create or edit more than 70 resource types using specific templates. Each resource type has its own kind of template, and each individual resource is characterized by its unique values within the template. Finally, if ResEdit doesn't have a special editor or a template for a resource (meaning it doesn't know about the resource's structure), it will present the resource to you as a sequence of characters in its hexadecimal editor. This book covers all the special editors and includes several chapters on templates. Appendix C covers the basics of working with hexadecimal numbers in the hexadecimal editor.

Sometimes resources are stored in compressed form to conserve space. ResEdit has to decompress resources in order for you to edit them, and it can't compress them again. That's why anytime you ask ResEdit to open a compressed resource, you'll see the alert shown in Figure 2-6. Duly informed of the situation, you'll usually just click

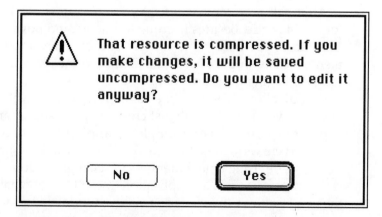

Figure 2-6. ResEdit alerts you when you're about to open a compressed resource.

"Yes" or press Return and go about your business. You can't make an omelet without breaking eggs, right? Besides, the increase in resource size is usually minimal. Of course there's no point in decompressing resources aimlessly, but if you're just browsing and make no changes, the resource will remain compact.

What You Can't Do with ResEdit

You can do a wide variety of things with ResEdit—that's what this whole book is about. But there are still a few things you can't do. You're bound to be happier as you customize your Mac if you keep in mind what ResEdit can't do and why.

You can change a resource's content, ID, name, and certain other attributes, but generally you can't change its type. That would be tantamount to software alchemy. You can't turn lead into gold, nor can you turn menus, pointers, icons, or dialog boxes into each other. Fortunately, the usual Macintosh magic still works where it makes sense, however. You can copy certain components of some resources to resources of other types. For instance, you can copy the bits that make up the image in one graphic editor and paste them into another graphic editor.

ResEdit only works on resources, so if an application doesn't use resources for the user interface components you want to change, ResEdit can't help you. The fewer resources an application uses, the more that has been "hard-coded," the less flexible and customizable an application is. (Register your complaints with the developer of the offending software.)

Although program code is stored in resources, ResEdit isn't useful for editing code. Besides needing to understand how to program a Macintosh, you need some sort of a software development environment (such as Apple's MPW, or Think C from Symantec) before you tackle changing program code.

ResEdit allows you to edit existing resources as well as create new ones. But you usually can't just create a new resource and expect an application to use it. For example, an application that doesn't have an animated cursor will just ignore the clever 'acur' resource you add. Likewise, devising a new menu won't change the functions an application can perform. The application doesn't know what to do with the new resource. In fact, it doesn't even know to *look* for the resource. Remember, applications look for resources by resource type and ID, so generally you can only substitute customized versions of existing resource types. You can either change the existing resource or substitute a new version. We'll tell you how to do that in the next chapter.

Summary

This chapter presents an overview of Macintosh resources: what they are, the advantages of using them, and how they're identified—by type and ID. We touch on the forked structure of Macintosh files, and how resources are stored in the resource fork. Finally, we describe in general terms how ResEdit works on the resource fork of a file and summarize the few things that ResEdit can't do.

Now that you're familiar with resources, you're ready to find out how to use ResEdit.

Chapter 3

 How to Use ResEdit

In most respects, ResEdit works just like any other Macintosh application, so you can forget whatever frightening or mystical references you may have heard. It's actually fairly simple: With word processing applications you create and edit text, with paint and draw programs you create and edit pictures, and with ResEdit you create and edit the resources found in most files. The important difference to remember is that rather than working on documents, you generally use ResEdit on valuable application files, so you have to be careful. Manipulating resources can be as simple as adding a keyboard shortcut for a common operation in your favorite application, or as complicated as editing a custom resource for an application you're writing. Although ResEdit behaves like a typical Mac application in most respects, it has some special characteristics because it does a unique job. This chapter describes ResEdit's features and tells you how to use it so that you'll feel comfortable taking it out for a spin.

One of the ways ResEdit differs from most Macintosh applications is that it can open any file. Text processing applications show you only text files in the standard file directory dialog, and graphics applications show you only graphics files. ResEdit isn't picky. It shows you every file because every file can have a resource fork, and it can open any of them. This ability gives ResEdit great power and utility, but it's also one of the reasons why careless joyriding with ResEdit can be dangerous. We recommend that you only open *copies* of files so that you don't accidentally damage important files and applications. Later, when you become a ResEdit pro, you'll know when you have to make a copy and when you don't. (Any time you wonder whether you should make a copy, you should.) We'll give more specific instructions for working on important files such as your System file in the next chapter.

Although ResEdit can open any file (or, more precisely, any file's resource fork), it can do so only if the file isn't already open. If you think about it, this is just as well. You wouldn't *want* to tweak an application's resources while it's running (unless you like living dangerously). However, there are two important files that ResEdit can open even though they're already running. ResEdit can open the System file's resource fork and it can open its own resource fork. (Of course, the System file is always open whenever your Mac is running.) Still, we recommend that you always work on copies of these files.

Starting ResEdit

When you open ResEdit you see a splash-screen that includes, in addition to the animated ResEdit Jack-in-the-Mac, the version number and other information. Virtually anything you do, such as pressing a key or clicking the mouse, causes the splash-screen to disappear so you can select a file to edit. While the splash-screen is displayed, ResEdit can also act on any Command keys that make sense, such as shortcuts that open files you work on frequently. Once you find the file (or preferably a copy of the file) you want to examine or edit, you can double-click and ResEdit will open it. But before you can find your way around in ResEdit comfortably, you need to understand how it presents information, so you should become familiar with its windows.

ResEdit's Windows

ResEdit has three general kinds of windows: pickers, editors, and info windows. Each kind of window has two or more subkinds. If you understand how ResEdit displays information, and know what you can and can't do from certain windows, you'll be able to accomplish more work with less wheel spinning. Figure 3-1 gives you a preview of how ResEdit's pickers and editors work together. The rest of this section introduces pickers, editors, and info windows in more detail.

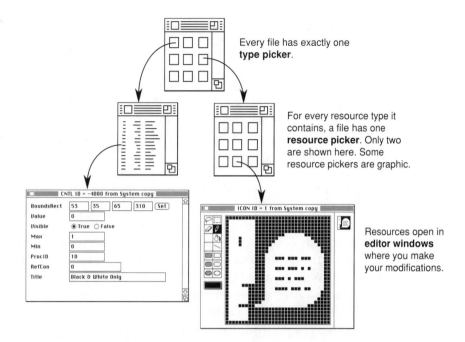

Every file has exactly one **type picker**.

For every resource type it contains, a file has one **resource picker**. Only two are shown here. Some resource pickers are graphic.

Resources open in **editor windows** where you make your modifications.

Figure 3-1. ResEdit's pickers and editors open in a predictable, hierarchical order.

Pickers

Pickers are windows that list text or icons, and they behave much like windows in the Finder. They have zoom boxes and size boxes so you can adjust their size and shape, and you can change how the window contents are displayed by choosing options from the View menu. You can also change the size characteristics of picker windows with the Preferences command on the File menu. Some commands apply only in pickers, such as the Edit menu's Select Changed item. There are two kinds of pickers: the type picker (one per file) and resource pickers (one for each resource type in a file). You pick the type of resource you want to edit from the type picker. You pick the individual resource you want to edit from the resource picker. Although there are many kinds of resource pickers, they all work similarly.

The Type Picker

The *type picker* is the first window you see any time ResEdit opens a file. The type picker lists the types of all the resources the file contains. You can view this list either by icon, as shown in Figure 3-2, or by resource type, as shown in Figure 3-3. As you can see in Figure 3-2, ResEdit has two generic icons that it uses for resource types for which it doesn't have editors. Such resources are either code resources, or resources you can edit using only the hexadecimal editor (see Appendix C). Any other icon represents a resource type for which ResEdit has a special editor, or a template you can fill in using the template editor.

In the By Type view you can see more information about the contents of a file. You see not only the four-character names of the resource types, but also how many resources of that type exist in the file. You can also tell ResEdit to show you the total size (in bytes) of the resources, as shown in Figure 3-4. This can be useful for analyzing the contents of a file, but sometimes displaying resource sizes can be slow. For example, on a Mac Plus, opening a file that contains a large number of resources can take several seconds or longer. Furthermore, any time ResEdit redraws part of a window (for instance, if you change the size of a window or scroll) it has to recalculate these sizes.

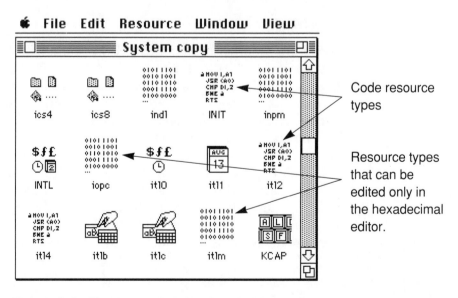

Figure 3-2. The type picker, view by icon. Some icons represent more than one resource type.

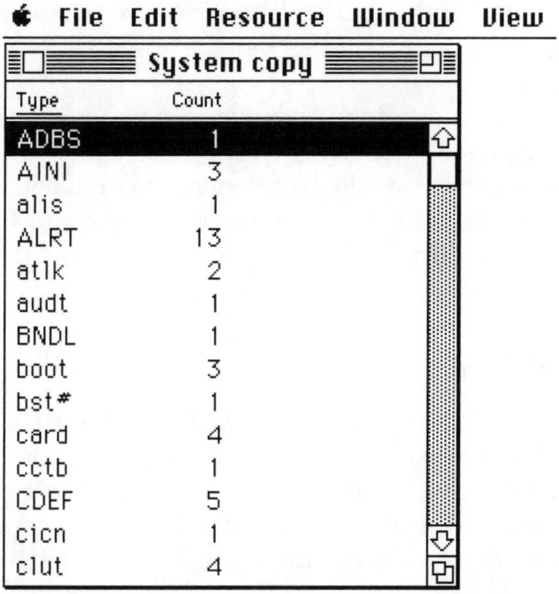
File Edit Resource Window View
System copy
Type Count
ADBS 1
AINI 3
alis 1
ALRT 13
atlk 2
audt 1
BNDL 1
boot 3
bst# 1
card 4
cctb 1
CDEF 5
cicn 1
clut 4

Figure 3-3. Type picker, view by type.

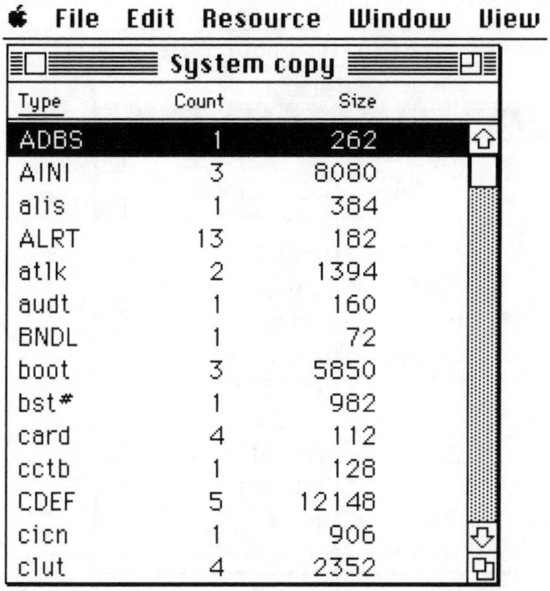
File Edit Resource Window View
System copy
Type Count Size
ADBS 1 262
AINI 3 8080
alis 1 384
ALRT 13 182
atlk 2 1394
audt 1 160
BNDL 1 72
boot 3 5850
bst# 1 982
card 4 112
cctb 1 128
CDEF 5 12148
cicn 1 906
clut 4 2352

Figure 3-4. The type picker, showing size (in bytes) with type.

If delays associated with displaying resource sizes become too annoying, simply turn off the Show Size With Type option on the View menu.

When you've found the resource type you want to open, double-click it or choose Open Pickers from the Resource menu. (The command's text varies slightly, depending on what's selected. Don't choose Open from the File menu or use Command-O—that opens files, not the resources within them.) The window that opens next is the other kind of picker—a resource picker.

Resource Pickers

Resource pickers show you all the resources of a particular type that are in a file. The list displays the ID, size, and name for each resource, as shown in Figure 3-5. In many cases resources don't have names, so the right side of the window is blank. The View menu for resource pickers gives you more options than the one available for type

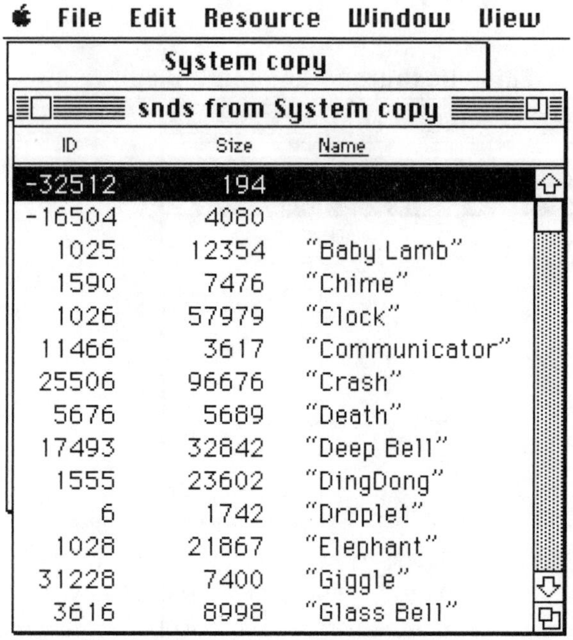

🍎   File   Edit   Resource   Window   View

ID	Size	Name
-32512	194	
-16504	4080	
1025	12354	"Baby Lamb"
1590	7476	"Chime"
1026	57979	"Clock"
11466	3617	"Communicator"
25506	96676	"Crash"
5676	5689	"Death"
17493	32842	"Deep Bell"
1555	23602	"DingDong"
6	1742	"Droplet"
1028	21867	"Elephant"
31228	7400	"Giggle"
3616	8998	"Glass Bell"

System copy

snds from System copy

Figure 3-5. The 'snd ' picker, a resource picker for 'snd ' (sound) resources.

pickers. You can sort resources by ID, Name, Size, or Order in File. Viewing by Order in File gives you a chronological list of resources, with the resource added to the file most recently listed first. You can also view some resource types in special pickers that give you more information. Pickers for graphical resources, for instance, default to a graphical view (sorted by ID) that shows you what each resource looks like. For example, the 'ICON' picker is shown in Figure 3-6. On some systems (notably the Mac Plus) the By Name and By Size views may be a bit slow.

The last item on the View menu is the Show Attributes command, which is available for any nonspecial view. Choosing this item tells ResEdit to display more detailed resource information, shown in Figure 3-7, that's generally useful only for programmers. You can't change this information here, but you can choose Get Resource Info from the Resource menu to change the attributes for any resource. (For more on resource attributes, see Chapter 22.)

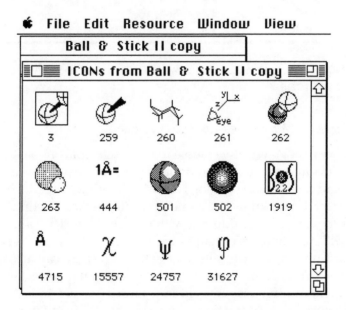

Figure 3-6. A resource picker, view by 'ICON'.

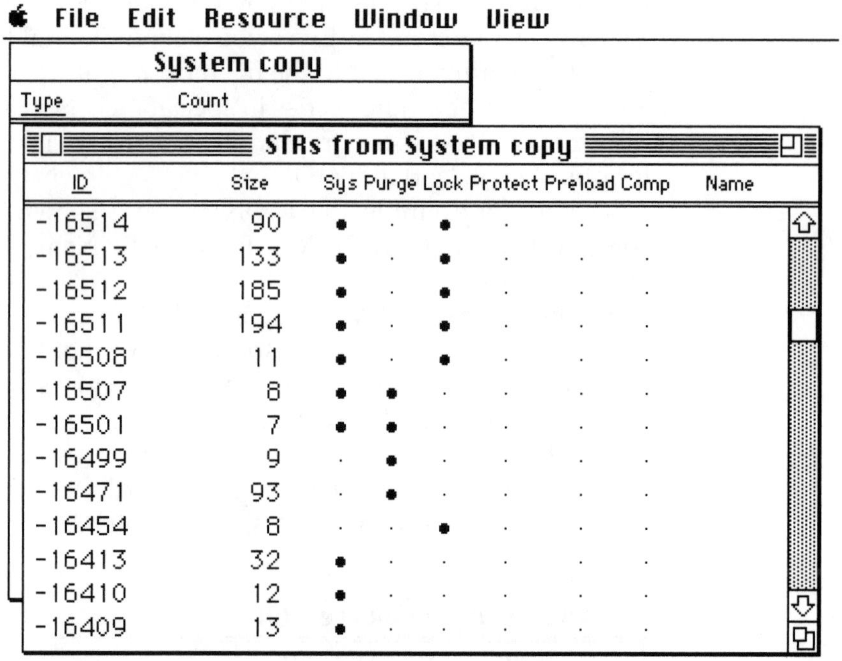

** & File   Edit   Resource   Window   View**

System copy	
Type	Count

STRs from System copy

ID	Size	Sys	Purge	Lock	Protect	Preload	Comp	Name
-16514	90	●	·	●	·	·	·	
-16513	133	●	·	●	·	·	·	
-16512	185	●	·	●	·	·	·	
-16511	194	●	·	●	·	·	·	
-16508	11	●	·	●	·	·	·	
-16507	8	●	●	·	·	·	·	
-16501	7	●	●	·	·	·	·	
-16499	9	·	●	·	·	·	·	
-16471	93	·	●	·	·	·	·	
-16454	8	·	·	●	·	·	·	
-16413	32	●	·	·	·	·	·	
-16410	12	●	·	·	·	·	·	
-16409	13	●	·	·	·	·	·	

Figure 3-7. Resource pickers can show the attributes of resources.

Hints on Making Selections in Pickers

You won't have any trouble making selections in pickers, but a few tricks and shortcuts could make your life easier. Just as in the standard file directory dialogs found throughout the Macintosh environment, if you know the name of what you want to find, you can just type it instead of fiddling with the scroll bar. The same trick works with ID numbers or names in resource pickers; just type them.

Knowing how to select more than one item can also come in handy. You can open multiple resource types from type pickers, and you can open multiple resources from resource pickers, too. The techniques generally work any time you see a list in ResEdit, which will mostly be in pickers. As usual in the Macintosh world, Shift-click extends a selection. To select items that aren't next to each other, use Command-click. If an item is already selected, Command-click deselects it without deselecting other items.

Editor Windows

After you select one or more resources from the resource picker, you can double-click or choose Open Resource Editor from the Resource menu to edit the resource(s). Each resource editor provides different features depending on the kind of information it handles. In many cases the editors look and behave similarly. For example, the 'ICON' and 'ICN#' editors are quite similar, and you can use the same editing techniques in both. You can think of each editor as a mini-application. It may have its own additional menus, and it may appear different from most other editors. Of course, many things are the same for all editors. We'll discuss editors in general terms here and cover individual editors in more detail in chapters devoted to them.

> **By The Way** As you browse files with ResEdit, you should be aware that color resource editors, such as 'cicn' and 'ppt#', open only on machines that have Color QuickDraw (for instance, SE/30s, Mac IIs, and up). Also, for those of you lucky enough to have two monitors, you can choose (in the Preferences dialog) which screen ResEdit's color pickers and editors use. If you decide to have them automatically open on the screen able to display the most colors or grays, that's where they open—even if that monitor isn't turned on. This can be confusing, but unfortunately the Mac doesn't have a mechanism for letting an application know whether a monitor is on.

ResEdit has many *graphical editors*, which let you manipulate visual representations of resources. Some examples are the editors that you use to work on menus, windows, alert and dialog boxes and their contents, and keyboard character maps. The graphical editors used for patterns, icons, fonts, and pointers (or cursors) are fatbits editors. These editors always give you at least two views of the resource you're editing—an enlarged fatbits editing area and at least one actual-size view. In addition, editors that work on list resources (such as the patterns in a 'PAT#' resource or the small icons in an 'SICN' resource) supply a method for selecting the item you want to work on from the list.

A handful of nongraphical editors allow you to edit all the remaining resources. The editors for date, time, and number formats ('itl0' and 'itl1' resources) resemble elaborate dialog boxes. The two most general editors, the hexadecimal editor and the template editor, can edit a wide variety of resources. In fact, if you know what you're doing, you can edit *any* resource using the hexadecimal editor. Most users won't find the hexadecimal editor very helpful, however, because it represents resources as a series of numbers. (For more on the hexadecimal editor, see Appendix C.)

The template editor is another story. This one editor comes with more than 70 templates, each one representing a different resource type (and you can add more). Although templates aren't graphical and may not be intuitively obvious, they're quite easy to edit. One example is the template used for animated cursors ('acur' resources). See Chapter 14 for more information on templates and the template editor.

Info Windows

The three kinds of info windows, which behave like dialogs, allow you to see and set a variety of characteristics for resources, files, and folders. For information about a file or a folder, you would choose the Get File/Folder Info item on the File menu. Programmers are most likely to use these windows, but customizers need them occasionally, too, and we've included several tips and tricks that use them. (For more programmers' information, see Chapter 22.)

To access the Resource Info window, choose Get Resource Info from the Resource menu. This command becomes available only after you've selected a resource. Like the other info windows, this window, which is shown in Figure 3-8, is most useful for programmers. But anyone serious about customization will find two fields in this window particularly useful. In experimenting with various resources you may have to change their ID numbers; this is where you do it. We guide you through the steps later in this chapter. You may also want to name some of the nameless resources you encounter as you browse through your files.

 File   Edit   Resource   Window

```
┌─────────────────────────────────────────┐
│            Finder copy                    │
│  ┌─────────────────────────────────────┐ │
│  │     acurs from Finder copy          │ │
│  │ ┌─────────────────────────────────────┐
│  │ │▤□▤▤▤ Info for acur 6500 from Finder copy ▤▤▤
│  │ │
│  │ │  Type:    acur          Size:  36
│  │ │  ID:    ┌─────────────┐
│  │ │         │ 6500        │
│  │ │         └─────────────┘
│  │ │  Name:  ┌──────────────────────────┐
│  │ │         │                          │
│  │ │         └──────────────────────────┘
│  │ │                        Owner type
│  │ │                      ┌──────────┬──┐
│  │ │   Owner ID: ┌──────┐ │ DRVR     │⬆ │
│  │ │             │      │ ├──────────┼──┤
│  │ │             └──────┘ │ WDEF     │  │
│  │ │   Sub ID:   ┌──────┐ ├──────────┼──┤
│  │ │             │      │ │ MDEF     │⬇ │
│  │ │             └──────┘ └──────────┴──┘
│  │ │  Attributes:
│  │ │   □ System Heap   ☒ Locked      ☒ Preload
│  │ │   □ Purgeable     □ Protected   □ Compressed
│  │ └─────────────────────────────────────┘
└──┴───────────────────────────────────────┘
```

Figure 3-8. The Resource Info window.

Hint Naming unnamed resources can be a big help as you peruse your files because the names appear in any nongraphic resource picker view. You won't have to waste time repeatedly opening resources just to find out which ones they are. Simply choose Get Resource Info from ResEdit's Resource menu and type a name in the Name field of the Resource Info dialog. You can do this either from resource pickers or from editors. But never change an existing name! Remember that sometimes applications look for resources by type and name rather than by type and ID, so play it safe and leave existing names alone. For this same reason, don't use a name already taken by another resource of the same type.

Using ResEdit's Windows

Working with ResEdit's windows will become second nature in no time. Just remember there's a hierarchy, as you saw in Figure 3-1. When you open a file with ResEdit, the first window you always see is the type picker for that file. From there (and only from there) you open the resource picker(s). Only after you've selected a resource in the resource picker can ResEdit open the appropriate editor. You can open as many windows as memory accommodates. Except for info windows, which you can open from more than one place, there's a predictable sequence to how the windows open.

Hint Closing a window also closes all the windows that were opened from it.

Finally, in your adventures with ResEdit, don't forget about the View menu and the Window menu. (There's more information about them later in this chapter, in the "Menus" section.) These menus exist to help you manipulate windows, so take advantage of them.

Clipboard Operations

At the beginning of this chapter we mentioned that ResEdit differs from most Macintosh applications in a few important ways. One difference is that it can open any file. Another is the way it handles the clipboard. In fact, in order to carry out its unique mission, ResEdit has to maintain its own clipboard to get around limitations of the Macintosh's main Clipboard. Fortunately, you don't have to worry about keeping track of clipboards—all that's taken care of for you. But you should understand a few important points about how clipboard operations work.

The Macintosh's main Clipboard can only contain one resource of each type because it doesn't keep track of ID numbers. To enable you to cut and paste multiple resources, ResEdit operates its own clipboard that can handle ID numbers. As long as you do your cutting, copying, and pasting within ResEdit, you shouldn't face any surprises because you're dealing only with ResEdit's clipboard. (See the Paste command in the "Menus" section later in this chapter for more details.)

You have to pay a little more attention, however, when you set out to move things to or from applications other than ResEdit because then you're using the main Clipboard. As you've probably surmised, you can't, for example, copy more than one 'PICT' resource at a time into your paint program, because the main Clipboard can only handle one resource of any type at a time.

The reverse situation, pasting a selection from an application into an open file in ResEdit, carries its own unique problem because many applications send more than one representation of a selection to the main Clipboard when you cut or copy. For example, MacDraw sends an 'MDPL' resource to the clipboard in addition to a 'PICT' resource. This approach works most of the time because when you paste from the Clipboard these applications look for their preferred representations. MacDraw looks for an 'MDPL' on the clipboard when you paste, but it will settle for a 'PICT'. ResEdit has no preferred representation, so if you're pasting into a type picker, it takes everything on the clipboard. Thus, you may get more than one resource when you paste to a type picker, and any extras will clutter up your file and take up space. If you know to look for them, you can purge any duplicate resources masquerading under assumed names—or more precisely, assumed *types*.

By The Way If you copy just one resource, ResEdit puts it on the Mac's main Clipboard. If you copy more than one, however, ResEdit *clears* the main Clipboard.

Hint How can you find all the aliases that a paste operation from another application gives you? One way is to first try pasting into a new, empty file temporarily created with ResEdit just for that purpose. Another approach is to choose Select Changed from the Edit menu, which shows you the resources that have changed since you last saved the file.

Of course, the best way around the problem is to avoid it altogether, if you can. If you know what resource type you're interested in, and you also know that the application you're copying from can give you that resource type, just paste it into the appropriate resource picker ('PICT' in the MacDraw example). When pasting to resource pickers, ResEdit pastes only resources of the corresponding type. For more information, see the Paste command discussion in the Edit menu section later in this chapter.

Resource Checking

When ResEdit opens a file, it automatically verifies the integrity of the resource fork. This preliminary checking is somewhat analogous to having a food taster check your food: If ResEdit tries to open a "poisoned" file, it may choke or die. Unlike the food taster, however, ResEdit's verification feature includes the ability to repair some damage—which not only prevents ResEdit from crashing, but also recovers resources from corrupted files!

The resource verification feature includes two levels of checking. You determine in the Preferences dialog whether ResEdit performs the brief or full check. If you click the "Verify files where they are opened" check box, ResEdit will always perform the full check. Also, the Verify command on the File menu lets you carry out a full check without opening a file.

By The Way The brief check verifies the basic structure of the resource fork. It checks the location of the resource map and checks to see that all the data fit within appropriate bounds. If any of the basic checks fail, the full test is automatically performed.

The full resource check does a more thorough walk through the resource map and verifies that the type list, the reference lists, and the name list are consistent, and that all resource data areas can be located and don't exceed the available space. It also checks for duplicate types and duplicate IDs within a type.

If you're familiar with Apple's MPW development environment, you may notice that the verification is similar to that performed by MPW's RezDet tool. ResEdit's resource verification feature can sometimes recover resources when RezDet can't even find a resource in the file. It can do this because it uses several techniques to locate the resource map, whose existence and location is critical to the resource recovery process.

Resource Fork Repair

ResEdit alerts you if it finds any damage upon opening a file and gives you the opportunity to repair it, as the alert shown in Figure 3-9 illustrates. You would see a similar alert, but without the Continue button, if you had checked the file using the Verify menu item. Most users should avoid the Continue button.

Warning Neither test can verify the contents of individual resources because only the structure of the resource fork is tested. When repairing damage, the integrity of individual resources can never be guaranteed, so you should always restore a backup of the file if you see a "damaged file" alert. The repair facility is intended as a last resort if you don't have any backups but still need to recover some resources.

When repairing a file, ResEdit doesn't do anything to the damaged file itself, but instead copies all the resources it can to a new file. It renames the damaged file with an extension of "(damaged)." ResEdit apprises you of its progress with a variety of alerts. If it can't extract all the resources in a damaged file, it tells you so. If only one resource can't be copied, ResEdit tells you its type and ID. Another possibility is that the file may be damaged beyond repair.

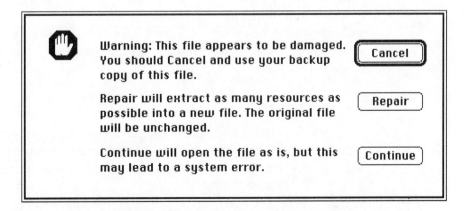

Figure 3-9. This alert warns you of possible damage encountered when opening a file and gives you the option of attempting to repair it. Most users should avoid the Continue button.

ResEdit does work directly on a damaged file in one situation: when a resource fork wasn't closed properly (perhaps the application bombed). Such damage is so minimal that ResEdit performs the repair without even asking your permission, but it informs you that it has done so.

Now you're familiar with how ResEdit presents information in its windows, how it deals with clipboard operations, and how it checks your files. Even though you're probably eager to take it out for a spin, you should first spend a few moments to become familiar with the controls on ResEdit's instrument panel—the menus.

The Menus: Once Over Quickly

ResEdit opens showing the four standard menus it always shows: File, Edit, Resource, and Window. But the menus and menu items available to you in ResEdit vary depending on the situation because ResEdit encompasses many applications in one. The changes aren't capricious but depend on where you are within ResEdit and what you're doing. For instance, why should you work around menus and commands having to do with color icons when you're modifying a dialog? We'll go over the basic menus here, and cover specific, resource-related menus in chapters devoted to those resources.

The File Menu

As you can see in Figure 3-10, most of the File menu's commands let you manipulate files or folders, and they're probably familiar to you from other Macintosh applications. However, a few of the commands are unique to ResEdit or behave a little differently than you might expect.

New

The New command displays the standard file directory dialog, which allows a new file to be created. This command behaves a bit differently from most applications because ResEdit asks you to name the new file before opening it.

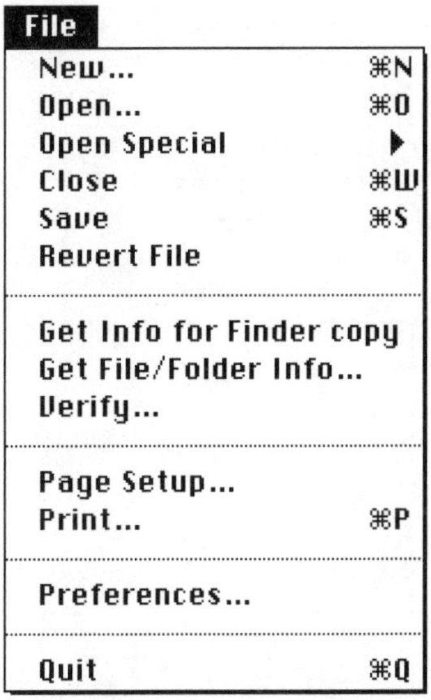

```
 File
   New...              ⌘N
   Open...             ⌘O
   Open Special         ▶
   Close               ⌘W
   Save                ⌘S
   Revert File
   ┈┈┈┈┈┈┈┈┈┈┈┈┈┈┈┈┈┈┈┈
   Get Info for Finder copy
   Get File/Folder Info...
   Verify...
   ┈┈┈┈┈┈┈┈┈┈┈┈┈┈┈┈┈┈┈┈
   Page Setup...
   Print...             ⌘P
   ┈┈┈┈┈┈┈┈┈┈┈┈┈┈┈┈┈┈┈┈
   Preferences...
   ┈┈┈┈┈┈┈┈┈┈┈┈┈┈┈┈┈┈┈┈
   Quit                 ⌘Q
```

Figure 3-10. ResEdit's File menu.

Open

The Open command works the same in ResEdit as in most other
applications. The only difference is that every file is visible in the
standard file directory dialog. Remember, ResEdit can open *any* file
that's not already open, not just ones of a specific type.

Open Special

If you get tired of sifting through the standard file directory dialog
every time you want ResEdit to open a certain file you work on
frequently, you'll like this item. The Open Special menu item displays
a hierarchical menu that you can customize by filling in the names of
files you work on frequently, as in the example shown in Figure 3-11.
To get going even more quickly, you can assign Command-key shortcuts that you can type as soon as ResEdit's splash-screen appears.
    When you first select the Open Special item, all you see on the
hierarchical menu is the Modify This Menu command. As you add
files, that command gets pushed further down. There's no limit—
within reason—to the number of files you can add. When you select
Modify This Menu, ResEdit displays the dialog shown in Figure 3-12.

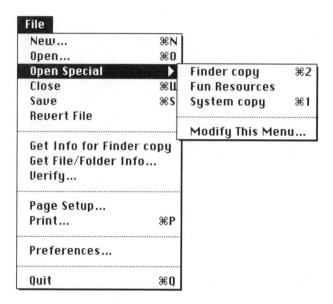

Figure 3-11. The Open Special menu item lets you create
custom shortcuts to files you work on frequently.

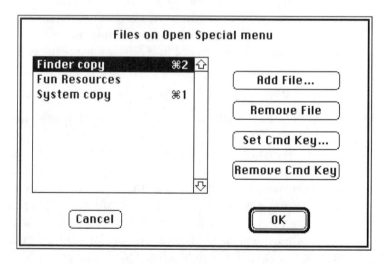

Figure 3-12. The Modify This Menu command displays this
dialog, which you use to change the files and Command-key
shortcuts on your Open Special menu.

This dialog contains everything you need to add and remove files and Command-key shortcuts on the Open Special menu.

When you click the Add File button, ResEdit displays a standard file directory dialog so you can locate the file you're after. Once you find it and double-click, ResEdit adds the file to the menu and remembers where to find it. ResEdit even lets you have two files with the same name on the menu. It keeps track of them by showing you the path it follows to get to each file. If you move a file or change its name, ResEdit will not be able to find it. (When this happens, ResEdit displays a fairly standard "File not found" alert.) The file remains on the Open Special menu, however, so before you can reteach ResEdit where the file is, you should remove the file name from the menu. To remove a file from the menu, simply select it and click the Remove File button.

Convenience is the whole point of the Open Special menu, so ResEdit also lets you assign Command-key shortcuts so you can quickly open the files you work on frequently. If you want to add a Command-key shortcut, first select the file, then click the Set Cmd Key button. ResEdit displays a dialog like the one shown in Figure 3-13. The dialog vanishes when you press a key, and you see your shortcut beside the file name in the Open Special dialog. If you press a key that's already in use, ResEdit warns you. (The warning gives you the option of using the key anyway, but we advise you to avoid double assignments.) To remove a Command-key shortcut from a file, simply select the file and click the Remove Cmd Key button.

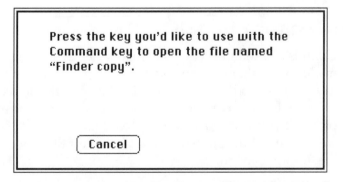

Figure 3-13. Clicking the Set Cmd Key button causes this dialog to be displayed.

By The Way You'll probably want to avoid using the Option key when you assign shortcuts. If you've checked Verify files when they are opened in the Preferences dialog, pressing the Option key when you open a file causes the file verification hidden diagnostic window to appear. (For more information, see Chapter 13.) There's nothing dangerous about this, it just slows you down a bit.

Close

Selecting this command is the same as clicking the active window's close box. If the active window is a type picker, ResEdit closes the file. If you haven't saved, ResEdit gives you the opportunity to do so before closing the file.

Hint Pressing the Option key when you close a window closes all windows for the file except the type picker. Also remember that closing a window closes all the windows you've opened from it.

Save

The Save command saves the file associated with the active window. If you have several files open, ResEdit saves only the file associated with the active window. It doesn't save individual resources within a file; it saves the whole file.

Revert File

Use this command if you have inadvertently deleted a resource or made some other change you're not happy with and want to get back to a known good file. This command reverts the active file to its last saved state. All open windows for that file will close except the type picker. If you want to restore only certain resources but you don't want to revert the entire file, use the Revert Resource command on the Resource menu.

Get Info for <Filename>

ResEdit provides a shortcut with this command. It works just like Get File/Folder Info (see next command), except that it automatically applies to the active file.

Get File/Folder Info

Unless you're a programmer, you probably won't need this command much (although there are a few tips and tricks in Chapter 13 that use it). It displays a standard file directory dialog that allows you to choose the file or folder you'd like to get information about. If you select a folder (you must use the dialog's Get Info button because double-clicking opens the folder), you get the Folder Info window. If you select a file (double-clicking works here), you get the File Info window. These windows enable you to set various attributes of files and folders. For more information, see Chapter 22.

Verify

This command displays a standard file directory dialog to let you select a file to verify. The selected file will be scanned to make sure that its resource fork is valid. For more information, see "Resource Checking" earlier in this chapter. If you're having trouble opening a file with ResEdit, try using this command to make sure the file hasn't been corrupted. To have ResEdit automatically verify files as they're opened, see the discussion of the Preferences command that follows.

Page Setup

The Page Setup command allows you to set the standard page setup information. This is where you tell your printer what size paper you're using, among other things. As usual, the dialog you get depends on the printer you're using.

Print

This command displays a standard print dialog that varies with the printer you're using. Here's where you tell your printer how many copies you want, and so on.

Printing in ResEdit is not intended to give you a beautifully arranged picture of your resource suitable for framing. You simply get a convenient record of the information you can refer to later. At least that's the intent. In many cases ResEdit just prints a copy of what you see in the active window and adds a title that's the same as the title of the window being printed, along with a page number if you print multiple pages. In a few cases ResEdit takes a slightly more sophisticated approach. For instance, printing from the hexadecimal editor gives you a copy of the whole resource. Similarly, printing from pickers gives you a listing of all the resources or types displayed by the picker. Try printing from the pickers or editors you're interested in and see what you get.

ResEdit accomplishes most printing by creating a bitmap that represents the window—taking a snapshot—and sending it to the printer, so if you're using a high-resolution printer, you may occasionally have some problems associated with printing bitmaps. The problem stems from discrepancies between screen resolution (usually about 72 dots per inch) and the resolution at which most laser printers print (300 dots per inch). If you have unusual results, try selecting Precision Bitmap Alignment in the Page Setup dialog. If that doesn't help, just remember that even though you may have a few stray bits on your picture, at least you have a record of the information you need.

For fancy output with headers, footers, and variable margins, you can copy the information from ResEdit and paste it into your favorite word processing application. The easiest way to do this is to take a screen snapshot using Command-Shift-3. This produces a file called Picture 1 in your root directory that you can open in your paint program. Then you can touch up the screen shot, select what you want of it, and paste it into your document.

Preferences

The Preferences command displays a dialog, shown in Figure 3-14, that lets you customize several ResEdit characteristics.

The Window at startup item lets you decide whether you want ResEdit to display the standard file directory dialog when it starts up. If you would rather have it start up with no dialog, click the None button. The next item lets you turn off ResEdit's splash-screen.

Because modifying the active System file or the version of ResEdit you're currently running can be disastrous if you make a mistake,

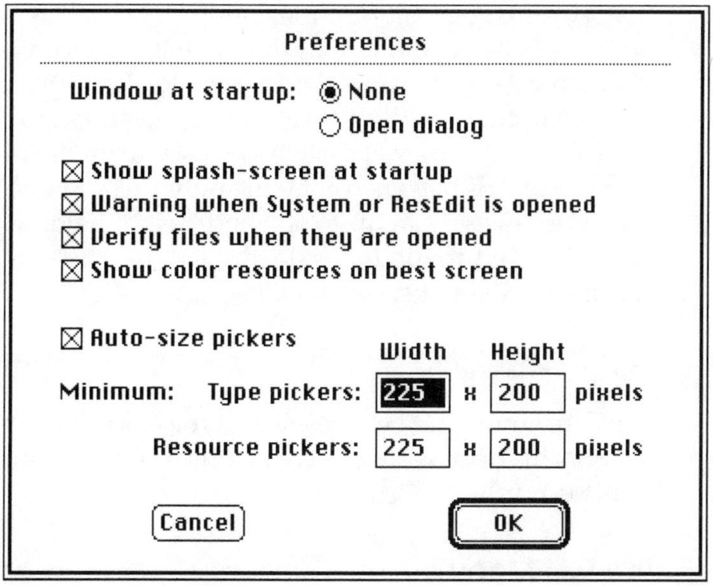

```
┌─────────────────────────────────────────────────────┐
│                      Preferences                      │
│ ....................................................  │
│  Window at startup:  ◉ None                           │
│                      ○ Open dialog                    │
│                                                       │
│  ☒ Show splash-screen at startup                      │
│  ☒ Warning when System or ResEdit is opened           │
│  ☒ Verify files when they are opened                  │
│  ☒ Show color resources on best screen                │
│                                                       │
│                            Width    Height            │
│  ☒ Auto-size pickers                                  │
│                                                       │
│  Minimum:   Type pickers:  [225] x [200]  pixels      │
│                                                       │
│           Resource pickers: [225] x [200]  pixels     │
│                                                       │
│   ( Cancel )                   (( OK ))                │
└─────────────────────────────────────────────────────┘
```

Figure 3-14. The Preferences dialog lets you adjust several ResEdit characteristics.

ResEdit displays a warning when you open either of these files. If you open these files frequently, and know for certain you won't mess them up, (such confidence!) you can turn off the warning. Simply click the check box in front of Warning when System or ResEdit is opened.

As you may remember from the "Resource Checking" section, ResEdit always performs a quick resource check when you open a file. If you want it to routinely carry out the more thorough check, simply click the check box in front of Verify files when they are opened. Selecting this option increases the length of time necessary to open files, but only slightly if they are on a hard disk. Opening files from floppy disks can take much longer, however, so if your files are on a floppy disk, you may not want to take advantage of this option.

The next item, Show color resources on best screen, is useful only for Mac owners with two monitors (in fact, the choice only shows up if you have more than one monitor). If it's checked, color pickers and editors automatically open on the screen capable of displaying the most colors or grays. If it's not checked, color pickers and editors always open on the same monitor as their parent window. This command applies only to those pickers and editors displaying resources that *require* color. Color-optional resources, such as 'MENU's, always open on the same monitor as their parent window.

When you check Auto-size pickers, ResEdit optimizes the size of picker windows, making them just large enough to show every item, or to show as much as possible, depending on the file and your screen size. For pickers containing only a few items, ResEdit uses the minimum sizes set in the Width and Height fields at the bottom of the dialog. If you turn off the Auto-size feature, these minimum sizes become the default sizes for all pickers.

Quit

The Quit command behaves like a typical Macintosh Quit command. It asks you if you want to save any files you have modified and then exits ResEdit.

The Edit Menu

The Edit menu, shown in Figure 3-15, behaves as you would expect it to behave in most Macintosh applications. An important point to keep in mind, however, is that the commands work differently depending on what kind of window is active. For example, if a type picker is active and a resource type is selected, Cut will cut all resources of that type. But if an editor is active, Cut applies only to selected resource components within the editor. Fortunately, because Cut, Copy, Paste, Clear, and Duplicate always work on a selection, it's always easy to tell what will be affected.

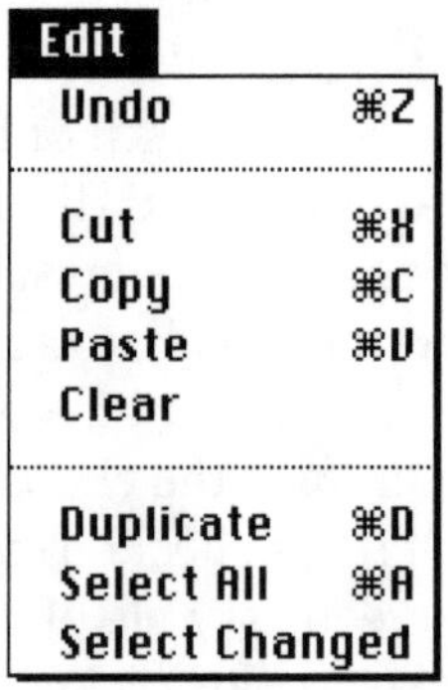

Edit	
Undo	⌘Z
Cut	⌘H
Copy	⌘C
Paste	⌘U
Clear	
Duplicate	⌘D
Select All	⌘A
Select Changed	

Figure 3-15. The Edit menu.

Undo

With few exceptions, the Undo command will undo the last editing command. There are a few cases in which Undo is not available and is dimmed in the menu. For example, you can't undo cutting and clearing in pickers. You can achieve the same result, however, with the Revert command on the Resource menu. Most of the special editors fully support Undo.

Cut and Copy

These commands put the current selection or a copy of it onto ResEdit's clipboard. If you cut or copy from a type picker, you'll get *all* the resources of the selected type(s). From a resource picker, you get only the resource(s) selected. If you don't want to replace the clipboard contents with a new selection, Option-Command-X and Option-Command-C append the selection to what's already on the clipboard. (Appending works with the menu commands, too; just be sure to press the Option key before you pull down the Edit menu.)

Paste

What happens with this command depends on what you're pasting and where. That sounds more iffy than it really is because, fortunately, what the Paste command does makes sense when you think about it. If you paste to a type picker, you'll get all the resources of any type from the clipboard. If you paste to a resource picker, you only get resources of the corresponding type. You can also paste certain resource components into editors. For instance, you can paste bits (which become 'PICT' resources when cut or copied) into any of the fatbits editors.

Clear

As in most of the Macintosh world, choosing Clear is the same as pressing the Delete key. Nothing goes to the clipboard and in many cases you can't undo it.

Duplicate

Duplicate is available from resource pickers and some editors. In resource pickers, this command makes a copy of each selected resource, but instead of sending them to the clipboard as Copy does, it gives the duplicates new ID numbers and puts them in the same window. In editors, the command makes a copy of the selected resource component and keeps it within the resource. For instance, you can duplicate a menu item in a 'MENU', or a pattern in a 'PAT#' pattern list.

Select All

When you know you want to select everything in a picker window, this is the command to choose. (It also works in a few editors.) If you want all but a few, choose Select All then deselect the ones you don't want by using Command-click.

Select Changed

The first time you close a file and ResEdit asks if you want to save, causing you to mistakenly exclaim, "But I didn't change anything!" you'll be glad you have this memory-jogging command. Available from picker windows, this command selects resources (in resource pickers) or types (in the type picker) you've altered since you last saved the file.

The Resource Menu

The Resource menu, shown in Figure 3-16, is ResEdit's most dynamic menu, but then resources are what ResEdit is all about. Although variable menu items may seem unsettling at first, they're intended to

```
Resource
  Create New Resource    ⌘K
  Open Resource Editor
  Open Using Template...
  Open Using Hex Editor
  ...........................
  Revert This Resource
  ...........................
  Get Resource Info       ⌘I
```

Figure 3-16. The Resource menu (as seen from a resource picker).

prevent confusion. ResEdit can perform such a variety of functions that generic commands would be almost meaningless. So, when necessary, menu items become more specific to let you know how they work in the current active window.

Create New Resource

What this command does in a resource picker is probably obvious—it creates a new resource of that type, gives it a unique ID, and opens it in the appropriate editor. In an editor, the command will either be dimmed, or it will allow you to create a new component to add to the resource you're editing. For example, in a pattern list ('PAT#') this command changes to Insert New Pattern. In templates it changes to Insert New Field.

From the type picker, this command displays the dialog shown in Figure 3-17, which lets you create any new resource type, whether or not that resource type already exists in the file. (Remember, this may not do you any good unless you can write some program code that uses the resource.) You can scroll through the list or you can enter the resource type in the editable field. ResEdit creates the new resource for you, gives it a unique ID, and opens it in the appropriate editor. ResEdit picks the first available number greater than or equal to 128 for the new resource ID. You can even create a completely new resource type by entering a unique four-character name. When ResEdit doesn't have a special editor for a resource type, it opens in the hexadecimal editor.

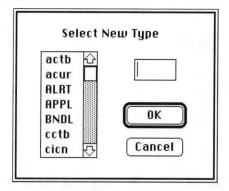

Figure 3-17. From the type picker, the Create New Resource command displays this dialog.

Open Resource Editor

When no resource type is selected in the type picker, this command is dimmed. As soon as you select a resource type, the item becomes available and the text changes to reflect your selection (Open 'MENU' Picker, Open 'ICON' Picker, and so on). If more than one type is selected, it becomes Open Pickers. The result of choosing this command remains the same—ResEdit opens the selected resource picker(s). Once you're in the resource picker, the command changes to Open Resource Editor. This item is also available from certain editors, where it will open an associated resource or a more detailed part of the same resource. For example, from the dialog ('DLOG') editor you can open the dialog item list ('DITL') editor, and from there you can open a dialog item. In short, this command (which is usually equivalent to double-clicking) gets you to the next deeper level, if there is one.

Open Using Template

This command, which is available from resource pickers and some editors, displays a dialog that allows you to choose a template from ResEdit's template list, which is shown in Figure 3-18. This dialog is similar to the one in Figure 3-17 for the Create New Resource command, except that the types list includes only template resources. Occasionally, you may want to open a resource as a template even if a

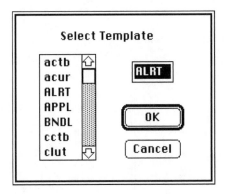

Figure 3-18. The Open Using Template command displays this dialog.

special editor exists, because sometimes you can edit infrequently changed parts in the template that you can't edit in the special editor. Option-Command-double-clicking a selection has the same result as choosing this command.

Open Using Hex Editor

The hexadecimal editor displays resources as a series of hexadecimal numbers. Programmers can open and edit any resource using the hexadecimal editor, but most users won't find it very helpful. This command is available from resource pickers and some editors. Option-double-clicking a selection has the same result as choosing this command.

Revert This Resource

If you've made a mistake and want to start over from the last saved version, choose this command. What this command affects depends on where you are when you invoke it, however. In resource pickers and editors, this item says Revert This Resource, or Revert These Resources, depending on how many resources you've selected. In the type picker this item changes to Revert <type> Resources, or Revert Resource Types if you've selected more than one type. Every change to all resources of the selected type(s) will be discarded. To revert more specifically, go to the resource picker, where you can revert individual resources.

Get Resource Info

Use this command, which is available from resource pickers and editors, to see or set a variety of resource characteristics. It displays the Resource Info window, shown in Figure 3-19, in which you can change ID numbers and names of resources. Generally, the rest of the fields, which are discussed in Chapter 22, are useful only to programmers.

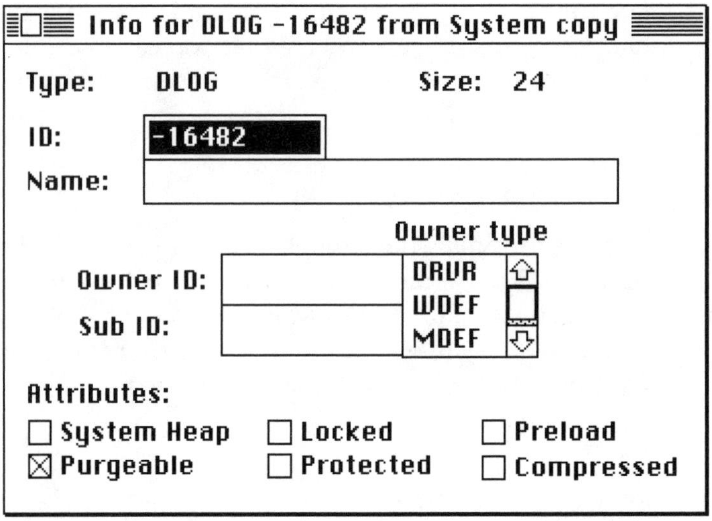

Figure 3-19. Unless you're a programmer, the Resource Info window is useful only for changing the names and IDs of resources.

The Window Menu

The Window menu can help you find your way around a screen plastered with lots of windows. It lists, in an organized way, all the windows you've got open, as in the example shown in Figure 3-20. Windows in the list are indented according to the order in which you opened them, with each subsequent window name appearing below and to the right of the name of the window from which you opened it. The most recently opened window in each category appears at the top. File and Folder Info windows are in a class by themselves and appear grouped at the top of the menu. A check mark designates the active window. Selecting a window name brings that window to the front, making it the active window. When you close a window, all the windows indented under it in the window menu (all the windows opened from it) also close.

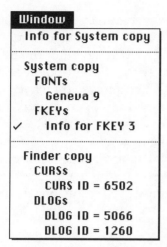

Figure 3-20. If you've got a lot of windows open, the Window menu can help you find the one you want.

The View Menu

The View menu, shown in Figure 3-21, lets you tell ResEdit how to display the contents of pickers. (The section on pickers earlier in this chapter describes much of this in more detail.) The View menu lets you display the contents of a type picker either by icon or by type. If you want to see resource sizes (in bytes), you can choose Show Size With Type.

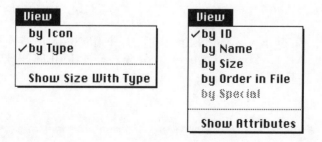

Figure 3-21. The View menu changes depending on whether the active window is a type picker (left) or a resource picker (right).

In resource pickers, the View menu lets you sort a list of resources by ID, Name, Size, or Order in File. You can also view some resource types in special pickers that give you more information. For instance, graphical pickers, such as those for icons or pointers, default to a graphical view (sorted by ID) that shows you what each of the resources looks like. The dimmed "by Special" item changes to the appropriate resource type, for instance, "by ICON." The last item on the resource pickers' View menu, the Show Attributes command, is available for any nonspecial view. Choosing this option tells ResEdit to display more detailed resource information that's generally useful only for programmers. (For more on resource attributes, see Chapter 22.)

Substituting Resource IDs

Now that you're familiar with ResEdit's windows and menus, you're ready to learn a simple procedure you'll use frequently. Often you'll want to substitute a custom resource for the original one. You can customize the original, of course, and doing that is often just fine. But the advantages of keeping the original are twofold: You have it for reference, and you can switch back to it if you need or want to. The more complicated the resource, the more important preserving the original becomes.

As you recall from the previous chapter, applications generally look for resources by type and ID. So if you want an application to use your custom resource, it has to have the right ID. Let's say you want to customize the Tweak menu in some application, and you want to keep the original version, too. Here's the easiest way to do it:

1. Open a copy of your application file with ResEdit, find the 'MENU' type in the type picker, and double-click it to open the 'MENU' resource picker.

Hint Remember a quick way to open any file is to drag and drop it on ResEdit's icon.

2. In the 'MENU' picker, find the Tweak menu, let's say it's ID 17, and duplicate it. (First select it, then choose Duplicate from the Edit menu.)

3. ResEdit makes a copy of the resource and, starting with 128, gives it the first available (unused) ID. Keep this one as your spare, and make your changes to ID 17.

4. To help you keep track of what you've done, and so you can find it later, why not label the spare? Simply click it, then choose Get Resource Info from the Resource menu. You'll see a dialog like the one you saw in Figure 3-19. Click in the name field and type "Original Tweak" or "Spare Tweak," or whatever makes sense to you. Similarly, you can label your custom Tweak menu. If the original resource had a name, you should preserve that name in your custom resource and rename the spare—just in case the application looks for resources by name instead of ID.

5. When you're through, close the file (saving your changes) and quit ResEdit. You can now try out your new menu in the application you changed.

If you want to switch back to the original Tweak menu and save your custom version, you'll have to shuffle both resource IDs around.

1. Open a copy of your application file with ResEdit, find the 'MENU' type in the type picker, and double-click it to open the 'MENU' resource picker.

2. In the 'MENU' picker, find your custom Tweak resource, ID 17, and select it.

3. Choose Get Resource Info from the Resource menu. Click the ID field and type in a number that hasn't been used, let's say 129. (ResEdit warns you if you pick a number that's taken.) Close the window.

4. Now select the original Tweak resource, ID 128, and once again choose Get Resource Info from the Resource menu. Click the ID Field and type 17. Remember, if the resource originally had a name, you should change it back, too.

5. Close the file (saving your changes) and quit ResEdit. Next time you use the application, you'll see the original Tweak menu.

The same steps apply no matter what resource type you're working with. Just be sure to remember what the original ID should be!

Summary

This chapter describes ResEdit's features and style of presenting information. ResEdit has three kinds of windows: pickers, editors, and info windows. You pick what you want to work on from pickers. There's one type picker per file, and one resource picker for every resource type in a file. You make your changes in the various editor windows. Info windows are specific dialogs that allow you to see or set a variety of file, folder, and resource characteristics. This chapter also provides a guide to ResEdit's menus. The menus are dynamic; ResEdit adds, changes, and removes options depending on what kind of window you're working in, so you'll understand how the commands apply in the given situation, and so you don't trip over menus or commands you don't need.

Now that you're familiar with ResEdit's features and instrument panel, you're ready for a test drive. In the next chapter we'll give you a few more rules of the road and describe how to safely cruise through changing familiar and vital files you'll probably return to frequently—the System and the Finder.

Chapter 4

 Editing the System, the Finder, and Other Files

Some of the most useful customization projects you can tackle involve resources found in important files, such as the System and the Finder, located in your System Folder. In fact, the System Folder and the Desktop database contain all the resources needed to initialize your Macintosh when you turn it on. Although the same rules apply to any application file, you must take special care when editing system files because a mistake can easily cripple your computer. With proper precautions, however, you can browse and modify to your heart's content. Table 4-1 lists selected System and Finder customization projects and the chapter that discusses the project. In this chapter we describe a few more basics for editing any kind of file; then we explain how the Macintosh uses the System and the Finder and how you can change them.

Table 4-1. Where to Find Some System and Finder Customization Projects

Chapter	Project
5	Changing your scroll bar pattern and permanently adding a desktop pattern to the Control Panel
6	Changing the animated watch pointer
7	Customizing icons in alert boxes
7	Replacing the Trash icon
9	Moving keyboard characters
10	Customizing the size of standard file directory dialogs
15	Speeding up your mouse response
15	Adding Command keys to Finder menus
17	Colorizing icons in alerts
18	Adding color to the user interface

Having a Rescue Disk

All Macintosh owners should take the precautions of maintaining backups and having a rescue disk. You should always have a floppy disk that you can use to start your Mac just in case disaster strikes. The easiest thing to do is to make sure you have a copy of the Disk Tools floppy disk that came with your Macintosh or your latest System software update. As you customize your System and Finder, you'll want to make backups of those files, to preserve your work.

Hint As you customize resources in the System and the Finder, why not save copies of your masterpieces in a special backup so that you can easily replace them when you update to a new System software release? Simply create a file with ResEdit, calling it something like "Custom System (or Finder) Resources." Then, whenever you customize a resource, paste a copy of it into your special file. After you update to new System software, you can copy your own resources into the new files.

Always Work on a Copy

When you first start to use ResEdit, and any time you're planning to make complicated changes, always make a copy of the file you're going to edit. ResEdit is a powerful program that has no limitations on the kinds of modifications you can make to resources. This power gives you the flexibility to change anything you want, but it also means you can destroy valuable data with the slip of a finger. Even though ResEdit can revert your file to the saved version, this only works if you catch your error soon enough. Mistakes using ResEdit can cause problems in a variety of ways. The most obvious mistake is to delete an important resource that the System or an application needs. Many more subtle problems stem from unforeseeable side effects of changes, due to complex interactions between resources and applications.

Hint Before you use ResEdit to open a file, use the Finder's Duplicate command to make a copy. You can also Option-drag the file to another folder or the desktop. For most files the methods are equivalent, but not for the System and the Finder. Here's the scoop. The Locked bit is set for the System and Finder, which makes their names unchangeable. If you use the Duplicate command, the name is not locked in the copy. (Obviously, the name must change for the Finder to be able to affix "copy" to the end). If you use Option-drag, the name remains unchangeable. By the way, there's nothing mysterious about the Locked bit—you can get to it using ResEdit's File Info window. (A tip in Chapter 13 tells you how.)

No matter which route you take, keep a spare copy of the file until you're sure your changes are working correctly and you want to keep them.

As you become more familiar with using ResEdit, you'll learn when you don't absolutely have to make a copy before editing. For example, if you're just going to change the location of a dialog box, you might decide not to work on a copy since you wouldn't be making any irreparable changes. Remember, you should always have a backup copy so you can restore the original contents of the resource if you decide you want to change back. Once you've tested your changes for a while and you're positive you like them and will never need the original resources, you should back up your customized file.

Until you have some experience using ResEdit, play it safe and work only on a copy.

Hint Avoid making dozens of changes at once. If a change turns out to be unstable, tracking down the culprit is easier to do when there are fewer changes. For the same reason, alter only one application at a time. That's especially true with the System and the Finder. If you alter them both and your changes turn out to be incompatible, you're much worse off than if you knew you had a stable situation before altering one or the other.

The System File

The System file is the brain, heart, and soul of your Macintosh. Without this file, the Mac won't even start. It contains part of the operating system (the rest is in ROM), keyboard layouts, pointers, icons, patterns, and many other resources you normally think of as integral parts of your Macintosh's personality. Many resources found here, such as the wristwatch pointer and the scroll bar definition, are provided for applications to use. Because the System file contains so many important resources, you'll find many of the most interesting resources to customize here. As you can surmise from Table 4-1, you'll find resources that control a variety of aspects of your Macintosh's appearance and behavior.

Your Mac needs this vital file to function, so you should be especially careful when making changes. It can mean the difference between a bootable or an unbootable Macintosh. *Always* work on a copy, keeping the original as a backup in case something goes wrong with the version you're using. You may remember that the System file is one of the two files that ResEdit can open even though it's already open. (Of course, the System file is open any time your Mac is on.) Although ResEdit will let you edit the active System file, *don't do it*.

The System file warrants special consideration, but don't be afraid to play with it just because it's an important file or you'll miss out on some of the most enjoyable and useful ways you can customize your Mac.

By The Way You may remember that under System 6 you could edit the active System file directly if you were careful. There were times when the risk was worth the convenience because you could try out your changes immediately without having to drag files around and restart. As soon as you saved the System file in ResEdit, your changes took effect. Of course it was much riskier because your changes might create conflicting demands on your Mac, causing it to freeze up in confusion.

Those days are gone. Under System 7.1 editing the active System is even riskier. The resource manager was changed to support resource overrides, in which several files act like one. This makes system enablers and the Fonts Folder possible without affecting the way applications look for resources in the

System Folder. While that's all very nice, it creates problems for resource editing applications like ResEdit. For instance, the active System file appears to contain resources that actually belong to other files. Changes can damage these files, the System file, and the way they work together—with unpredictable but depressing results. In short, the convenience is no longer worth the risk.
Never edit the active System file.

Editing the System File

Since the System file is indispensable, you must make a copy before making changes. Never edit your active System file! Follow these steps to modify your System file.

1. Use Option-drag to make a copy of the System file. You can drag it out onto the desktop, or you can drag it to a folder.

2. Use ResEdit to modify the System copy, not the active System.

3. When you're done making your changes, save the file and quit from ResEdit.

4. Drag your original System file out of the System Folder and onto the desktop or into a folder named "Original System," depending on where you Option-dragged the copy you modified. (You can't have two files with the same name on the desktop.)

5. Drag your modified System into your System Folder.

6. Restart your Mac to activate your new System file.

7. If everything works as you planned, you can throw your original System file into the Trash. Better yet, hold on to it for a backup just in case your changes misbehave in the future.

There's another variation. You can use the Finder's Duplicate command instead of Option-drag. If you do, you still have to swap files and restart, but there's an extra renaming step and the System file you end up with will not have the Locked bit set. Of course you can set it in ResEdit's File Info window, but that's yet another step. (Steps 2, 3, 6, and 7 are the same as in the first method.)

1. Use the Finder's Duplicate command to make a copy of the System file. You can leave it in your System Folder.

2. Use ResEdit to modify the System copy, not the active System.

3. When you're done making your changes, save the file and quit from ResEdit.

4. Drag your original System file out of the System Folder and onto the desktop (or into a folder named "Original System" or whatever makes sense to you).

5. Rename your System copy file "System."

Hint Pay attention when you rename your System file! Be sure you don't leave any extra spaces in the name when you rename "System copy" to "System." If there are any spaces, it's misspelled and your Mac will have trouble finding the file—and starting up.

6. Restart your Mac to activate your new System file.

7. If everything works as planned, you can throw your original System file into the Trash. Better yet, hold on to it for a backup just in case your changes misbehave in the future.

8. If you want to lock the System's name again, start ResEdit and choose Get File/Folder Info from the File menu. Select your System file in the dialog that appears and click the Get Info button. In the info window that appears, click the Locked box in the upper right. Close the window and save.

Hint Some people are under the impression that you can't have two System files on the same disk. They'll tell you to put your inactive, backup System file on another volume altogether, to avoid confusing your Mac. The goal is noble—a confused Mac is usually a painful sight—but your Macintosh isn't that dumb. The thing to avoid is multiple System Folders, and there's more to it than the name. The only place you should ever have both a Finder and a System in the same folder is in your one-and-only active System Folder. Don't store backup Finders and Systems in the same folder.

The Finder

When you're not using any other application, you'll always find
yourself using the Finder, the application that manages your desktop.
It helps you use your Mac by providing such things as folders and
desktop icons, and housekeeping services such as emptying the
Trash, copying or renaming files, and restarting your computer.
Although substitute applications have been developed to replace the
Finder, in this book we assume you're using the Apple Finder that
came with your system software. You can customize many aspects of
the Finder and one of the features of System 7 is that personalizing
the Finder became easier. Still, there are some changes you just can't
make without ResEdit.

Under System 6 you could turn off MultiFinder, and when you
launched ResEdit your current Finder would no longer be active.
That was handy for minor tweaks, but it's not possible any longer.
Under System 7, MultiFinder is always running, and under
MultiFinder, the Finder is always running. Remember that, with the
exceptions of itself and the System file, ResEdit can't open files that
are already open. So, you can't edit the active Finder, which shouldn't
upset you because you should work only on copies anyway.

Editing the Finder

Since the Finder is an indispensable system application, and because
it's always running , you must make a copy before making changes.
Follow these steps to modify your Finder.

1. Use Option-drag to make a copy of the Finder. You can drag it
    out onto the desktop, or you can drag it to a folder.

2. Use ResEdit to modify the Finder copy.

3. When you're done making your changes, save the file and quit
    from ResEdit.

4. Drag your original Finder out of the System Folder and onto the
    desktop (or into a folder named "Original Finder," depending
    on where you Option-dragged the copy you modified. (You
    can't have two files with the same name on the desktop.)

5. Drag your modified Finder into your System Folder.

6. Now press Command-Option-Escape and click Force Quit in the dialog that appears. This causes the active Finder to quit, and when it relaunches, your modified version becomes active. (You can also restart your Mac to activate your new Finder, but that takes longer.)

7. If everything works as planned, you can throw your original Finder into the Trash. Better yet, hold on to it for a backup just in case your changes misbehave in the future.

As with the System file, there's another variation. You can use the Finder's Duplicate command instead of Option-drag. If you do, you still have to swap files and restart, but there's an extra renaming step and the Finder you end up with will not have the Locked bit set. Of course you can set it in ResEdit's File Info window, but that's yet another step. (Steps 2, 3, 6, and 7 are the same as in the first method.)

1. Use the Finder's Duplicate command to make a copy of the Finder itself. You can leave it in your System Folder.

2. Use ResEdit to modify the Finder copy.

3. When you're done making your changes, save the file and quit from ResEdit.

4. Drag your original Finder out of the System Folder and onto the desktop (or into a folder named "Original Finder" or whatever makes sense to you).

5. Rename your Finder copy "Finder."

Hint Pay attention when you rename your Finder file! Be sure you don't leave any extra spaces in the name when you rename "Finder copy" to "Finder." If there are any spaces, it's misspelled and your Mac will have trouble finding the file—and starting up.

6. Now press Command-Option-Escape and click Force Quit in the dialog that appears. This causes the active Finder to quit, and when it relaunches, your modified version becomes active. (You can also restart your Mac to activate your new Finder, but that takes longer.)

7. If everything works as planned, you can throw your original Finder into the Trash. Better yet, hold on to it for a backup just in case your changes misbehave in the future.

8. If you want to lock the Finder's name again, Start ResEdit and choose Get File/Folder Info from the File menu. Select your Finder in the dialog that appears and click the Get Info button. In the info window that appears, click the Locked box in the upper right. Close the window and save.

Updating the Desktop Database

System 7 did away with the Desktop file, replacing it with a Desktop database that's considerably faster, especially on large volumes storing lots of applications (and therefore lots of icons). The Finder uses the Desktop database (actually it's two files, Desktop DB and Desktop DF) to store information about which kinds of documents belong to which applications. When you double-click a document, the Finder looks in the Desktop database to determine which application to launch. The Desktop database contains the desktop icons for any application that has ever been on the volume, as well as the icons for each application's documents. Each mountable volume (such as a floppy disk, a hard disk, or a server volume, if you're connected to a network) has its own Desktop database that stores information about applications and files it has encountered. You haven't seen these files lying about anywhere because the Finder makes them invisible. They're also the only system files (files necessary for startup) not stored in the System Folder. Instead, they're located at the "root," or top level (not in any folder) on each volume. You can see them from within ResEdit, but you can't change them.

Just about the only time you'll have to think about the Desktop database is if you fiddle with Finder icons, discussed in Chapters 7 and 17. When you edit an application's icons, you do that in the application file itself and then update the Desktop database. The Macintosh User's Guide recommends that you rebuild your desktop once a month or so. However, when you update your Desktop file, you lose any comments you've entered into the Finder's Get Info windows. If you only store short comments (one or two lines), try putting them in 'vers' resources instead of the Finder's Get Info windows. These resources survive when the Finder rebuilds the

Desktop database. For more information, see "Adding Version Information to Documents" in Chapter 13.

Here's how to get the Finder to rebuild a disk's Desktop database for you:

1. Hold down the Command and Option keys when you restart your Macintosh (or when you insert a floppy disk). Keep pressing the keys until you see a dialog asking if you really want to rebuild your desktop. Click OK. That's it.

Summary

This chapter describes a few precautions to take before editing files, and discusses two of the most important files stored in your Macintosh—the System and the Finder. Some of the most enjoyable and productive customization projects you can undertake involve resources in the System and the Finder. We discuss rescue disks, and remind you to always work on copies of files you edit. The System file is the brain, heart, and soul of your Mac, so you should be especially careful when editing System resources. Editing the Finder, another vital file, is similar. The Desktop database is important to the Finder, and we describe how to update it.

Customizing
Your Macintosh

Chapter 5

 Playing with Patterns

Without patterns, the Macintosh wouldn't be the Macintosh. They're everywhere. The desktop and scroll bars are filled with patterns. In some cases tones—such as the white, black, dark gray, gray, and light gray that are always available to any application on the Mac—are also generated using patterns. Then, of course, there are all the designs and pattern possibilities available in paint and draw programs.

Patterns, along with other graphical resources such as icons, fonts, and mouse pointers, are some of the most fun and rewarding resources to customize. You edit these graphical resources in fatbits, and ResEdit provides more than ten fatbits editors. These editors have so much in common that once you know how to use one fatbits editor, you'll have a good grasp of all of them. (We'll cover specific features unique to the color fatbits editors in the color section.) This chapter introduces the fatbits editors in general, then tells you about pattern resources and what you can do with them.

Using the Fatbits Editors

Figure 5-1 shows two representative editors, the 'ICON' editor and the 'PAT ' editor. Fatbits editors always give you at least two views of the resource you're editing—an enlarged fatbits editing view, and one or more actual-size views. A tool palette runs along the left side of the window. In addition, editors that work on list resources (such as the

71

patterns in a 'PAT#' resource or the small icons in an 'SICN' resource) supply a scrolling selection panel so you can select the item you want to work on from the list. A dark outline around the list tells you when the list is active so you know when the Edit menu commands apply to the list instead of to the fatbits editing area. Fatbits editors also add the Transform menu to the menu bar. We discuss these features in more detail in the following sections, but first let's clarify a few details about how copying, cutting, and pasting work in fatbits editors.

Copying, cutting, and pasting fatbits resources will work without a hitch if you're clear about the difference between copying resources and copying selections of bits from resources. When you choose Copy from an editor or picker, the selected resource is copied to the clip-board *as a resource* of a certain type. You can paste that resource into a type picker, or a matching resource picker, but you can't paste it into another resource. On the other hand, if you have fatbits selected in an editor when you choose Copy, your selection goes to the clipboard *as bits*. ResEdit handles a selection of bits as a 'PICT' resource, just as paint programs do. You can paste those bits into any fatbits editor or into a paint program document. So, although you can't paste an 'ICON' into an 'ICN#', for example, you can paste the bits from an 'ICON' into an 'ICN#'. You can find the tools you need in the tool palette.

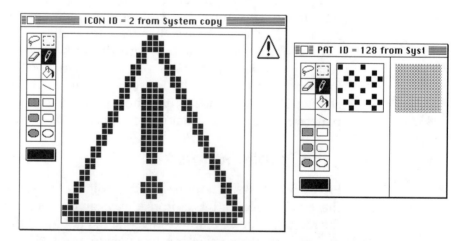

Figure 5-1. These representative examples illustrate some common features of the fatbits editors: an enlarged fatbits editing view, at least one actual-size view, and a tool palette.

The Tool Palette

Most of the standard tools in the palette probably look familiar to you. The top two, the lasso and selection rectangle, are for selecting irregularly shaped and rectangular sections of bits, respectively. The eraser comes in handy for getting rid of lots of black bits, while the pencil lets you click black bits white or white bits black in a more precise fashion. The paint bucket pours black or white bits, or a selected pattern, into an enclosed area. The gray-filled shapes tools work the same as the empty shapes tools, except that the shapes you draw will be filled with the selected pattern.

Hint The tool palette has some built-in shortcuts that may already be familiar to you from paint and draw programs.

- Double-clicking the rectangle selection tool gives the same result as Select All on the Edit menu—the entire editing area becomes selected.
- Double-clicking the eraser clears the entire view.
- Pressing the Shift key constrains several of the tools. For example, the rectangle tools draw only squares when you press the Shift key. Similarly, you can constrain ovals to circles, and lines to 45- or 90-degree angles. The eraser's action is constrained to a straight line. (*Wanting* to constrain the paint bucket or lasso makes no sense.)

The Pattern Palette

The swatch under the tool palette tells you what color (black or white, except for color editors) or pattern the filled shapes and paint bucket tools will use. To change the pattern setting, click the swatch and the pattern palette pops up, as shown in Figure 5-2. Simply drag the mouse pointer to the pattern you want to use, and then release the mouse button. The swatch under the tool palette reflects your choice. You can also "tear off" the pattern palette and move it to any convenient spot on the screen. Just click the palette's close box when you're through.

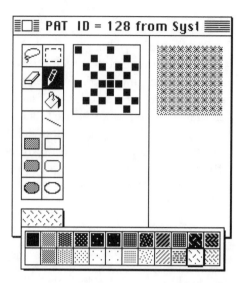

Figure 5-2. Pull down the swatch under the tool palette to select a pattern from the tear-off pattern palette.

> **By The Way** ResEdit lets you add or change patterns in the pattern palette. Simply open a copy of ResEdit and open its 'PAT#' type, where you see all the patterns in the palette. By the end of this chapter you'll know how to edit this resource type. If you significantly customize the patterns, you might want to consider copying the 'PAT#' resource to the ResEdit Preferences file in your System folder. That way you won't lose all your work when you update to a new version of ResEdit.

The Transform and PAT or PAT# Menus

To give you more ways to manipulate the bits and images you're working with, the fatbits editors add the Transform menu, shown in Figure 5-3, to the menu bar.

The Flip, Rotate, and Nudge commands all work on selections, so they're dimmed until you've selected something for them to work on. Flip Horizontal flips the selection so that what was on the right appears on the left and vice versa. (The flip axis is vertical, but the

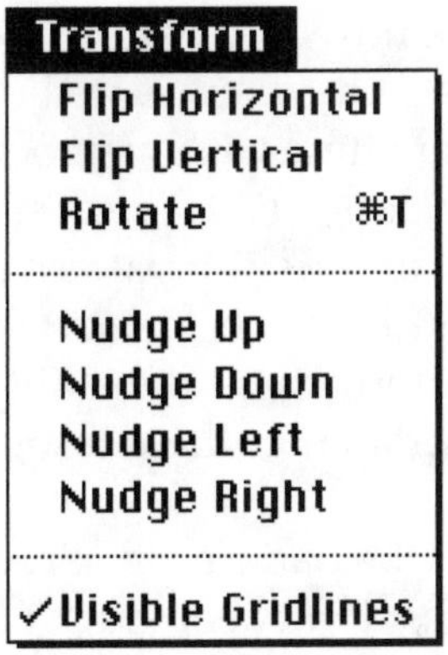

```
┌─────────────────────┐
│ Transform           │
├─────────────────────┤
│ Flip Horizontal     │
│ Flip Vertical       │
│ Rotate        ⌘T    │
│ ·················   │
│ Nudge Up            │
│ Nudge Down          │
│ Nudge Left          │
│ Nudge Right         │
│ ·················   │
│ ✓Visible Gridlines  │
└─────────────────────┘
```

Figure 5-3. The commands on the Transform menu help you manipulate selections in a fatbits editor's window.

fatbits move horizontally.) Flip Vertical flips bits from top to bottom and vice versa. Rotate moves the selection counterclockwise. You can always move a selection by dragging it with the hand pointer, but the Nudge commands offer finer shifts. They move the selection by one bit in the chosen direction. The arrow keys do the same thing.

When you have the Visible Gridlines option turned on (indicated by the presence of a check mark), each bit is outlined by a tiny strip of white space. This white grid lets you see exactly where the bits are so you can position the editing tools more easily.

ResEdit adds one other very simple menu, PAT or PAT#, depending on which editor you're in. This menu has one item, Try Pattern, a toggle which temporarily substitutes the pattern you're editing for the desktop pattern so you can see more of it.

That's all you need to know about the fatbits editors. Now you're ready to edit patterns.

Pattern Resources

A *pattern* is an 8-by-8-bit image used to define a repeating design (such as stripes or plaid) or tone (such as gray). They can draw lines or fill areas. When the Mac draws patterns, it aligns them so that adjacent areas of the same pattern blend into a single continuous pattern with no seams. (If only wallpaper worked as well!)

There are two kinds of black-and-white pattern resources. In the 'PAT ' type each resource is a pattern, whereas in the 'PAT#' type each resource is a list or collection of patterns. (Remember that resource types are always four characters long. 'PAT ' has a space at the end.) 'PAT#' resources come in handy for offering pattern options and flexibility to users. Applications generally use 'PAT ' resources to store only a few consistently used patterns when flexibility is not a concern. We discuss the color versions of these resources, 'ppat' and 'ppt#', in Chapter 18.

How do applications keep all the patterns in a 'PAT#' resource straight? Remember, applications don't keep track of individual patterns—that would defeat the purpose of using a resource. Instead, they keep track of position in the list. If you rearrange patterns or add new ones, you alter the order of the patterns, so it's a good idea to add new patterns to the end of a 'PAT#' list.

'PAT ' Resources

As you would expect, opening the 'PAT ' type from the type picker opens the 'PAT ' resource picker, shown in Figure 5-4. Simply double-clicking the pattern you want to alter opens the 'PAT ' editor, which you've already seen in Figures 5-1 and 5-2. The 8-by-8-bit editing field sits beside a sample field that shows you the results of your changes.

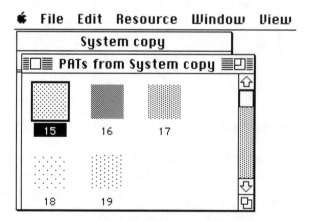

Figure 5-4. The 'PAT ' resource picker.

If you browse through your applications using ResEdit, you may
not find many 'PAT ' resources. Most programs that use patterns use
'PAT#' resources so that they can offer users flexibility. One way the
System uses a 'PAT ' resource is to fill scroll bars. (In Figure 5-4 compare ID 17 to the scroll bar.) Of course with ResEdit, you can change
them. We'll show you how later in the chapter.

> **By The Way** On Classics, SEs, and other 68000 machines, the
> System stores the current desktop pattern in 'PAT ' ID 16.

'PAT#' Resources

If you open a copy of your System file with ResEdit and open the
'PAT#' resource, you'll see a window that looks something like Figure
5-5. This is the 'PAT#' picker, but in this case there's only one 'PAT#'
resource, one pattern list, to pick. Some paint programs may have
more than one, so the window would look somewhat different, as
shown in Figure 5-6.

You can enlarge the window or click the zoom box to show more of
the patterns, but 'PAT#' resources can be so long that you may not be
able to see the whole list unless you have a large screen. That's OK,
because you can browse through all the patterns in the 'PAT#' editor.

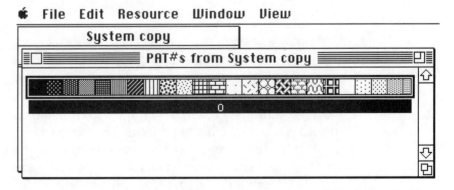

**Figure 5-5. The System file has only one 'PAT#' resource, but it
contains dozens of patterns.**

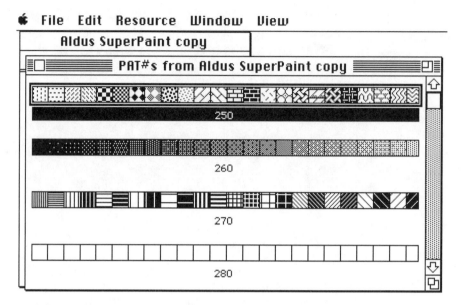

Figure 5-6. Some paint programs have more than one 'PAT#'
resource.

Hint As you work on patterns in the 'PAT#' editor, remember that
Revert applies to the whole resource—the whole list of patterns—
not just the pattern you're currently working on. If you're planning
a multipattern editing session, saving after changing each pattern
would be a good idea.

To open the 'PAT#' editor, double-click the patterns list, or select
Open Resource Editor from the Resource menu. The editor always
opens on the first, or leftmost, pattern, so it doesn't matter where on
the list you double-click. This editor, shown in Figure 5-7, is similar to
the 'PAT ' editor, except that it also has a scrollable panel on the right
to help you scan the list of patterns. The pattern that's first, or leftmost, in the resource picker becomes the topmost pattern in the
scrollable list. The selected pattern has an outline around it. If you
want to select another pattern, simply scroll to it, click it, and it will
fill the editing field.

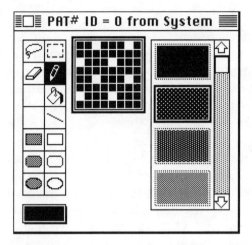

Figure 5-7. The 'PAT#' editor.

Hint You can select more than one pattern in the list for copying, cutting, or deleting (but not for editing, obviously). Also, you can move a pattern in the list simply by dragging it around in the scrollable selection panel. Of course, if you do this you'll rearrange the order of the list, which could create surprises later, depending on the application.

In addition to editing existing patterns, you can create entirely new ones. Simply scroll to the bottom of the pattern list, select the last pattern, and choose Insert New Pattern from the Resource menu. You can insert a new pattern anywhere you want to, but you might change something like the About the Finder box (and who knows what else) if you add to the first part of the list. If you want to keep both the original and modified versions of a pattern, copy the original pattern, paste it at the end of the list, then modify. The next section gives more details about working with patterns.

Copying and Pasting Patterns

Maybe you found a nifty pattern in HyperCard or somewhere else that you'd like to add to your paint program or spread across your desktop. Or perhaps you stumbled across an interesting visual effect in your paint program by airbrushing a pattern or overlapping two patterns—in effect creating a new pattern without going to a pattern editor. Although paint programs may offer you the option of creating or editing patterns, in some cases the custom pattern stays with the document. Even if you can create new default patterns, copying a pattern from another application may not work. With ResEdit you can copy patterns within and between applications, and preserve swatches of new patterns as resources.

ResEdit allows a great deal of flexibility for moving patterns around in files. Normally, if you want to copy one fatbits resource image into another fatbits resource type, you have to select and copy the bits. With pattern resources, ResEdit makes an exception. You can copy a pattern from a 'PAT ' picker into the scrollable selection panel in the 'PAT#' editor. Picking up a swatch of a pattern from a paint program is easy, too. Just use a selection tool to grab a chunk of the desired pattern and copy it. Keep in mind that you're pasting it into an area only 8-by-8-bits square. If you paste a selection larger than 8 by 8, you can slide it around in the editor to position it. Once you deselect it, it's trimmed to 8 by 8.

Pasting and positioning patterns can be slightly trickier, but fortunately these operations work basically the same in both of ResEdit's pattern editors.

1. Once you've copied the pattern you're interested in, use ResEdit to open the appropriate pattern resource in the application to which you want to add it.

2. If you're pasting bits, you have to create a new, blank pattern in which to paste them. To do this, choose from the Resource menu either Create New Resource (from the 'PAT ' picker) or Insert New Pattern (from the 'PAT#' editor). If you fail to first insert a new pattern and click in the empty editing window, the bits will end up pasted into the currently selected pattern.

3. Choose Paste from the Edit menu. If you copied bits, the pattern you copied will appear in the editing field surrounded by a selection marquee. (The marquee may be hidden if the pasted selection is larger than 8 by 8 bits, but the mouse pointer will be the grabber hand.) As long as the marquee or hand pointer is present, you can slide the pattern about in the editing field using the mouse, the Nudge commands, or the arrow keys.

Hint You can create brand-new patterns just by repositioning patterns and selections in the editors. Because patterns repeat, almost any change can make a pattern look different.

As you're playing with patterns, remember that any time you'd like to see your new creation spread over your desktop (temporarily), all you have to do is choose Try Pattern from the PAT or PAT# menus.

Changing Your Scroll Bar Pattern

Follow these steps to change the pattern in your scroll bar to something like that shown in Figure 5-8, or any other pattern you like.

Hint If you make your scroll bar black or mostly black, you won't be able to see the scroll box outline moving along with your pointer during repositioning. If you don't miss that feedback and really want a dark scroll bar, go ahead.

1. Open a copy of your System file with ResEdit and open the 'PAT ' resource type. If you think you might want to return to the original scroll bar pattern, duplicate resource ID 17 first. (Choose Duplicate from the Edit menu.)

2. Double-click pattern ID 17 to open the 'PAT ' editor.

3. Arrange and rearrange the bits to your heart's content.

4. When you're satisfied with your results, save your changes and quit ResEdit.

5. Now, simply reinstall the copy of your System file. (If you need a refresher, see Chapter 4.)

After you restart, you should see your new scroll bars. Try moving the scroll box and clicking the up and down arrows. Remember that scroll bars also work horizontally. If your eyes cross or your stomach turns when the scroll box moves over your new pattern, you can just repeat these steps to edit and test the pattern until you're pleased with your results.

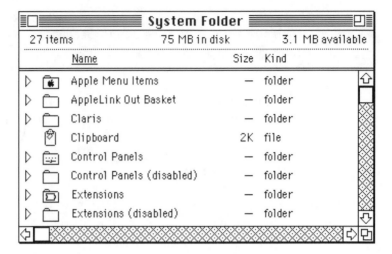

Figure 5-8. Your scroll bar can have any pattern you like.

Adding a Desktop Pattern

Not everybody uses the variety of desktop patterns available from the General Controls Control Panel. If you always keep the same desktop pattern, you might want to skip this part. This task is for those people who not only like to switch among the desktop patterns provided, but who also long to permanently add custom patterns.

Have you ever created a desktop pattern that you wanted to keep but didn't necessarily want to look at all the time? Maybe you have festive seasonal desktop patterns, like those shown in Figure 5-9, that you don't want to have to recreate every year before the holidays. Under System 6, as soon as you switched from your custom pattern, it was lost. Under System 7, you can add a pattern by double-clicking the miniature desktop in the General Controls Control Panel, but that doesn't seem to work on all machines. Besides, ResEdit offers much better editing tools anyway.

Now, before you can plunge in, you have to figure out which pattern resource type your Mac uses for desktop patterns. Classics, SEs, PowerBook 100s, and other machines that have a 68000 micro-processor (which can't use Color QuickDraw) use the strictly black-and-white 'PAT#' resource you saw in Figure 5-5. On most other machines, System 7 presents you with a smaller range of choices from a 'ppt#' resource, which includes both color and black-and-white versions of every pattern. In Chapter 18 we describe the 'ppt#' editor and how to add that sort of desktop pattern.

Here's how to add patterns to the 'PAT#' resource your Mac uses for drawing the desktop.

1. Open a copy of your System file with ResEdit and open the 'PAT#' resource.

2. Double-click anywhere on the patterns list (the bar of patterns) in the 'PAT#' picker to open the 'PAT#' editor.

3. Scroll to the end of the patterns list, and choose Insert New Pattern from the Resource menu.

4. Now you're ready to create a new pattern by clicking fatbits or to paste in a pattern copied from somewhere else. Remember that dragging a selection can create new patterns and visual effects. And don't forget about the Try Pattern command on the PAT# menu.

5. Once you're satisfied with your results, just reinstall the copy of your System file.

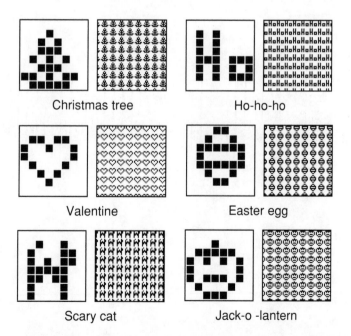

Christmas tree

Ho-ho-ho

Valentine

Easter egg

Scary cat

Jack-o-lantern

Figure 5-9. You don't have to recreate your festive seasonal desktop patterns every year.

Summary

This chapter introduces ResEdit's fatbits editors and describes their common features. They always give you at least two views of the resource: an enlarged, fatbits editing view and at least one actual-size view. They have a tool palette and a tear-off pattern palette. The commands on the Transform menu, which these editors add to the menu bar, are also explained. Then we discuss the two types of pattern resources, 'PAT ' and 'PAT#', and their editors. We describe how to change your scroll bar pattern and how to permanently add desktop patterns to your Control Panel.

Chapter 6

 Personalized Pointers

The mouse is so integral to the Macintosh user interface that you probably don't think that much about it anymore. Just point and click, or click and drag. No big deal, right? Right! But as with so much about the Mac, you can customize aspects of the mouse user interface.

The small icon that indicates the mouse position is called the *pointer*. People often call it a cursor and, in fact, pointers are stored in 'CURS' resources. Pointers come in many different shapes but only one size, 16 by 16 bits. You can find them in applications, the System file, and the ROM. You can't modify the most common pointer, the arrow, because it's in the ROM. But you can modify three other common pointers—the wristwatch, I-beam, and crosshairs—because they're in the System file. You've no doubt encountered a variety of pointers in various Macintosh applications, so the examples in Table 6-1 probably look familiar.

As with many other types of resources, you have to keep a few things in mind when you set out to change a pointer. Not all applications use standard resources. Some (such as MacPaint) have their own copies of the pointers stored in the application. Others (such as Microsoft Word) don't use resources for their pointers. Still, you can modify most pointers you encounter.

Table 6-1. Some Macintosh Pointers

Pointer	Use
▶	The arrow is the standard pointer.
I	The I-beam is used with text.
✍	The hand is used to move things.
?	The question mark indicates that a help mode is active.
⌚ ✹	Some pointers indicate that an application is busy.
+ ✎ ◨ ◗	Graphics applications use a wide range of pointers.
☺ ⬚ ✖	Other pointers can be substituted just for fun.

By The Way If you look in HyperCard 2.1, you'll notice that there's a 'CURS' resource for the hand pointer. However, HyperCard doesn't use this for its hand pointer. The hand is actually stored in a font resource (an 'NFNT'). So, to modify HyperCard's hand pointer, you actually need to modify ASCII character number 152 (ò) in HyperCard's font resource. For more details, see Chapter 13.

The 'CURS' Editor

The 'CURS' editor is one of ResEdit's fatbits editors. (Even if you don't want to play with patterns, flip to the first part of Chapter 5—if you haven't already done so—for an introduction to the fatbits editors.) When you open a 'CURS' resource you see a window like the one shown in Figure 6-1.

This editor is a little more complex than the pattern editors because a 'CURS' resource includes three parts—the pointer, the mask, and the hot spot. Each of these is a separate, editable entity. The fatbits view can display either the pointer itself or the shadowlike *mask* that

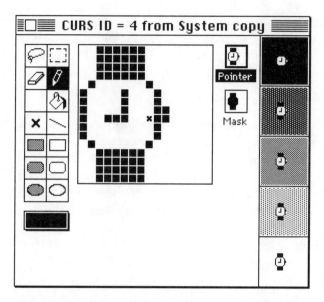

Figure 6-1. The 'CURS' editor.

determines how the pointer looks on various backgrounds. Immediately to the right of the editing area you see actual-size views of the pointer and the mask. Just click the one you want to edit. The dark outline and inverted name indicate which one is displayed in the fatbits view. To create a mask, simply drag the pointer view down onto the mask view. ResEdit makes a copy of the pointer and fills in all the enclosed areas. In most cases, this default mask will meet your needs. In any case, it's a good mask to start from. Along the right side of the window the pointer appears on different backgrounds, to give you an idea of how it will look in various situations.

The fatbit marked with an X shows the hot spot. The *hot spot* embodies the whole purpose of a pointer—it's the bit that positions the results of the pointer's actions. It's where the pointer truly points. You position the hot spot by using the hot spot tool (the X-shaped tool on the tool palette) to click the bit you want to set as the hot spot.

The 'CURS' menu, which appears when the 'CURS' editor opens, has only one command on it. Try Pointer lets you test drive the pointer you're working on. ResEdit substitutes your pointer for the arrow it normally uses so you get to see how it feels and looks moving over various backgrounds. You can even edit your pointer during your test drive. When it's over the fatbits view, the pointer turns into the selected tool, as you would expect. But when you move the pointer outside the editing area, you can see the results of your changes. You can switch back to the normal arrow pointer by choosing Try Pointer again or by closing the editor window.

Mask Hints

The mask determines how the pointer looks as it passes over nonwhite backgrounds on the screen. The only parts of the background affected are those where either the pointer or the mask contains black bits. That's why a pointer without a mask can look transparent; the background hasn't been masked, so it shows through. You can obtain interesting effects by altering the mask, but usually you'll want the mask to be the filled-in copy of the pointer that ResEdit automatically makes for you when you drag the pointer down onto the mask.

If you're careful, you can creatively modify the mask to improve a pointer's usefulness and visibility on various backgrounds. For example, if you make the mask one bit bigger than the pointer in all dimensions, the pointer will always have one bit of white around it. This white halo makes the pointer stand out much better against most backgrounds, as shown in Figure 6-2.

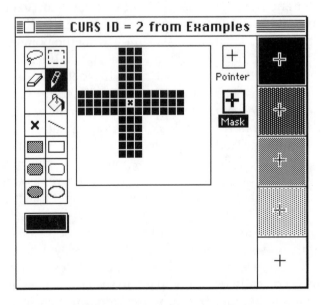

Figure 6-2. By altering the mask, you can make a pointer and its hot spot more visible.

Putting a hole in the mask allows one bit of underlying data to show through. If the hole corresponds to the location of the hot spot, as is the case in Figure 6-2, you'll be able to position the pointer more precisely. This trick is particularly useful in graphics applications where you want to know exactly which bit you'll select when you press the mouse button.

You can also eliminate the mask entirely. The crosshairs and I-beam pointers stored in the System file don't have masks. A pointer is normally drawn by erasing the bits covered by the mask and then inverting all the background bits that correspond to black bits in the pointer. If there's no mask, the black bits in the pointer will be white on a black background, as Figure 6-3 shows, or black on a white background. Such a pointer can be confusing on varied backgrounds, such as text and some patterns.

Some pointers can give unexpected results when you drag the pointer onto the mask view to create an automatic mask. ResEdit makes a copy of the pointer and fills in all enclosed areas. But with a pointer like the hand (𝄞), ResEdit simply produces a copy of the pointer that's not filled in. How can it fill the hand with bits if they all

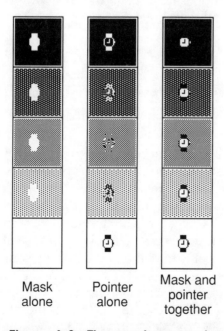

Mask alone   Pointer alone   Mask and pointer together

Figure 6-3. The mask erases background bits, and the pointer inverts background bits. When they're combined, the mask makes a hole in the background first, then the pointer is drawn.

leak out the wrist? To avoid this, simply draw a line across the
bottom of the hand, create the mask (which will now be filled in),
then remove the extra line in the pointer. For any type of pointer, just
make sure the picture forms an enclosed area before creating the
mask. If the enclosed area in the pointer is filled in, however, or if the
pointer is identical to the mask, it can disappear on black backgrounds. You can solve this problem by turning some enclosed bits
white in either the pointer or the mask, or by making the mask larger.

Hot Spot Hints

The fatbit marked with an X in the 'CURS' editor shows the location
of the business part of the pointer—the hot spot. It's the bit that
indicates the exact spot pointed to when you click the mouse. For
example, the hot spot on the arrow pointer is at its tip. Interestingly,
every pointer has a hot spot, even if you can't use it for positioning
the mouse's actions. The familiar watch and other special pointers
that some applications display while they carry out lengthy operations illustrate this point. Essentially, these pointers say "please wait."
Because the application is busy, you can't *do* anything with such
pointers, but they still have hot spots.

By The Way You can locate the hot spot anywhere in the 16-by-
16-bit field. It doesn't have to correspond to a black bit in either
the pointer or its mask.

Moving a pointer's hot spot can make your interactions with an
application less frustrating. Sometimes the pointer just doesn't
position your mouse click's action exactly where you think it should.
For instance, do you ever run into situations where the insertion
point ends up in the wrong place after you click the mouse? The
I-beam pointer that text processing applications use illustrates this
problem. If the hot spot is too high in the I-beam, sometimes you end
up putting the insertion point on the line above the one you were
aiming for. You can fix this easily enough by simply editing the
pointer and moving the hot spot toward the center of the I-beam.
(Unfortunately, if you use Microsoft Word, you're stuck with the
I-beam Microsoft thinks you should have. Remember, Word doesn't
use resources much, so you can't customize it with ResEdit.)

Hint Have you ever wished you could flip certain pointers (the pencil, for instance, or other tool palette pointers) to make them left-handed? You can! Just use the Flip Horizontal command on the Transform menu. Don't forget to move the hot spot, too.

Personalizing the Watch Pointer

You're probably familiar with the watch that many applications display to indicate that they're busy. That watch is set at 9:00. What if that's not your favorite time of day? Here's how you can reset the hands, put stripes on the watchband, or even change the pointer to an hourglass, shown in Figure 6-4.

1. Use ResEdit to open a copy of the System file, and then open the 'CURS' type.

2. From the 'CURS' resource picker, select the watch pointer (it should be ID 4) and duplicate it (from the Edit menu). Having a duplicate means you can easily restore it later if you don't like your new creation.

3. Double-click the original watch cursor (ID 4), which opens in the 'CURS' editor and should look something like Figure 6-1.

4. Edit the pointer to suit yourself.

5. You can edit the mask, too, but ResEdit creates a mask automatically if you drag the actual-size view of the pointer straight down onto the actual-size view of the mask. If you're only resetting the watch's hands, the original mask will still work.

6. You can move the hot spot by selecting the hot spot tool and clicking the bit of your choice, but there's not much point since you can't use this pointer for selecting things anyway.

7. If you choose Try Pointer from the 'CURS' menu, you can test-drive your new pointer. Return to the normal arrow pointer by choosing Try Pointer again, or by closing the editor window.

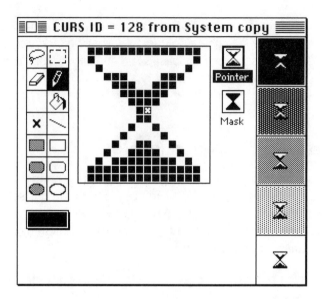

Figure 6-4. You can create an hourglass—or anything else you like—and substitute it for the watch pointer.

8. When you're happy with your pointer, save your work, quit ResEdit, and reinstall your System file. Your new pointer should appear in place of the watch pointer in any application that uses the System file's 'CURS' resource.

Power Up Your PowerBook I-Beam

Do you love your PowerBook but hate hunting for that pesky, disappearing I-beam? Why not fatten it up so you can find it better? This isn't as straightforward as it sounds because you'll have to do a ROM override to make your Mac use the change.

1. Use ResEdit to open a copy of the System file, and then open the 'CURS' type.

2. From the 'CURS' resource picker, select the I-beam and duplicate it (from the Edit menu). Having a duplicate means you can easily restore it later if you don't like your new creation.

3. Double-click the original I-beam, which opens in the 'CURS' editor. (Click Yes when asked if you want to save the resource uncompressed.)

4. Edit the pointer to suit yourself. Try adding a row of bits on each side at the top and bottom. If you leave it thin in the middle, you'll still be able to aim it accurately.

5. There's no mask to worry about so you can take your pointer for a test drive if you'd like, or just close the 'CURS' editor and go back to the type picker.

6. Now open the 'ROv#' resource type and open ID 1660. It opens in the template editor. (For more about templates, see Chapter 14.) Scroll to the bottom of the window and click on the last item, a row of five asterisks.

7. Choose Insert New Fields from the Resource menu (Command-K). Two new blank fields appear, labeled Type and Resource ID. In the Type field, enter CURS (all caps) and in the ID field enter 1.

8. Quit ResEdit and save all your changes. Swap System files and restart.

You'll see your new I-beam in the Finder and any applications that use the System file's pointers. Some applications have their own 'CURS' resources, so you may want to browse through copies of your applications and see if they have any I-beams you want to modify.

Animated Pointers

Some applications take the watch pointer one step further—they display an animated pointer when performing a lengthy task. For example, the Finder displays a watch with a rotating hand, and some other applications display a rotating beach ball. In most applications, you can easily modify these animated pointers to display any animation you can fit into a series of 16-by-16-bit pointers. If you get annoyed with an application's performance, why not change its pointer to a rotating pig face, such as the example in Figure 6-5?

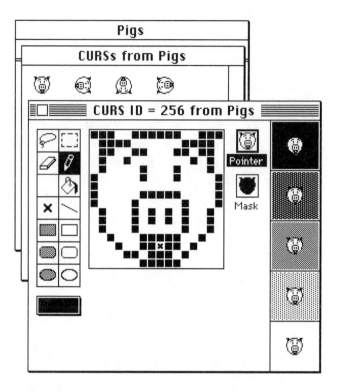

Figure 6-5. You can change an animated pointer to a rotating pig face, or any other animation sequence you design.

An 'acur' (Animated CURsor) resource controls pointer animation. (Remember, you can only modify existing 'acur' resources; you can't add an animated cursor to an application that doesn't already have one.) This resource determines how many 'CURS' resources the animation sequence uses and lists their ID numbers in the order they should be displayed.

The Finder's Animated Watch

Let's look at the Finder's animated watch to see how this works. Like any 'acur' resource, the one that controls the Finder's animated watch uses several ordinary 'CURS' resources to make up the animation sequence. Figure 6-6 shows the Finder's 'CURS' resources.

The Finder's 'acur' resource, which is shown in Figure 6-7, organizes these pointers into the sequence we recognize as animation. The 'acur' resource is an example of a template resource. You can

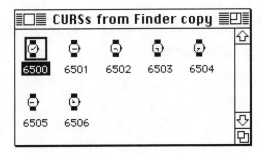

Figure 6-6. The Finder uses these watches for its animated pointer.

learn more about using templates in Chapter 14. The first field contains the number of individual pictures or *frames* used in the animation sequence, in this case, eight. The second field controls the speed of animation; smaller numbers produce faster animation. Next, the IDs of the frames are listed in order. The first frame follows the last frame, and the sequence plays over and over until the application returns to the usual pointer.

By now the wheels are probably starting to turn in your head. Yes, all you have to do to make the hand rotate backwards is reverse the order of the pointers' IDs in the 'acur'. (This will not make time go backwards, of course, but you already knew that.) You can also substitute a completely different animation sequence. Perhaps you liked a series of pointers or other 16-by-16-bit images you saw in one of the miscellaneous resource collections you downloaded from a bulletin board. Or maybe you'd like to develop your own animated cursor.

One way to devise your own animated sequence is to go to the 'CURS' editor and create a series of pointers that advance some action a little bit with each successive image. (The Rotate command on the Transform menu comes in handy for pointers that rotate.) Perhaps you'd like to follow up on the hourglass pointer. The first frame would have all the sand at the top, and successive frames would show more and more sand flowing to the bottom. Finally, in the last frame, the sand fills the bottom and the top is empty. If you really want a fancy hourglass animation sequence, rotate the hourglass at the end so the part full of sand is on top again. You can create and store this set of frames in the (copy of) Finder's 'CURS' resource type, or you can create an "Experimental Resources" ResEdit file and work on the project in there.

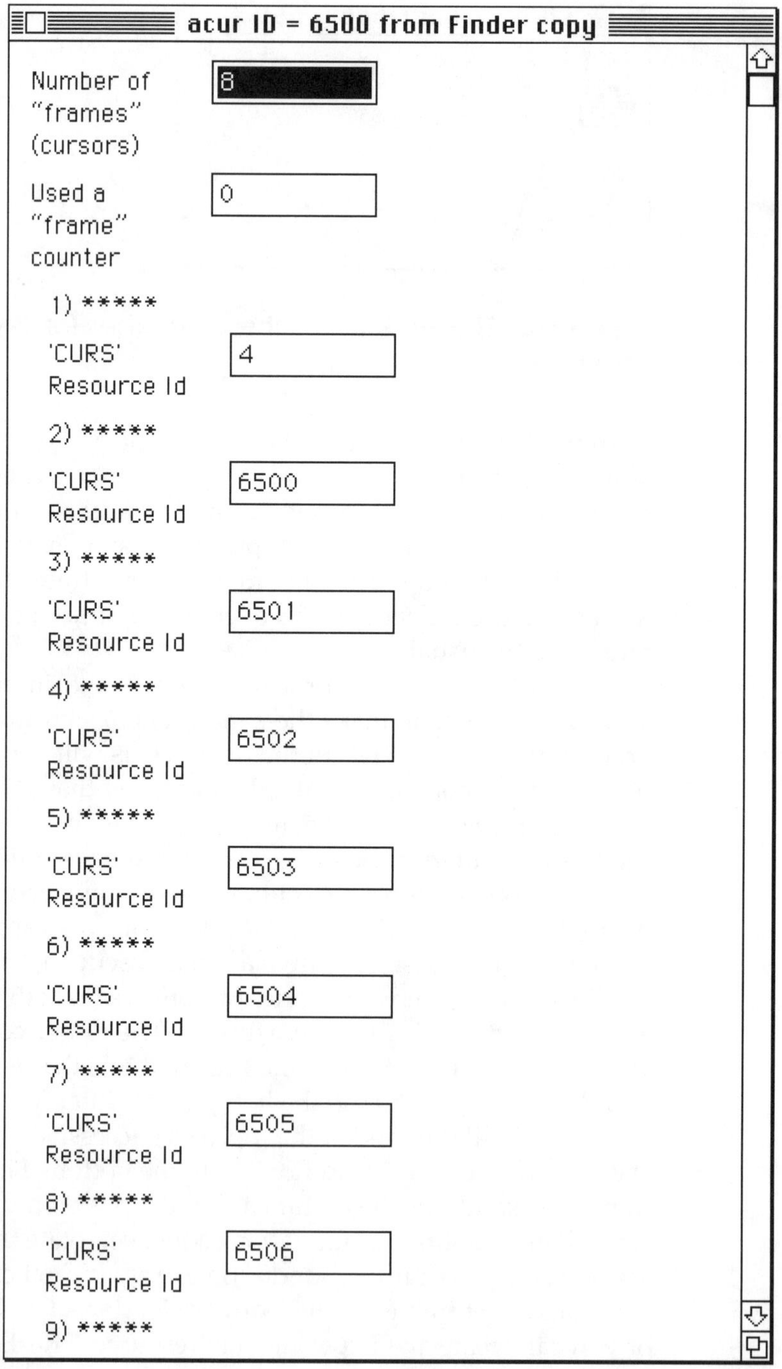

Figure 6-7. An 'acur' resource organizes the series of pointers used in an animated pointer sequence.

By The Way You've probably noticed that although the 'acur' resource uses eight pointers, only seven watches appear in the Finder's 'CURS' picker. The first pointer in the 'acur', ID 4, is the old familiar 9:00 watch. "But I just changed that to an hourglass (or something)!" you cry. Relax. You don't have to worry about ruining the Finder's animation sequence. You may remember from Chapter 2 that System resources usually override ROM resources. However, in this instance the Finder reprioritizes to make sure that it gets the watch from the ROM.

Customizing the Finder's Animated Watch

Follow these steps to substitute the animation sequence you've designed for the Finder's rotating watch hands. (See Chapter 4 if you need to refresh your memory before modifying the Finder.)

1. Use the Finder's Duplicate command to make a copy of the Finder itself, and leave it in your System Folder.

2. Use ResEdit to open your copy of the Finder and open the 'CURS' resource type. You should see the seven watches shown in Figure 6-6. If you created your new pointers in this file, you'll also see them, and you can skip the next step.

3. If you created your animation sequence in another file, paste the new pointers you want the Finder to use into the 'CURS' picker. You may want to switch back to using the watches later, so be sure you don't overwrite any of them. (ResEdit will warn you if any of your new pointers happen to have the same ID as the watch pointers. Just be sure to click the Unique ID button in the dialog.)

4. Select all the pointers you just added to the Finder and choose Get Resource Info from the Resource menu. Make sure that the Locked and Preload check boxes are checked in the Resource Info window for each pointer, as shown in Figure 6-8. This guarantees that the Finder can always find the pointers when it needs them.

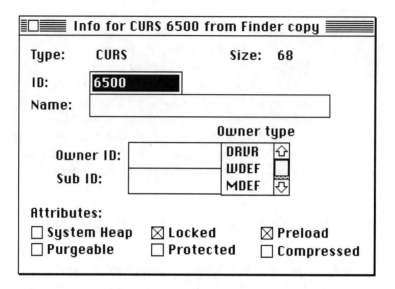

Figure 6-8. Make sure the Locked and Preload check boxes are checked for each 'CURS' resource you use in your animation sequence.

5. Make a note of the resource ID for each of your pointers and also the order in which they should appear.

6. Open the Finder copy's 'acur' picker and duplicate the 'acur' with ID 6500. You should now have two 'acur's—one with ID 6500, and one with ID 128. The one with ID 128 will be your spare if you want to return to using the watches. (You can label it as such by giving it a name with Get Resource Info on the Resource menu.)

7. Open the 'acur' resource with ID 6500 and change it so that it contains the appropriate number of frames and the IDs of your new pointer resources. List your pointers' IDs in the order you want them to appear. If you need to remove items, select the row of five asterisks (*****) above the item to be removed and press the Delete key. If you need to add items, select the last group of five asterisks and choose Insert New Field(s) from the Resource menu. (For more information about using templates, see Chapter 14.)

8. Close the Finder copy, save your changes, and quit ResEdit. Drag your current Finder to the desktop, and rename your copy (it should still be in the System Folder) "Finder."

9. Restart, and you should be able to see your new animated pointer whenever the Finder performs a lengthy operation.

10. Once you have restarted, you can throw the old Finder (the one on the desktop) into the Trash.

Restoring the Watch Pointer

If you decide you're tired of your new pointer, you can easily restore the Finder's original rotating watch.

1. Make a copy of the Finder.

2. Open the copy with ResEdit, and open the 'acur' resource type.

3. Select the 'acur' resource with ID 6500 and choose Get Resource Info from the Resource menu.

4. Change the ID to 129 (or the next available number).

5. In the same way, change the ID of the 'acur' with ID 128 (you did save it, didn't you?) to 6500. If you left all the watch pointers in the file, you shouldn't have to worry about them.

6. Reinstall your new Finder and restart.

By The Way A delightful shareware desk accessory called CursorAnimator lets you have animated cursors in every application. The program includes a large collection of clever animated cursors to suit every taste, and it even lets you add your own. With ResEdit and CursorAnimator you'd never be at a loss for animated cursors. CursorAnimator is available on most electronic bulletin boards and from many Macintosh user groups.

Summary

This chapter introduces pointers, the small icons that indicate mouse position. They're often called cursors, and are stored in 'CURS' resources. A 'CURS' resource has three editable parts: the pointer, the shadowlike mask that determines how the pointer looks on various backgrounds, and the hot spot—the bit that positions the pointer's actions. To handle this added complexity, the 'CURS' editor has a few more parts than the pattern editors, but it's still an easy-to-use fatbits editor. We show how to change the watch pointer that many applications use to indicate they're busy. Some applications use animated pointers, which are stored in 'acur' resources. The Finder's watch with its rotating hand is one example. We describe how to substitute your own animation sequence for the Finder's animated watch.

Chapter 7

 Ideal Icons

As you customize your favorite applications, why not customize their icons, too? Modifying icons is one of the most popular and rewarding things you can do to personalize your Mac, and you've probably been itching to dig in. Changing icons can not only satisfy your urge to personalize, but it can also add information. An application's Finder icon can include a version number, your initials, or any other identifying information you're clever enough to fit into the space you've got. Icons play an important role throughout the Macintosh environment. You're familiar with their use in the Finder to represent files and devices such as disk drives. These icons can show up on the desktop or within folders. Icons also appear in dialog and alert boxes, and occasionally in menus.

The Mac uses many different kinds of icon resources. Ultimately, they all describe a set of bits that are copied to the screen, but each resource type contains slightly different information. Icons come in two basic sizes, large (32 by 32 bits) and small (16 by 16 bits), except for one type of color icon ('cicn'), which can vary in size. Table 7-1 briefly lists all the icon resource types.

To handle all these icon types, ResEdit has five editors. Each of the first four icon types listed in Table 7-1 has its own editor. The last five icon types are related, so you can edit them all in one editor, the icon family editor. We'll talk about the color icon editors ('cicn' and icon family) in Chapter 17. Similar editing methods work in all the icon editors, so we'll review a few techniques first, then progress through the icon types, and give you some ideas for what you can do with them.

Table 7-1. Types of Icon Resources

Type	Description
'ICON'	32-by-32-bit icon used in dialogs, alerts, and menus.
'SICN'	16-by-16-bit small icon lists used in menus and some applications.
'ICN#'	32-by-32-bit icon the Finder uses on the desktop. Includes a shadowlike mask.
'cicn'	Color icon. Size can vary (from 8 by 8 to 64 by 64 bits). Can include a black-and-white version that's used when color isn't available. Used in dialogs, alerts, and menus, but only on machines with Color QuickDraw (Classic II, LC III, etc.).

These came into existence along with Finder 7.0:

'icl4'	32-by-32-bit icon, 16 colors.
'icl8'	32-by-32-bit icon, 256 colors.
'ics#'	16-by-16-bit icon, black and white, includes a mask.
'ics4'	16-by-16-bit icon, 16 colors.
'ics8'	16-by-16-bit icon, 256 colors.

Hint Although System 7 lets you change Finder icons by pasting a new image in the Get Info window, ResEdit gives you more options and more control over your results. For instance, you have complete control over the mask, and you can create the whole icon family if you want to. You can also copy and use images you wouldn't be able to access otherwise, such as patterns, pointers, and 'cicn's. And, if you're willing to accept the Finder's mask and small icon scaling, there's a shortcut for turning any fatbits or fatpixels image into a Finder icon. Simply select all by double-clicking the selection rectangle in ResEdit's fatbits or fatpixels editors, copy, then paste in the Finder's Get Info window.

Creating and Editing Icons

Almost any time you want to create a totally new icon, you can head for the first item on the Resource menu, Create New Resource. The command isn't available from editors, so you may have to go back to the icon picker. (Creating new icons within 'SICN's is a little different, but we'll explain that in the section on 'SICN's.) If you're working in a file that doesn't have the icon type you're interested in, you'll have to go back to the type picker and create the icon type there. But first, decide whether this makes sense. Remember, with rare exceptions, you can't just create a new resource type and expect an application to use it. Whether you do it from the type picker or the resource picker, ResEdit creates a new resource, gives it a unique ID, and opens it in the editor. Now you can happily click away using normal fatbits techniques. (For a refresher on how to use ResEdit's fatbits editors, see the first section of Chapter 5.)

You might also want to create an icon in a paint program. Maybe you find drawing easier in paint and draw applications (just remember the icon size you're limited to). Or perhaps you've come across part of a picture you'd like to turn into an icon. Once you've got the desired art, use a selection tool to grab the picture and copy it. You don't have to worry about trying to select an area exactly the size of the icon because you'll have a chance to position things later. Next, use ResEdit to create a new icon resource in your target file and paste your selection into the blank editor. If the selection was too large, or if you only want an edge of it, use the Nudge commands on the Transform menu (or the arrow keys) or the mouse to slide the selection to where you want it. When you deselect it (for instance by selecting another tool), any bits not visible in the editor are discarded.

Why not try out these basic editing techniques on one of the simplest types of icons, the 'ICON' resource.

'ICON' Resources

With a few clicks in the 'ICON' editor, you can make the talking head in dialogs friendlier, as shown in Figure 7-1. You can find this icon, along with several others you may want to change, in the System file.

Figure 7-2, which shows the System file's 'ICON' picker, gives you an idea of the 'ICON's the System file contains. HyperCard has tons of icons you may want to copy or modify. When you double-click an

Figure 7-1. In the 'ICON' editor you can change the icons you see in dialogs, alert boxes, and some menus.

'ICON' resource, ResEdit opens it in the 'ICON' editor, shown in
Figure 7-3. The editing field is just the right size to hold a 32-by-32-bit
image, and the editor works just as you would expect. The next
section describes how to use this editor to change icons in alert boxes.

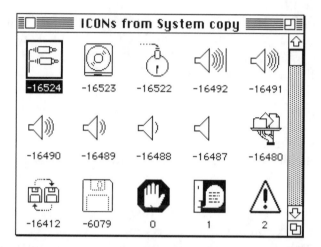

Figure 7-2. The System file has many 'ICON's you might want to
change.

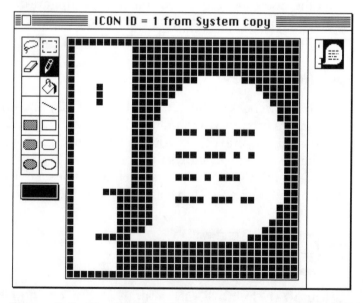

Figure 7-3. The 'ICON' editor is a prototypical fatbits editor.

Changing Icons in Alert Boxes

You can easily modify any of the alert icons shown in Figure 7-4. (In Chapter 17 we'll show you how you can make them appear in color!)

 Note

 Caution

 Stop

Figure 7-4. Alert boxes can employ one of these three icons from the System file.

By The Way Macintosh applications generally use four kinds of alert boxes. One kind contains no icon. For the other three, the icon indicates the type of alert, as shown in Figure 7-4.

If you're not experienced with modifying the System file, now would be a good time to flip to Chapter 4 to review procedures and precautions.

1. Use ResEdit to open a copy of your System file.

2. Open the 'ICON' picker. You should see something similar to the icons you saw in Figure 7-2.

3. Select the icon you want to alter and duplicate it. That way you'll always have a copy of the original in case you need to start over or want to switch back.

4. Double-click the icon you just duplicated to open the 'ICON' editor. (If you work on the original instead of the duplicate, you won't have to change IDs.)

5. Edit the icon until you have exactly what you want.

6. Close the file, save your changes, and quit ResEdit.

7. Install your modified System file and restart to see your changes.

Small Icon Lists ('SICN' Resources)

Applications can use 'SICN' (Small ICoN) resources in a variety of places, but you're most likely to see them in menus or palettes. Each 'SICN' can contain any number of small (16-by-16-bit) icons. (This is an example of a list resource that doesn't have a pound sign (#) in the resource type.) Although many applications don't use any 'SICN's at all, others have quite a few. So, if the icon you want to modify is small and doesn't seem to have a big counterpart, checking the file's type picker for the 'SICN' resource type could prove worthwhile.

By The Way Until the 'cicn' and Finder 7.0 small icons came along, the only way applications could have a small icon was to use an 'SICN' resource. The icons the System 6 Finder used for its small icon view weren't 'SICN's; they were reduced 'ICN#' icons—which is why they sometimes looked clumpy. System 7 got around this problem by defining a whole new set of icons, which includes both small black-and-white and small color icons. For more information on this icon family, see Chapter 17.

Like a typical picker for a list resource, the 'SICN' picker displays the first several icons for each 'SICN' in the file, as shown in Figure 7-5. Some 'SICN' lists are short enough to fit, but others may be much longer. You can enlarge the picker window or click the zoom box to show more of the icons if you need to, but 'SICN' resources can be so long you may not be able to see the whole list even if you have a large screen. That's OK, because you can browse through all the icons in the 'SICN' editor.

When you open an 'SICN' resource, you see the first icon in the list in the fatbits editor window, and a list of actual-size icons displayed along the right side in a scrollable panel, as shown in Figure 7-6. Where you double-click an 'SICN' resource doesn't matter, the editor

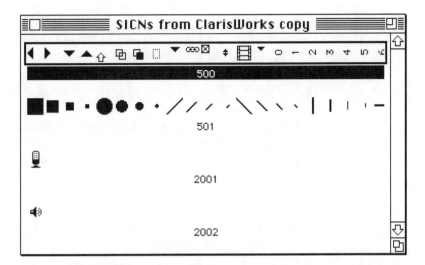

Figure 7-5. ClarisWorks has only four 'SICN' resources, but two of them contain numerous icons.

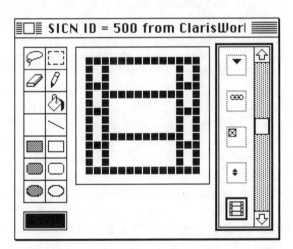

Figure 7-6. The 'SICN' editor displays a fatbits view of the selected icon and a scrollable list.

always opens on the first (leftmost, or topmost) icon in the list. Use the scrollable list along the right to select the icon you want to modify. The selected icon has a dark box around it. To edit a different icon, simply click it. An outline around the scrollable list tells you when it's active, meaning the Edit menu's commands apply to it instead of to the fatbits editing area.

You may remember from the introduction to list resources in
Chapter 2 how an application decides which icon to use in an 'SICN'
resource. Applications don't keep track of specific icons—that would
defeat the purpose of using a list resource. Instead, they keep track of
position in the list. Therefore, be careful not to rearrange icons or
otherwise alter their order because that can lead to chaos. When an
application fetches and displays the wrong icons, you quickly realize
how much you depend on these little pictures. Any substitutions or
rearrangements should be the result of a conscious effort, not an
accident.

By The Way If you're familiar with the pattern list resource
('PAT#'), some of this may sound familiar. However, there's an
important difference in the way applications employ these two list
resource types. Generally, applications make patterns available
for users to use, but they use 'SICN's themselves. So, patterns
might exist in 'PAT#' resource lists without ever being used, but
any icon that exists in an 'SICN' resource has a purpose, presum-
ably, or it wouldn't be there. That's why you don't want to take a
cavalier attitude toward rearranging icons in 'SICN' resources.

Choosing Insert New SICN from the Resource menu adds a new
small icon just after the currently selected one. Of course, that
rearranges the order of icons in the resource, but if you're a programmer, we're assuming you'll figure out how to make your application
do the right thing. Even if you're not a programmer, you can still add
new icons if you keep the list in order by adding them at the very end.
A question probably just sprang to your mind: "What good does it
do me to add icons to the end of the list if the application won't use
them anyway, because it won't know they're there?" Icons at the end
of the list can serve as "extras." For example, you can keep the
original icon handy while you put your modified version into service.
Even though you've got a backup copy of the file (you do, don't
you?), storing the spare icon in the same resource is awfully
convenient if you want to switch back. The end of the list is also a
great place to store or create experimental icons.
OK, so maybe it makes sense, but how do you go about it? You can
scroll to the very last icon, select it, and choose Duplicate (from the

Edit menu), or choose Insert New SICN (from the Resource menu). Either way you end up with a spare spot to play around with. Keeping track of where the list of "real" or in-service icons ends might be a good idea. You can do that any number of ways, but just leaving a blank icon as a spacer easily does the trick.

Hint As you work on icons in the 'SICN' editor, keep in mind that, as with all list resources, Revert This Resource applies to the whole resource—the whole list of icons—not just to the icon you're currently working on.

Hint Remember to pay attention to the location of the dark outline in the editor (either around the fatbits editing area or the scrollable list) so you'll know whether you're copying a whole icon or a selection of bits from an icon. When you paste an *icon* (that is, when you've copied it from the scrollable list), ResEdit pastes it just after whatever icon is currently selected. When you paste a selection of *bits* (that is, when you've copied bits from any of the fatbits editors or from a paint program), ResEdit pastes the selection into the currently selected icon, thus overwriting it. If you're pasting bits, create a new empty icon to paste into. Menu item text also gives you clues as to what will happen. For example, the Edit menu says "Paste PICT" for bits and "Paste Icon" for an icon.

Finder Icons

Some of the most prominent icons you work with are those displayed on your desktop, including the Trash, file, and folder icons, and the specific icons associated with applications. These icons are stored in 'ICN#' resources, and, because the Finder is responsible for drawing and keeping track of them, people sometimes call them Finder icons. Most applications have their own special icons, but you can personalize them to make them uniquely yours.

ResEdit can edit 'ICN#' resources in two different editors, but which one you see depends on your Macintosh. On the smaller, one-piece Macs up through the Classic, 'ICN#' resources open in the

'ICN#' editor, a strictly black-and-white editor. But if your Mac's
ROM has Color QuickDraw (which SE/30s, Classic IIs, and all LCs
and above do), 'ICN#' resources open in the Icon Family editor,
discussed in more detail in Chapter 17.

When you open an 'ICN#' resource you see a window containing a
magnified view of the icon, and several actual-size views along the
right side of the window, as shown in Figure 7-7 for the 'ICN#' editor
and Figure 7-8 for the Icon Family editor. The fatbits view can display
either the icon itself or the shadowlike *mask* that determines how the
icon looks on various backgrounds. Immediately to the right of the
editing area you see actual-size views of the icon and the mask. To
select the one you want to edit, simply click it. A dark outline and a
highlighted label indicate which one is displayed in the fatbits view.
The mask determines how the icon looks when drawn on various
backgrounds and in various states. (More on this in a minute.) You
can edit the icon and mask using normal fatbits techniques.

Along the right side of the window you see the selected icon as it
would appear in several different states. As the labels indicate, the
top views show the icon in its normal state (closed), the middle views
show it open, and the bottom views show it offline (ejected but still
mounted).

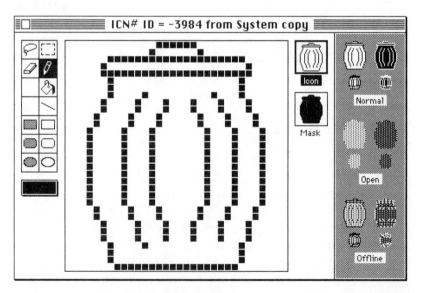

**Figure 7-7. The 'ICN#' editor can show the icon or its mask in
fatbits, and combines them in actual size to show how the
Finder would draw them in various situations.**

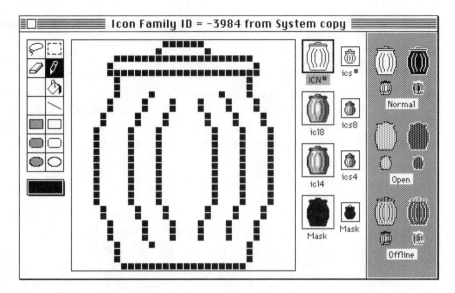

Figure 7-8. On Macs with Color QuickDraw, you edit 'ICN#' resources in the Icon Family editor.

In each case, the left side shows the icon unselected and the right side shows it selected. Underneath you see the shrunken version of the icon. You can change the background on which the samples are drawn to white, gray, black, or your current desktop pattern with the aid of the 'ICN#' (or Icons) menu.

By The Way When the Finder needs a small icon for its small icon view, it simply shrinks the large icon (and its mask) by half unless it can find a related (by ID) small icon.

Creating the Mask

You may be wondering how the mask works. In a nutshell, when the Finder draws an icon, it uses the shape of the mask to erase a hole in the background, then draws the icon in the resulting hole. An icon without a mask may become transparent—or even disappear altogether—depending on the background and the state of the icon (for instance, selected or not). So when you change an icon, remember to change its mask, too. The only mask guaranteed to work properly under every circumstance is a filled in version of the icon itself. You can easily create such a mask by dragging the boxed icon (just to the right of the editing panel) straight down onto the box labeled "Mask." (If you're working in the Icon Family editor, grabbing and dragging also works for creating color icons. See Chapter 17 for more details.) Of course, you can also experiment with trying to get interesting effects by altering the mask. Browsing through your applications' icons may give you more ideas for techniques to try.

Hint If the icon you design contains open shapes, you may be puzzled over the results you get when you drag the icon down onto the mask box. To create a mask, ResEdit makes a copy of the icon, then fills it in, which works fine with a closed shape. But if the shape of the icon is open, ResEdit can't fill it in—all the bits leak out! This doesn't have to cramp your creative style, however. Simply close up the icon before you make the mask, then open it again afterward. (You can also enclose areas of the mask using the pencil tool, then fill them using the paint bucket.)

Changing an Application's Icons

Changing the icons of your applications or data files can be fun as well as informative. For example, you could add the version number of an application to its icon. If you want to add a document icon to an application, or if you're a programmer creating your own application, refer to Chapter 21.

Hint An easy way to find all the 'ICN#' resources an application uses is to open the 'BNDL' editor. See Chapter 21 for more information.

1. Use ResEdit to open a copy of the application whose icon you want to change.

2. Open the 'ICN#' type and select the icon you want to change. Duplicating the original icon before you make changes is a good idea just in case you want to switch back later.

3. Make your changes (to the original, not the duplicate, so you won't have to change IDs).

4. Close the file and save it.

As you can see, changing an icon is relatively easy. Getting the Finder to use your new icon can be somewhat trickier. Before you can convince the Finder to use your new icons, you need to know a little about how it interacts with icons.

Understanding Finder Icons

Clearly, the Finder can't magically know the icons for every application possible, so it has a mechanism for acquiring and keeping track of these icons. Applications generally supply icons for themselves and for the documents they create. The Finder uses these icons to represent the application and its documents, and it stores them in its invisible Desktop database.

By The Way When you use the Finder's Get Info Window to paste a custom icon on a file, the Finder creates the whole family of icon resources and stores them within the file. When you paste a custom icon on a folder, the icon resources are stored in an invisible file within the folder called "Icon." You can open this invisible file from within ResEdit.

How the Finder Finds Icons—Type and Creator

To link icons with their appropriate files, the Finder makes use of two identifiers. These identifiers, which every file has, are four-letter codes called the *Type* and *Creator*. Applications always have the Type APPL, but their Creators give each application a unique signature. For example, ResEdit's Creator is RSED and MacPaint's is MPNT. A document has the same Creator as the application that created it, so the Finder knows where to look for its icon. The Finder uses the Creator to associate a document with the appropriate application.

An application's documents may have various Types, and these tell the Finder which icon of the application's set of icons to use for which type of document. The Finder uses file types to display different icons for each kind of file. Table 7-2 lists some examples to illustrate these relationships. For more information about associating icons with file types, see Chapter 21.

Table 7-2. Types and Creators Used to Match Icons and Files

Icon	Type	Creator	Kind of File
	APPL	MWPR	MacWrite Pro application
	MWPd	MWPR	MacWrite Pro document
	sWPd	MWPR	MacWrite Pro stationery
	TEXT	MWPR	MacWrite Pro text file
	APPL	BOBO	ClarisWorks application
	CWPT	BOBO	ClarisWorks paint document
	sWPT	BOBO	ClarisWorks paint stationery
	PICT	BOBO	ClarisWorks PICT file

Although the Finder gets icons and information from applications, it doesn't repeat the fetching process every time it encounters a file. Instead, it maintains a list of every application it has ever encountered. This list includes every application's icon for itself and the icons for all its documents. The Finder stores this roster in an invisible file known as the Desktop database. Thus, the Desktop database contains a history of every Type and Creator that has ever resided on the disk.

When the Finder encounters a file, for example, when you copy a file to a disk, it checks the file's Creator and Type. Then it checks the Desktop database to see if the copied file is related to anything it has ever encountered before. If the file is a document, the Finder determines whether it has ever encountered the creator application, and if it has, it uses the icon previously stored in the Desktop database. The process is similar for a previously encountered application—the Finder uses the icon from the Desktop database. When the Finder encounters a new application, it adds the new icons, Type(s), and Creator to the Desktop database's roster. When it can't find specific icons, the Finder uses generic icons to represent files. It uses its generic document icon when it encounters a document whose creator application has never been on your disk, or whose creator application doesn't specify a special document icon. The Finder uses the generic application icon when an application doesn't contain an icon for itself.

You may be wondering why the Desktop database is invisible. It prevents tampering and keeps the desktop tidier. Most of the time nobody needs to see it or do anything to it. But the Finder won't use your custom icons until you make it update the Desktop database.

Updating the Desktop File

Now you know why the Finder seems to ignore your new icon masterpieces. Actually it doesn't ignore them, because it doesn't even look for them. It continues to use old stored versions until the Desktop database is updated. Fortunately, as discussed in a little more detail in Chapter 4, the Finder does the dirty work for you. If you hold down the Command and Option keys when you restart your Macintosh (or when you insert a floppy disk), the Finder automatically rebuilds the disk's Desktop database and includes any new icons you've added. (To be sure the Finder uses your new icon, don't leave the original copy of the file on the same volume. Move the original to a different disk.) Unfortunately, the Finder also throws away any comments you've added to the Get Info windows.

Hint If you only store short comments (one or two lines), try putting them in 'vers' resources instead of in the Finder's Get Info windows. These resources survive when the Finder rebuilds the Desktop database. For more information, see "Adding Version Information to Documents" in Chapter 13.

Personalizing Other Desktop Icons

In addition to application icons, the Finder draws numerous other icons commonly found on the desktop. It gets these icons, shown in Figure 7-9, from the System file, and they are obvious targets for customization. Many people play with the Trash Can, making it overflow, turning it into a toilet, or turning it into an IBM PC. Figure 7-10

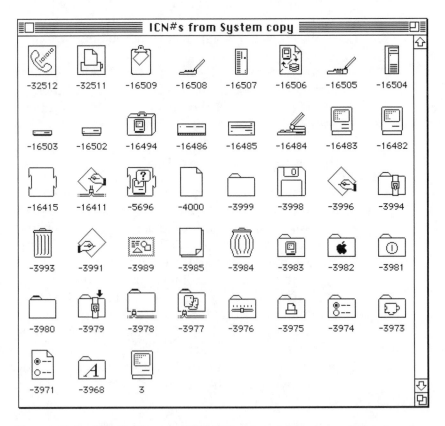

Figure 7-9. The System's 'ICN#' resource type contains many familiar desktop icons.

shows fatbits versions of some possible Trash substitutes. Before you edit the Finder's icons, review the procedures described in Chapter 4.

Remember to create a mask before saving the icon. (Drag the icon straight down onto the box labeled "Mask.")

By The Way Whatever substitute you choose for the Trash, you may be able to carry the metaphor further. Let's say you substituted a toilet icon. You can modify the Finder's Special menu so that it says Flush instead of Empty Trash. You can also change all the Finder's messages that refer to the Trash by searching in the 'STR ' and 'STR#' resources. For information about modifying menus, see Chapter 8. For information about changing string resources ('STR ' and 'STR#'), see Chapter 15.

Figure 7-10. Here are some potential substitutes for the Finder's Trash can. You can copy these or create your own.

Summary

This chapter discusses three types of icon resources and how they're used and edited: 'ICON', 'SICN', and 'ICN#'. 'ICON' resources often appear in dialogs, alerts, and menus, and we show you how to customize the ones that appear in alerts. Applications use 'SICN' resources in menus, palettes, and other parts of the user interface. The Finder keeps track of desktop icons—'ICN#' resources—in its Desktop file. We also describe how to change an application's desktop icons and how to update the Desktop file so that the Finder will use the new icons.

Chapter 8

Modifying Menus

One of the best features of the Macintosh is that the user interface remains the same from one application to another. Mostly. But let's face it—not all software developers follow the same user interface guidelines. One result is that menus tend to vary and keyboard shortcuts are inconsistent—even within an application type, such as text processing. As you become more familiar with the programs you use frequently, keyboard shortcuts can speed up your work. But some of your most-used menu commands might not come equipped with Command-key equivalents. Plus, you can run into problems if Command-P means "Plain Text" in WizzyWrite, "Print" in FingerPaint, and "Propagate" in ZowieCalc. If you absentmindedly type Command-P without remembering where you are, you could end up with unsettling results—and increased appreciation for Command-Z (which is always Undo).

In many cases, you don't have to put up with annoying menus or keyboard shortcuts. With ResEdit you can add menu icons and Command-key shortcuts. You can also modify the names, text style, and colors for menu items to increase consistency between applications, to streamline your work, or just to suit your style, as Figure 8-1, a rather extreme example, shows.

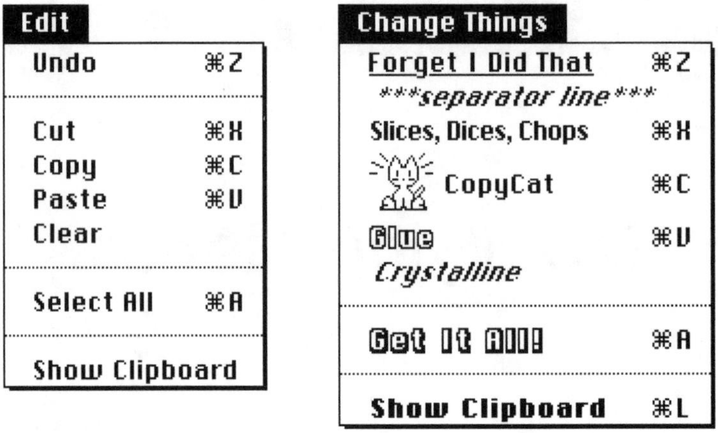

Edit	
Undo	⌘Z
Cut	⌘H
Copy	⌘C
Paste	⌘U
Clear	
Select All	⌘A
Show Clipboard	

Change Things	
Forget I Did That	⌘Z
separator line	
Slices, Dices, Chops	⌘H
CopyCat	⌘C
Glue	⌘U
Crystalline	
Get It All!	⌘A
Show Clipboard	⌘L

Figure 8-1. With ResEdit you can customize menus to suit yourself.

Macintosh Menus

Much of your communication with Macintosh applications is through menus, which tell applications what operation to perform next. Whether or not they use resources for their menus (most do), applications work with the Macintosh's Menu Manager, the user interface middleman that sets up and manages menus. When you select a menu item, either by pulling down on a menu or by typing a keyboard equivalent, the application calls the Menu Manager, which highlights that menu's title (by inverting it), and does all the other things that make menus behave like menus. The application doesn't know which menu item you chose until the Menu Manager tells it. The split-second interchange goes something like this:

Application: Yo, Menu Manager? The user just typed "Command-X." What is this?

Menu Manger: OK, I'll check into it so I can do some user interface stuff and get back to you. Let's see . . . that's menu 3, item 2.

Application: Item 2 on menu 3? Gotcha. The user wants to cut.

In other words, applications can't read menus, and the Menu Manager doesn't understand application commands. The bottom line is that you can't add new commands to menus just by typing them into 'MENU' resources. You can't rearrange the order of menu commands either. Moving the *text name* of a menu command doesn't change the instructions the application associates with that *location* in the menu. For example, if you swap the names of Cut and Copy in the Edit menu, the application will still cut when you select the second menu item, even though you made it read "Copy."

By The Way Applications written with newer versions of MacApp will have 'CMNU' (Command MeNU) resources instead of 'MENU' resources. With 'CMNU's, each menu item has a unique command number associated with it, and that number is what counts. 'CMNU's allow you to rearrange items in menus, and even move items to different menus, because all that counts is the command number. When you find 'CMNU's in your applications, you can edit them with ResEdit just as you would edit 'MENU' resources. The 'CMNU' editor looks almost the same as the 'MENU' editor, except for the addition of a field that allows you to specify a command number.

ResEdit won't let you get at every menu, and there are some you can't or shouldn't try to modify. For example, you can't do much that's useful to the Apple menu, or to various Font and Size menus, because they're designed to contain information that varies. In these cases the application has to get that changeable information from somewhere else, usually your System file. (For a tip on rearranging Font menus—by changing font names—see Chapter 12.) Finally, some applications (such as Microsoft Word) don't use any menu resources; they employ special code for their menus instead. You won't be able to change such menus with ResEdit.

By The Way With the birth of System 7 came the death of easy-to-customize Finder menus. Now the Finder's menus are stored in 'fmnu' resources instead of 'MENU' resources. But you can still edit them with ResEdit. You can either use the hex editor (confusing) or the special 'fmnu' template we've included on the disk with this book (much easier). We'll tell you how to do it in Chapter 15.

Command-Key Shortcut Considerations

Perhaps one of the most popular uses for ResEdit is assigning keyboard equivalents for menu commands. Some people like to create Command-key shortcuts for the Finder's Special menu, such as Command-R for Restart and Command-S for Shutdown. Of course, if you get distracted, you could wind up turning off your machine instead of saving the file you *thought* you were in. Fortunately, as usual, the Macintosh protects you from such blunders by asking if you want to save before quitting, so you won't lose anything. You'll probably realize your mistake, click Cancel in the Save dialog, and continue working. Then, some time later, when you quit from the application, your Mac will shut down. Surprise!

Which brings up an important point. To try to avoid surprises, consider Command-key shortcuts carefully before implementing them. Generally, it's a good idea to try to avoid confusing yourself or your Mac. As you contemplate your modifications, keep several things in mind.

First, get an overview of your existing keyboard commands so you don't inadvertently duplicate key combinations you already have. Clearly, you need to check the application you want to tweak, but also remember that desk accessories may have hot keys assigned, and you may have created global shortcuts in a macro utility. When faced with conflicts, what does your Mac do? Let's take an example from the old days, when the System 6 Finder menus were in 'MENU' resources. Say you added Command-E to the Finder's Special menu so you could quickly Empty Trash. But Command-E was already taken by Eject on the File menu. How would your Mac decide whether to empty the Trash or stick its floppy out at you? The Menu Manager looks at Command-key shortcuts from right to left across the menu bar, and from top to bottom on the menus, taking the first command equivalent it sees, so Command-E would work for Empty Trash, not Eject.

Once you figure out which Command-key shortcuts are already taken, you can get down to the business of assigning some new ones. Ideally, the keyboard shortcuts you choose should make sense to you so they'll be easy to remember and use. You can use almost all the letters and numbers on the keyboard for Command-key shortcuts. However, the Menu Manager ignores the Shift key, so Command-+ is the same as Command-=. Consequently, you *can not* use most punctuation characters for keyboard equivalents because they're Command-Shift-number combinations. Recall, for example, that Command-Shift-1 and -2 eject disks, and Command-Shift-3 takes a screen snapshot no matter what application you're running. These key combinations are not handled by the Menu Manager, so it can't return any information to the application. (If you really want to use punctuation, Chapter 9 contains a solution to this problem.)

Even though you can't use the Shift key, you still have the Option key. Check the Chicago font in the Key Caps desk accessory if you want to get an idea of the possibilities. (Menus use the System font, which is Chicago unless you change it. To find out about changing the System font, see Chapter 15.) Let's say you use Save As frequently in an application, and want a keyboard shortcut. Command-S is taken for Save, but you can add Command-Option-S to that application's File menu. Option-S gives you a "ß" character, so you'll see "⌘ß" after Save As on your customized menu. Bear in mind that some keys just give you an empty box character when pressed with the Option key. Seeing "⌘□" on the menu won't help much if you forget the key you assigned.

By The Way Having an extended keyboard doesn't extend your range of options. All the function keys put the same character— an apple—in your menus, which doesn't help much. Look into macro utilities, such as QuickKeys, for an alternative.

Before you set to work, with a gleam in your eyes, to assign and change Command-key shortcuts, remember that sometimes you may wish you had left well enough alone. While it's true that you'll probably be able to change things back (assuming you have the suggested copies and backups), that's sort of like saying you can heal after you shoot yourself in the foot. Consider, too, that most Macintosh users are familiar with certain standard Command-key shortcuts. If you aren't careful, the more you customize your Macintosh or your applications with nonstandard "improvements," the more likely you are to flummox yourself up with inconsistencies and bewilder other people who may someday use your software and equipment. It's your system, and customization is one of the major benefits of the Mac and ResEdit—just try to think through your modifications.

Finally, for cosmetic reasons, always type in capital letters when assigning keyboard shortcuts. Even though the Menu Manager doesn't distinguish between capitals and lowercase (because it ignores the Shift key), lowercase letters will look out of place in the menus.

'MENU' Resources

Besides Command-key shortcuts, you can modify menu items in a variety of other ways. You can change a menu item's name or text style so that it stands out or makes more sense to you. Maybe an icon to the left of a menu item would provide a helpful visual reminder of that item's function. Exploring the 'MENU' editor will give you an idea of the possibilities, but first you need to know a bit more about 'MENU' resources. Then, after some examples, you can branch out on your own.

To find the menu resources you want to edit, you first have to start ResEdit and use it to open up (a copy of) the application you're interested in. Find the 'MENU' resource type and open it. ResEdit opens the 'MENU' picker, shown in Figure 8-2, which displays the top of every menu in the file. Searching through the 'MENU' picker for the particular menu you want to modify takes almost no time, but you need to remember a few things. You may find that some applications contain more than one 'MENU' resource for the same menu. ClarisWorks, for instance, has four 'MENU' resources for its Format menu. Also, an application might have more menus to sift through than just what's along the menu bar because some dialog boxes use 'MENU' resources for pop-up menus. So, sometimes you may have to open a 'MENU' resource before you know you've found the right one. If you've got the right one, you're ready to work. (If it's not the right one, just click the close box and choose the next likely candidate from the 'MENU' picker.)

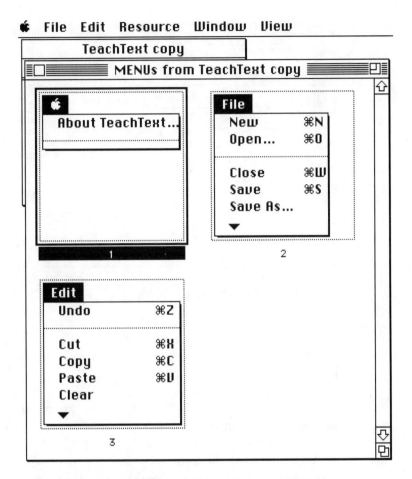

Figure 8-2. The 'MENU' picker, view by 'MENU'.

The 'MENU' Editor

The 'MENU' editor, shown in Figure 8-3, opens showing a likeness of the selected menu with the menu's title already highlighted. If you wanted to change the menu's title, you could do that now by typing the new name into the Title field. Programmers use the radio button with the Apple icon when they're creating the Apple menu for an application, but most users won't have much reason to click it. For programmer information about the Enabled box, see Chapter 20. If you want to add color to your menus, see Chapter 18. Off to the right

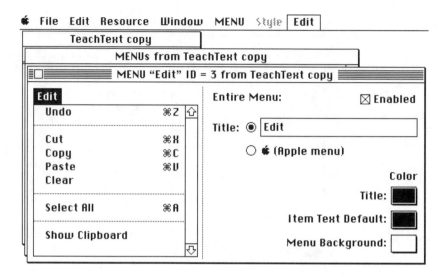

Figure 8-3. The 'MENU' editor with a menu title selected.

on the menu bar ResEdit displays a test version of the menu you're modifying. You can pull it down as you edit to see the effect of your changes.

To edit a menu item, simply click it. But be careful not to drag menu items around within the editor! Remember, moving the *text name* of a menu command doesn't change the instructions the application associates with that *location* in the menu. As Figure 8-4 shows, the 'MENU' editor offers more options for modifying menu items than it does for menu titles. The Style menu becomes available, allowing you to change menu item text to any combination of seven text styles. The Choose Icon item in the 'MENU' menu (see the next section) also becomes available. Unless you are a software developer, however, you won't use the other available options. You'll want to confine your modifications to four areas: setting Command-key shortcuts with the Cmd-Key field, changing the text name and style of menu items, adding icons, and changing the colors used to draw the menu.

In other words, stay away from the Enabled, has Submenu, and Mark boxes. For more information on these boxes, see Chapter 20. Also, be careful not to click the radio button that could obliterate a

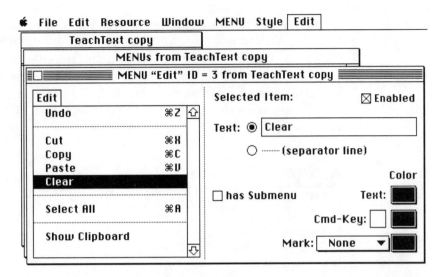

Figure 8-4. The 'MENU' editor, with a menu item selected. Menu items have more options for customization than menu titles do.

menu command with a separator line. (You can, however, change an existing separator line into a "command" that does nothing. We're not sure why you'd want to do this, but it seems relatively harmless, so here's how: Simply click on the separator line to be replaced, click the radio button by the Text field and type in "Bogus" or whatever name you choose. Don't use hyphens to start the text—they automatically change the text back to a separator line.)

The menus in some applications have submenus, and you can modify those, too. To edit a submenu, double-click the menu item that the submenu is attached to. Another 'MENU' editor window opens containing the submenu, which you can edit just as you would any other menu.

The 'MENU' Menu

When the 'MENU' editor opens, it adds a new menu, shown in Figure 8-5, to ResEdit's menu bar. Programmers use the first item, Edit Menu & MDEF ID, when they are developing the menus for an application. (For more information, see Chapter 20.) This item has no customization potential, and, in fact, unless you're developing software, you should leave it alone. You can use the next two items, Choose Icon and Remove Icon, to add and remove icons in your menus. We'll talk more about menu icons a bit later in this chapter. The last two items, Remove Colors and Use Color Picker, are useful when you're working with color in your menus, which is described in Chapter 18.

MENU

> Edit Menu & MDEF ID...
> Choose Icon...
> Remove Icon
> Remove Colors
> ⋯⋯⋯⋯⋯⋯⋯⋯
> Use Color Picker

Figure 8-5. The 'MENU' editor adds its own menu to ResEdit's menu bar to help you modify 'MENU' resources.

Changing Menu Item Text

To modify the text of a menu item, click in the Text field. You don't have to select the text to apply styles. If the blinking insertion point is in the text field, ResEdit applies whatever text style(s) you choose from the Style menu to the text of the entire menu item. You can't apply styles to individual words within a menu item. The change will show up to the left within the editor window and in the test menu to the right on the menu bar, but not in the text field. If you don't like what a menu item says, select the existing text and type in something you like better. The 'MENU' editor's Text field allows you to type in more characters than you'll ever need or want. Once you get beyond 15 to 20 characters, or overflow the Text field, further text won't show up within the 'MENU' editor. The Menu Manager can make menus as big as necessary, however, so you can check the test menu to see how your lengthy menu item looks.

Assigning Command-Key Shortcuts

Adding or changing Command-key shortcuts is a snap. Simply click the menu item you want to change, click the Cmd-Key box, and type in the character you desire. Remember: Use capital letters, for cosmetic reasons. Also, you can't use Command-Shift-number combinations because they're already taken for built-in Fkeys; for example, Command-Shift-3 takes a screen shot no matter what application you're using. (If you must use punctuation characters, see Chapter 9.)

Adding Menu Icons

Icons, which appear to the left of menu item text or alone if there is no text, can give valuable visual clues about the function a menu command performs. Figure 8-6 illustrates how icons can help. Few applications use them, perhaps because they can take up so much space, but any menu item can have an icon. You can add three types of icons to menus. Normal icons are 'ICON' resources, which are 32-by-32-bit pictures. Reduced icons are normal icons reduced to 16-by-16-bit pictures. Small icons are 'SICN' resources, which are also 16-by-16-bit pictures. For more information, see Chapter 7. Normal icons sometimes look too big and can give the menu an off-balance appearance, so reduced or small icons may look better. But if you also want a keyboard equivalent for your illustrated menu item, you have no choice: You have to use a normal icon. You can't have a Command-key shortcut with reduced or small icons.

By The Way Menus on the original Macintosh didn't include provisions for small or reduced icons. To add this capability, another part of the 'MENU' resource had to be reassigned. You guessed it: The Command-key shortcut lost its place. Reduced and small icons can be used only in System 5.0 or later.

By The Way Actually, you can add four types of icons to menus. If you're interested in color icons, you can substitute a 'cicn' for an 'ICON'. See Chapter 17.

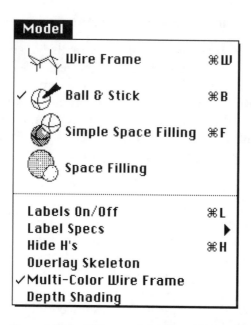

Figure 8-6. This menu from Ball & Stick, a chemistry molecular modeling program, shows a good use of menu icons.

Menu icons can come from a number of places. You can use an existing icon, create an icon from scratch in ResEdit, or copy a picture from a paint or draw program. Whichever way you choose, you'll need to become familiar with the Choose Icon dialog and the icon editors.

When you select Choose Icon from the 'MENU' menu, ResEdit displays the dialog shown in Figure 8-7, which asks you to do just that. What you see next depends on the application. ResEdit shows you all the 'ICON' (but not 'ICN#') resources in that application or the first icon in each 'SICN' list it finds. The dialog defaults to show Normal Icons, but you only have to click the radio buttons to move between the three types of icons. Most icons you see will probably be dimmed, indicating that you can't use them because they don't have suitable ID numbers. In menus, you can only use icons with IDs from 257 to 511. Then again, you may not see any icons. MacPaint, for example, doesn't have any icons of the types used in menus. TeachText has only two small icons, and they're dimmed. (Of course, if there aren't any Normal Icons, there won't be any Reduced Icons either, since both come from the same 'ICON' resources.)

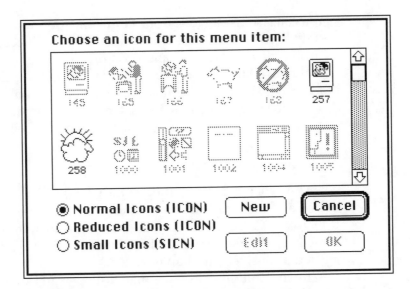

Figure 8-7. You select icons to add to menus from the Choose Icon dialog.

Using Existing Icons

If you happen to come across an icon you like and it's not dimmed, simply double-click it, and ResEdit will add the icon to the currently selected menu item—you're all set. If you want to use an icon that's dimmed, you can copy it and give it a suitable ID. Here's how.

1. Go back to the type picker.

2. Look for the 'ICON' or 'SICN' type, whichever type matches the icon you're after, and open it.

3. Find your icon in the icon picker and select it (click once). Duplicate the icon (from the Edit menu), and give the duplicate an ID between 257 and 511 (using Get Resource Info from the Resource menu). If you need to brush up on how to use the Resource Info window to change IDs, see Chapter 3.

When you go back to the 'MENU' editor and select Choose Icon, your icon won't be dimmed, so you'll only have to double-click it.

You can also use an icon from a different application. Just use ResEdit to copy it from the icon picker of the original application into the icon picker of the application you're modifying, giving it an appropriate ID if necessary. (Be careful not to cut or delete icons!) When you go back to the 'MENU' editor, you'll be able to edit the icon or add it to your menu as is. Icons don't appear in the 'MENU' editor window, so you'll have to check the test menu to see how it looks.

Creating and Editing Icons

When you click the New button in the Choose Icon dialog, or select an icon and then click the Edit button, ResEdit opens either the 'ICON' or 'SICN' editor, depending on the radio button selected. These two editors behave like ResEdit's other fatbits editors and are covered extensively in Chapter 7.

Actually, ResEdit does more than just open an icon editor when you click the New button; it creates an icon and assigns it an ID number in the appropriate range. In other words, from within the 'MENU' editor you create an icon resource. If you never click one fatbit, you'll still have a new, all-white icon, which will precede the menu item text. If you fiddle with the fatbits a while and then decide you don't want the icon after all, you can't just throw it away from here. Remove Icon on the 'MENU' menu only takes the icon off the menu item you're editing, but there will still be an icon resource cluttering up your file. Revert This Resource on the Resource menu applies only to the 'MENU' resource open, not the icon ('ICON' or 'SICN') resource. You can select Revert File from the File menu, but of course that throws away all the changes you've made to any resources in that file.

So it's a little easier to make messes than it is to clean them up. Fortunately, throwing out an icon isn't very hard. Simply go back to the type picker and double-click the appropriate icon type ('ICON' or 'SICN') to open that icon picker. You can toss unwanted icons from there, or choose Revert This Resource to get rid of your changes. If you're planning a major icon-editing session, you might consider going directly to the icon editor via the icon picker instead of the 'MENU' editor.

Adding a Command-Key Shortcut to ResEdit

Why not modify one of ResEdit's menus by adding a keyboard short-cut to the Revert This Resource item on ResEdit's Resource menu? Such a shortcut will probably come in handy as you play around with ResEdit. This is one of the rare occasions when you don't have to make a copy first—*if* you follow the steps exactly and don't make any other changes, and if you have a backup in case of disaster.

"Use ResEdit on itself?!" you exclaim. Sure, it's a little like doing brain surgery on yourself, but hey—ResEdit's a powerful program.

1. Start up ResEdit and use it to open ResEdit. You'll see a warning dialog that reminds you to be careful. Click OK and remember to be careful.

2. Find the 'MENU' resource type and open it.

3. From the 'MENU' picker, open the resource for the Resource menu (ID 128, Named "Resource"), and ResEdit will open the 'MENU' editor. You might notice that the Enabled box is not checked. That's OK; leave it alone. (The Resource menu remains disabled—dimmed—until a resource is selected/opened. At that point, ResEdit enables the menu.)

4. Click the Revert This Resource item in the 'MENU' editor's window (not the one on the menu bar). Next, click the Cmd-Key box and type a capital R.

Warning Be careful not to click and drag items around within menus! Remember, moving the text name of a menu command doesn't change the instructions the application associates with that location in the menu.

5. Close all ResEdit's windows or just quit, making sure to save. Next time you start ResEdit, you can try out your new shortcut as you poke around an application's resources.

Now you're armed with a quick way to revert resources as you embark on customizing menus—or any other resources you tackle.

Summary

This chapter describes 'MENU' resources and briefly explains how the Macintosh works with them. With ResEdit's 'MENU' editor you can add or change Command-key shortcuts, edit the names of menu titles and commands, alter the text style of menu items, and add icons to menu items. (Changing the colors used to draw menus is discussed in Chapter 18.) We conclude the chapter by showing you how to add a Command-key shortcut to one of ResEdit's menus.

Chapter 9

Modifying Your
Keyboard Layout

There has never been and there will never be a keyboard layout that can please everyone. Most people probably wish they could move at least one character. The good news is that ResEdit lets you move characters around to your heart's content. The bad news is that moving the physical key caps is not nearly as easy. In fact, it's almost impossible to move most key caps because they're difficult to remove without breaking and because they're sculpted to fit their location, so they wouldn't feel right even if you could move them.

But even without moving the key caps, you can make some useful changes to the keyboard layout. Wouldn't it be nice if you could type "P.O. Box" without having to release the Shift key for each period? Or how about making the curly (printer's) quotes more accessible? You can make small changes such as these without worrying about moving key caps. If you're interested in more radical changes, such as converting your keyboard to a Dvorak layout (a layout that minimizes the distance your fingers need to travel for common characters, thus enabling you to type five to ten times faster), you should look for a new keyboard instead of trying to remap the keys. (If you just want to try out a Dvorak keyboard layout, a customized keyboard layout is available from many user groups and bulletin boards.)

First, a bit of definition. As we're using it here, a "key" is a physical key on the keyboard labeled with a symbol, such as "A." A "character" is what your application receives when you press a key. A key in a given keyboard location can be labeled differently and can produce different characters, depending on what country's System software you're using and what changes you've made to the resources we'll describe shortly. For example, on the U.S. keyboard, the first key in the second row of keys produces a *q* character, whereas in France it produces an *a* character.

To allow for many different keyboards and languages, the translation of a key pressed on your keyboard into a character that can be displayed by your application involves a couple of steps, each controlled by a different resource. Figure 9-1 shows the path a character takes from the keyboard to the application. The 'KMAP' resource maps the key pressed to a "virtual" keycode that's independent of the kind of keyboard being used. The 'KCHR' resource is next in line. It translates the virtual keycode into a character that an application can use. Because of this, you can take advantage of the 'KCHR' resource to change the layout of your keyboard. In fact, the 'KCHR' resource is used to customize the Macintosh for different countries. No matter what country you live in, you can probably modify your 'KCHR' resource to make your life a bit easier. We'll mention a couple of modifications for U.S. keyboards here.

The 'KCHR' resource determines keyboard and character assignments—which key on your keyboard produces which character. This is a complex resource, but ResEdit's editor allows you to avoid most of the complexity if you only want to make simple changes. Because it was designed to allow Apple to change the keyboard layout for different languages and countries, the 'KCHR' editor can handle complex situations you'll never encounter while customizing. This chapter first explains the 'KCHR' resource and how the editor works

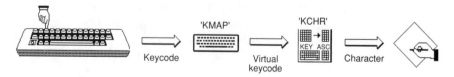

Figure 9-1. A character's trip from the keyboard to your application.

and then gives some examples of how you can remap your own keyboard. We've included more detailed information at the end of the chapter for those of you who want to make more significant changes.

By The Way Each country has its own 'KCHR' resource provided by Apple. The name of the resource is usually the same as the name of the country or region that uses the resource. The resource ID is the same as the country's Country Code (a unique number assigned to each country by Apple). For example, the 'KCHR' for the United States has an ID of 0 and is named "US," whereas Switzerland has two 'KCHR's, either ID 18 ("Suisse Romand") or 19 ("Deutsche Schweiz"). If you have more than one 'KCHR' resource, you can use the Keyboard Control Panel to choose which 'KCHR' your Mac uses.

The Main Window

The main 'KCHR' window is divided into five parts, as shown in Figure 9-2. You'll mainly be concerned with the character table and the keyboard, so we'll only briefly mention the other parts of the window. You can find more information about the modifier key tables later in this chapter.

This editor adds a few menus to help you manipulate the resource. Because most of the commands on the KCHR menu aren't useful for customization projects, we'll discuss only the pertinent commands. The Font and Size menus come in handy for changing the character table, which we discuss next.

Character Table

The character table contains a spot for each of the 256 characters that a font can contain. Most fonts don't define every possible character, and you'd probably have trouble remembering all the key combinations even if they did. The font shown in the character table doesn't matter—you're mapping the keyboard, not the font. But if you're looking for a certain special character, you can switch to the appropriate font and size. The character table is initially filled in with the characters from the default application font (usually Geneva), but

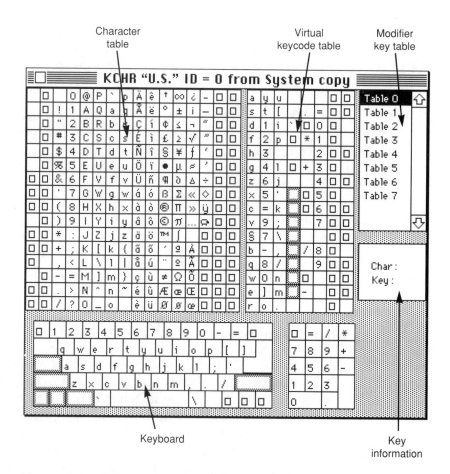

Figure 9-2. The 'KCHR' window has five parts.

you can use ResEdit's Font menu to switch to any available font. It's from the character table that you get the characters to assign to keys on the keyboard.

Hint The 'KCHR' window is normally displayed using the application font (usually Geneva). You'll notice, however, that many of the characters in the character table aren't defined (they just contain a box character). If you use the Font menu to change the font to Helvetica, the empty spots in the table will be filled in with all the special characters supported by the Apple extended character set.

Keyboard

The keyboard area of the window shows a picture of a keyboard. You can change to a different keyboard picture by selecting the View As command from the 'KCHR' menu. The View As dialog is shown in Figure 9-3. The keyboards listed in the dialog correspond to the 'KCAP' resources found in your System file. (The 'KCAP' resources contain the physical layouts of the keyboards displayed by the Key Caps desk accessory.) As you can see in Figure 9-3, not all of the keyboards are named. If you don't see your keyboard listed, simply try the unnamed ones until the editor displays one that matches. Remember, no matter what keyboard you display, you're still editing the same 'KCHR' resource, so you can't set it up differently for each keyboard. Pressing a key on your real keyboard, or clicking a key in the keyboard area, highlights the associated fields in the editor's tables.

Hint If your keyboard isn't named in the View As dialog and that annoys you, why not name it? The View As dialog gets the names from a 'KBDN' resource within ResEdit. Let's say you have Apple's ergonomic, adjustable keyboard and figure out that it's ID 16. Go to the 'KBDN' resource in a copy of ResEdit and create a new resource (Command-K). Don't bother typing anything in the window that appears. Go to the Resource Info window (Command-I) and change the ID to match the ID of your keyboard, in this case, 16. Type the keyboard name in the name field. You can leave off the word "keyboard" because it's automatically added to the name you type. Before you close all the windows, saving your changes, be sure to click the Purgeable box in the Resource Info window. (There's no point in having a 'KBDN' tying up memory after ResEdit is done with it.) When you run your modified ResEdit, you'll see your keyboard's name listed in the View As dialog.

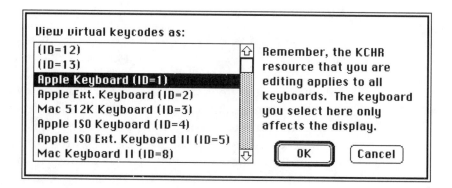

Figure 9-3. The View As dialog lets you pick a keyboard layout.

Modifier Key Tables

Each 'KCHR' resource contains several modifier key tables that are used to translate virtual keycodes to characters. Every keyboard has several modifier keys, such as the Shift, Command, Caps Lock, Option, and Control keys. They are outlined in gray in the keyboard area. Each modifier key combination is associated with one of the tables. For example, there is one table for the Shift key and one for the Shift-Option key combination. Several modifier key combinations (such as Control, Control-Shift, and so on) can share the same table.

Warning Don't click on the table numbers! Clicking on a table number in this list changes the table used for the current modifier key combination. There's more information about how to use these tables later in this chapter.

Virtual Keycode Table

The virtual keycode table shows the translation from virtual keycode to character for the current modifier key table (the one that's high-lighted in the list). (Remember, virtual keycodes are just numbers that represent the keys on the keyboard. They're "virtual" because they're independent of the keyboard used.) Each spot in the table corresponds to a different virtual keycode and can contain any character from the character table. For example, the first position in the table corresponds to the virtual keycode for the key labeled *A* on the U.S. keyboard. In Figure 9-2, this entry in the table contains the character *a*.

Key Information

The Key Information field shows the ASCII code and the virtual keycode of any key you press.

Making a New 'KCHR' Resource

If you have more than one 'KCHR' resource in your System file, you can use the Keyboard Control Panel to switch to the one you want to use. This is convenient if you work with different countries or if you want to make your own customized keyboard layout. If you're going to modify your 'KCHR' resource, it's convenient to make a copy of the original resource so you can switch back to it if you have any problems with your modified version. Here are the general instructions for making your own 'KCHR' resource.

1. Use ResEdit to open a copy of your System file.

2. Select the 'KCHR' resource. (Its name should be the same as the name of your country or region.)

3. Duplicate the resource using the Duplicate command on the Edit menu.

4. Select the new resource and choose Get Resource Info from the Resource menu.

5. Change the name to something new, like "My KCHR," then close the Info window.

6. Edit your new 'KCHR' resource to suit yourself. The following tasks contain some suggestions.

7. Close and save the file. Swap and rename your System files as described in Chapter 4, then restart.

8. Open the Keyboard Control Panel. You should see your new resource listed under the "Keyboard Layout" label.

Changing Shift-Period to a Period and Shift-Comma to a Comma

Shift-period is usually a > character, and Shift-comma is usually a < character. If you're like most people, you don't use these characters very often, and you might like not having to release the Shift key to type periods within abbreviations like U.S.A., P.O., and D.C. Here's a simple way to make better use of these keys.

1. Use ResEdit to open a System file copy.

2. Open the 'KCHR' resource you created in the previous task, "Making a New 'KCHR' Resource." You should see a window similar to the one shown in Figure 9-4. (Table 1 won't be selected until you press the Shift key.)

3. If the picture of the keyboard doesn't look like your keyboard, select the View As command from the 'KCHR' menu. You'll see a dialog listing keyboards, and you can pick the one you're using. (If you don't see your keyboard named, pick unnamed ones until the picture you see matches your keyboard.)

4. Press the period key and notice where the period character is in the character table (it's in the lower-left part of the character table).

5. Now press and hold the Shift key. While you hold the Shift key down, drag the period from the character table and drop it on the key on the keyboard displaying the right angle bracket character, as shown in Figure 9-4.

You've now replaced the > character (Shift-period) with a period, and you can follow the same procedure to replace the < with a comma. Of course, now you have no way to type the < and > characters. If you think you might occasionally need these characters, you should map them to some other key combination. A good place might be Option-Shift-period and Option-Shift-comma since most fonts don't use those key combinations.

Reinstall the modified System copy as your current System file and restart. Now all you have to do is select your new 'KCHR' in the Keyboard Control Panel to make your changes take effect.

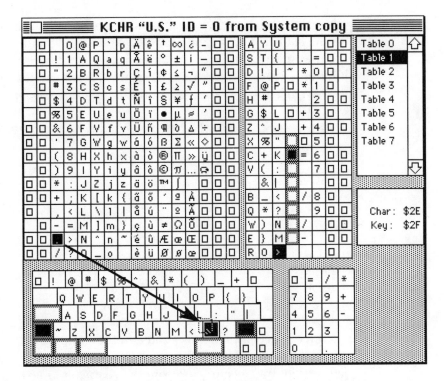

Figure 9-4. Changing the > character to a period.

Making Curly Quotes Easy to Type

A document looks more professional if you use "curly" (smart) quotes instead of the common "straight" quotes. These characters are always available on the keyboard but aren't very convenient. Normally, you can use the curly quotes by typing these key combinations:

- Option-[for open double quote (")
- Option-Shift-[for close double quote (")
- Option-] for open single quote (')
- Option-Shift-] for close single quote or apostrophe (')

If you're like most people, you probably don't use the straight ([and]) and curly ({ and }) bracket characters very often, so why not put the curly quote characters there, where you can get to them easily? Even if your word processing program has an automatic curly quote feature, you might wish you could type them more easily in all your applications. Since the curly quotes already use the Option-] and Option-[keys, you can just switch the quotes and the brackets, as shown in Table 9-1, and you'll still have access to all the characters.

Table 9-1. Suggested Character to Key Assignments

Key	Character Produced
{	"
}	"
[	'
]	'
Option-[	[
Option-Shift-[	{
Option-]	]
Option-Shift-]	}

You can accomplish this switch in the same way described for Shift-period—just hold down the modifier keys you want to use while you drag a character from the character table to the key on the keyboard.

Using the Modifier Key Tables

So far we've talked about some simple changes you can make to your keyboard. But what if you want to make more complex changes? Since the 'KCHR' resource was designed to support the myriad differences between languages and keyboards in different countries, chances are it will support any change you want to make. For example, you might want to make the punctuation characters (such as ! and *) available for use as Command-key equivalents. Or you might want to change the special accent characters (generated by the so-called dead keys described shortly) to get to extra characters in a font.

When you press the *A* key or Option-*A*, your Mac has to have some way of deciding what character it should send to the application. Since a keyboard has many modifier keys (Command, Option, Control, Caps Lock, Shift, and so on), the translation from virtual keycode to character is a complex process. (Remember, the keycode from the keyboard is translated into a virtual keycode using the 'KMAP' resource.) The Macintosh performs the translation using the Modifier Key Table that corresponds to the modifier keys held down when the key is pressed. For example, when you press Option-*A*, your Mac finds the Modifier Key Table for the Option key and looks up the *A* virtual keycode. The character it finds in the table is the one it sends to your application. Every key on the keyboard has a spot in the table that contains the character to be generated when that key is pressed. (To find the spot in the table, just press the key.) The tables are kept in the 'KCHR' resource and are displayed in the Modifier Key Tables section of the 'KCHR' editor window you saw in Figure 9-2.

The same table is often used for several key combinations, as you can see in Table 9-2.

By The Way There's no way to find out which modifier key combinations have been assigned to a particular table, other than pressing all combinations in turn and seeing which tables are selected. Also, remember that you shouldn't click the table numbers because that reassigns them.

Table 9-2. Modifier Key Tables and Their Use in the U.S. 'KCHR'

Table Number	*Modifier Key Combinations*
Table 0	Command, Command-Shift, Command-Caps Lock, Command-Shift-Caps Lock, or none
Table 1	Shift, or Shift-Caps Lock
Table 2	Caps Lock
Table 3	Option
Table 4	Option-Shift, Command-Option-Shift, Option-Shift-Caps Lock, or Command-Option-Shift-Caps Lock
Table 5	Option-Caps Lock
Table 6	Command-Option, or Command-Option-Caps Lock
Table 7	Control with or without any other modifier key(s)

These tables can be confusing to use, but they're worth the small extra effort it takes to understand them. Remember, the selected table is the active table for the modifier keys you've pressed. You can't select a table to see what it contains; if you click a table, you'll reassign it. For example, in the U.S. 'KCHR' resource, if you press the Option key, Table 3 is selected. If you click Table 4 while still pressing the Option key, you'll reassign the Option key to use Table 4 instead of Table 3. The virtual keycode table area of the window shows the contents of the current modifier key table, as shown in Figure 9-2. (In the figure, no modifier keys are pressed.)

Now that you understand something about how the modifier key tables work, you can safely change them a bit.

Making the Punctuation Characters Available for Menu Commands

Adding extra Command-key equivalents to your menus is often convenient (see Chapter 8 for details about how to do this), but you may quickly run out of meaningful characters. When that happens, you can start using Command-Option characters like Σ or f, but will you really remember how to type them? The problem with such characters is that pulling down the menu doesn't help remind you of the shortcut because it doesn't indicate which keys to type. To solve this problem, you can use the number keys, but sometimes the punctuation characters (such as ! and *) might be easier to remember. You can't use Command-Shift numbers because they're already defined to be Fkeys (such as print screen) by the System, but you can make these characters available from Command-Option number. Here's an example of how it would work. To type the @ you would still press Shift-2, but to use @ as a keyboard shortcut you would press Command-Option-2. Option-2 would still produce the ™ character; you would have changed only what Command-Option-2 produces.

1. Use ResEdit to open a copy of your System file.

2. Open the 'KCHR' resource you created earlier. (Use the Duplicate command to make a copy of the 'KCHR' resource, if you haven't already.) You should see a window similar to the one shown in Figure 9-4, except that Table 0 will be selected.

3. If the picture of the keyboard doesn't look like the keyboard you're using, set the correct keyboard from the View As item on the 'KCHR' menu.

4. Press the Command and Option keys and choose Duplicate Table from the 'KCHR' menu. This makes a duplicate of Table 6 (since it was selected) and names it Table 8. If you want to duplicate a different table, hold down the set of modifier keys that selects that table before choosing Duplicate Table from the 'KCHR' menu.

5. Now hold down the Command and Option keys (which causes Table 6 to be selected) and click the new table in the table list. An alert appears asking if you're sure you want to switch tables. Click the OK button.

6. You now have a new table, but it behaves exactly the same way as the old one since it's a duplicate table. Hold down the Command and Option keys and drag the punctuation characters from the character table to the corresponding number keys on the picture of the keyboard. The standard characters are: !, @, #, $, %, ^, &, *, (, and).

> **Hint** You can locate the characters in the character table by holding down the Shift key and pressing the appropriate key on the keyboard. For example, hold down Shift-1 and you see that the ! character is in the upper-left part of the character table.

7. Close and save the System copy.

8. After you install the copy in your System folder and restart your Mac, you can activate your new 'KCHR' by selecting it in the Keyboard Control Panel.

Changing Dead Keys

Even on a U.S. Macintosh you can use many accented characters, such as é or â. You enter these characters by pressing two keys in succession: The first key tells your Mac what accent you want and the second key tells it what character to accent. So, for example, to type the é character you type Option-e followed by e. The first key (Option-e in this example) is called a *dead key* because it doesn't produce any character by itself, but instead modifies the character generated by the next key typed. In general, there's one dead key for each accent mark. Dead keys are indicated by a dark outline in both the virtual keycode table and the keyboard picture (the gray outlines indicate the modifier keys). The U.S. 'KCHR' resource uses the Option key for all the dead keys, as shown in Figure 9-5. 'KCHR' resources for other countries may use other modifier key combinations to access the dead keys.

Your Mac needs some way of knowing what the final accented character should be. It finds out by looking in a dead key table. Each dead key has its own table that indicates which characters can have the indicated accent. To see a dead key's table, just press the dead key or click it in the picture of the keyboard. A window similar to the one shown in Figure 9-6 appears, to let you edit the dead key. You can also select the dead key you're interested in from a list if you choose the Edit Dead Key command from the 'KCHR' menu.

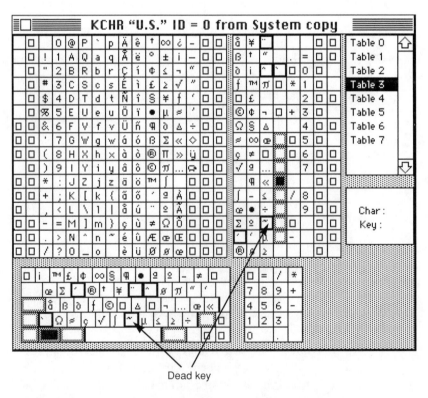

Dead key

Figure 9-5. Dead keys in the U.S. 'KCHR' resource.

The substitution character table contains the pairs of characters that determine what character is produced by the dead key. For example, if Option-~, the dead key shown in Figure 9-6, is followed by a character from the first column of the substitution character table, the result will be the character shown in the second column. To change either part of a substitution pair, just drag a character from the character table to the appropriate spot in the substitution character table. If you want to create a new pair, just drag a character into one of the empty gray squares. If you want to delete a pair, drag either character into the Trash.

If a dead key is followed by a character that's not found in the substitution character table, the No Match character is used instead. This character is shown in the upper-right part of the dead key window and can be changed by dragging a new character over the existing one.

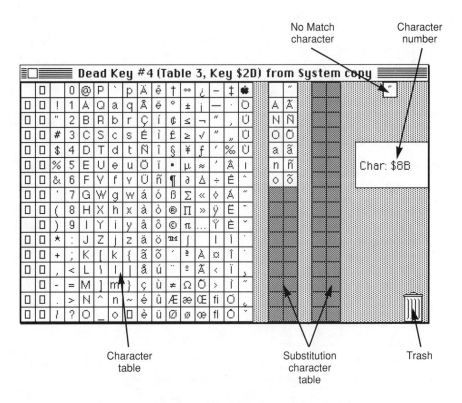

Figure 9-6. The dead key editor window for Option-~.

Summary

This chapter explains how the 'KCHR' resource is used to translate a key typed on your keyboard into a character that appears in your application. We explain the parts of the 'KCHR' editor window and show you how to make some commonly used characters easier to type by modifying the 'KCHR' resource in your System file. Next, we explain the modifier key tables and show you how to make a new table so you can use punctuation characters for menu shortcuts. Finally, we discuss dead keys—the keys that modify other keys so you can type accented characters.

Chapter 10

 Customizing Windows,
Dialogs, and Alerts

The ways that you can customize windows, dialogs, and alerts may not rate as the flashiest, but they definitely rank among the most practical. If you continually find yourself moving a certain window that always opens in the same awkward place on your screen, change its default location and save yourself some time and annoyance. If you wish you could see more file names in the standard file directory dialogs, you can enlarge the dialog's list box so you'll spend less time scrolling. If you're always using the mouse to click the Yes button in a certain alert, change the default to Yes so you can simply press Return. This chapter tells you how you can do all these things.

The editors for windows, dialogs, and alerts are closely related, and we suggest you read about them in order because the discussion for each successive editor builds upon the last. In other words, understanding how to edit windows, or 'WIND' resources, helps you learn the basics for editing dialogs ('DLOG'), which in turn helps you understand how to work with alerts ('ALRT'). Dialogs and alerts get their contents from a fourth resource type, called a dialog item list ('DITL'), and this chapter covers that editor, too. Some of these are no doubt more familiar to you than others, so we'll start with some brief definitions.

- A *window* defines a rectangle's size and location on the screen and can include a bit of other associated information, such as a title.

- *Dialogs* appear when an application needs more information from you in order to carry out a command. Dialogs may or may not be *modal*. A modal dialog is one you must respond to before you can do anything else. Modeless dialogs behave pretty much like document windows. A dialog consists of a rectangle that defines the dialog's size and location, an optional title, and the ID of a 'DITL' (Dialog ITem List) resource.

- Applications use *alerts*, a special subset of dialogs, to report errors or give warnings. They're always modal. Alerts contain only buttons, some text, perhaps an icon, and sometimes a sound signal. There are no fancy controls and no boxes or fields to fill in.

- A *dialog item list* is a collection of the various items a dialog or alert contains, such as text, pictures, icons, buttons, check boxes, and other controls. The 'DITL' specifies a size and window-relative location for each item.

With these definitions to build upon, you're ready to dive in.

Windows

Windows are relatively simple resources, so there are only a few ways you can customize them. Changing a window's default size and location are the two most useful changes you can make. (You can also change a window's colors. See Chapter 18 if you're interested.) If you have a large screen, you can change the window size in your favorite application so you can use all that space. If a certain window always appears in the same awkward place, you may be able to change where it appears.

As with most resources, you need to remember a few caveats. Because the Macintosh provides other, more convenient, ways of drawing windows, many applications avail themselves of those methods instead, and you can't customize those windows. Applications that do use 'WIND' resources may already enlarge some windows automatically to take advantage of bigger screens. They may also keep track of where you last left certain windows, in effect automatically resetting the default. You can still make useful changes in some applications, however, once you know how.

The 'WIND' Editor

The 'WIND' editor, shown in Figure 10-1, is pretty easy to understand. Across the top of the editor window, under the title bar, you see a row of small pictures of windows. These pictures are actually buttons that allow you to choose from a variety of window types. You would simply click a different picture to choose that window type. In most cases, however, you'll want to leave the window-type buttons alone, unless you're a programmer. Choosing a new window type with a size box or a close box won't do you any good, anyway. You'll see the boxes, but they won't work unless the application has been designed to support them.

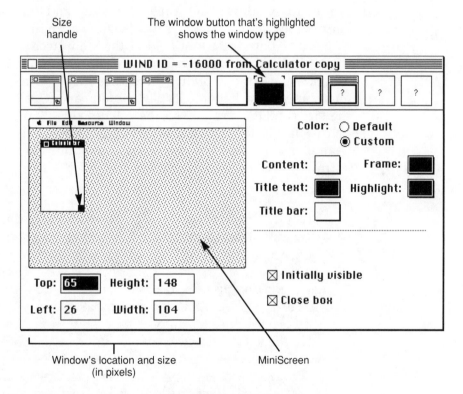

Figure 10-1. The 'WIND' editor, scaled for a Classic screen, showing the 'WIND' resource for the Calculator DA.

By The Way The Calculator DA is an example of an application that keeps track of where you left the window (by updating the 'WIND' resource). Also, it's one that you should not change the size of, because the contents (the calculator) won't fit right if you do. The only thing you can customize is the window title.

Beneath the window-type buttons on the right are the radio buttons that allow you to control window colors. You can learn about them in Chapter 18. Unless you're a programmer, you'll want to stay away from the two check boxes in the bottom right. (For more information, see Chapter 19.) Four fields in the bottom-left corner of the editor window allow you to set the size and location of the *content area* of the window. (In other words, the space a title bar takes up is "extra.") Above these four fields is the MiniScreen, a miniature likeness of a Macintosh screen, complete with menu bar. You can change the size and position of the window on the MiniScreen in two ways. You can simply drag it to its new location and resize it by pulling on its size handle. As you do so, the values in the size and location fields are updated. Alternatively, you can type in new size and location values, and the window changes size and jumps to the new spot. The arrow keys can change position, too.

Hint If you want to use the size and location fields, it helps to understand that the top-left corner of the screen is defined as the origin (0,0), and everything is measured from there in pixels. The menu bar covers the first 20 pixels down from the top (in most Western languages), so remember to position tops of windows at 21 or more pixels. Also keep in mind that the values in these fields indicate the size and location of the *content area* of a window, so a title bar or other window frame needs extra space. (Title bars vary but generally take up about as much space as the menu bar.)

It is important to remember that if you change the position of the top of the rectangle without also changing the position of the bottom, you squash the window. If that particular window has contents, they probably won't fit properly anymore. You can avoid squashing the window if you choose Show Height & Width (instead of Show Bottom & Right) from the 'WIND' menu. Or you can just drag it to its new position.

This editor adds two menus to ResEdit's menu bar. You can set characteristics of the MiniScreen using the MiniScreen menu. The 'WIND' menu lets you control a variety of characteristics of the 'WIND' editor and the resource you're editing.

The MiniScreen Menu

ResEdit uses the same MiniScreen menu, shown in Figure 10-2, for the 'WIND', 'ALRT', and 'DLOG' editors. The MiniScreen defaults to a Classic screen, but you can change it to any of the standard Apple monitor sizes listed. Their dimensions are shown in pixels. If you have a monitor that's not listed (or if you want to create a screen so you can see magnified details), choose Other from the MiniScreen menu. You see the dialog shown in Figure 10-3, which allows you to set another screen size (in pixels), and even add it to the menu if you wish. The editor appropriately scales the MiniScreen and the window it contains to whatever screen size you select, as shown in Figure 10-4. When you set the MiniScreen size for any one of the 'WIND', 'ALRT', or 'DLOG' editors, you set it for all of them because ResEdit saves your choice in its Preferences file.

```
MiniScreen
✓512 x 342   - Classic
 512 x 384   - 12" RGB
 640 x 400   - Portable
 640 x 480   - B&W or 13" RGB
 640 x 870   - Portrait
 1152 x 870 - Two-page
..............................................
 Other...
```

Figure 10-2. The MiniScreen menu lets you set the scaled screen size displayed in the 'WIND', 'ALRT', and 'DLOG' editors.

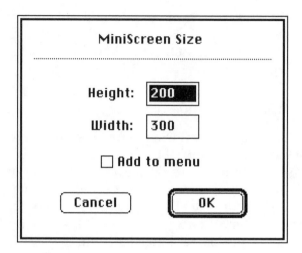

Figure 10-3. This dialog, which is displayed when you choose Other from the MiniScreen menu, allows you to set a custom screen size.

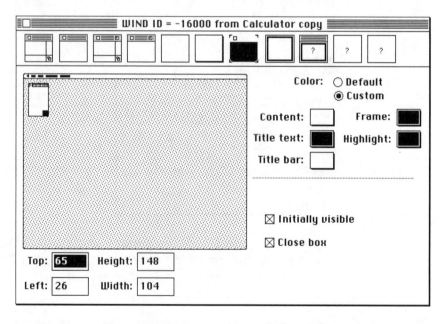

Figure 10-4. The 'WIND' editor showing the 'WIND' resource for the Calculator DA, scaled for a two-page screen. (Compare with Figure 10-1.)

The 'WIND' Menu

The 'WIND' menu, shown in Figure 10-5, allows you to control certain characteristics of 'WIND' resources and the 'WIND' editor. The first item, Set 'WIND' Characteristics, causes the dialog shown in Figure 10-6 to be displayed. If you want to change the title of a window, perhaps changing the "Calculator" DA to the "Abacus" DA,

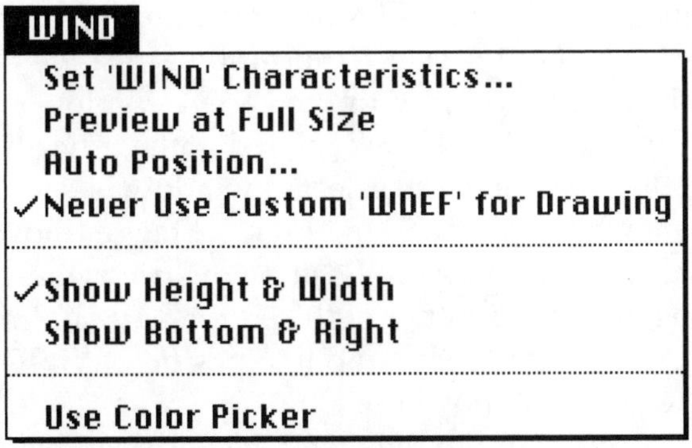

Figure 10-5. The 'WIND' menu helps you manipulate resources in the 'WIND' editor.

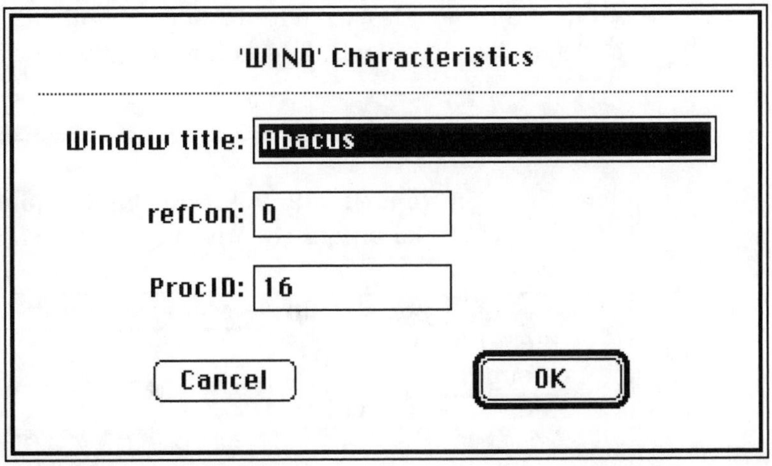

Figure 10-6. This dialog, which is displayed when you choose Set 'WIND' Characteristics, allows you to edit the title of a window.

here's where you make the change. Unless you're a programmer, you should leave the other two editable fields alone.

The Preview at Full Size command temporarily displays the 'WIND' you're editing at full size and in the location specified. Clicking the mouse or typing a key makes the preview disappear.

The Auto Position command displays the dialog shown in Figure 10-7, and as indicated, this feature only works with System 7.0 or later. The pop-up menu on the left in the dialog determines the positioning, and the three choices in the pop-up menu on the right determine whether the selected position is relative to the Main Screen, the Parent Window, or the Parent Window's Screen. If you choose Center, the 'WIND' is centered both vertically and horizontally, relative to the selected window or screen. Alert Position is also centered left to right, but higher. Stagger moves the 'WIND' down and to the right. Auto Position overrides the default position set in the bottom left corner of the editor, so if you're using System 7, experiment with this command to reposition 'WIND's (also 'DLOG's and 'ALRT's) that annoy you.

The next command in the menu, Never Use Custom 'WDEF' for Drawing, is a Programmers Only item. For more information, see Chapter 19. One of the next two items on the 'WIND' menu is always checked—checking one unchecks the other. They let you choose how to display the size of the 'WIND', either in terms of the location of its bottom and right sides, or in terms of its height and width. We discuss the last command, Use Color Picker, in Chapter 18.

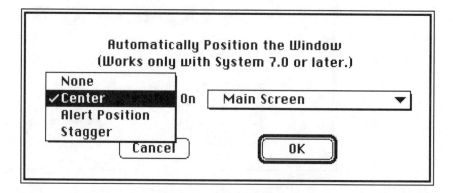

Figure 10-7. The two pop-up menus in the Auto Position dialog let you tell System 7 how to automatically position a 'WIND'.

Changing Where a Window Appears

Not many applications have 'WIND' resources but they are some-times used for fixed windows, such as Clipboard, Header, and Footer windows. They tend to appear in the same place on your screen, which might not be exactly where you'd like them. You have to move them every time. And they tend not to automatically take advantage of a larger screen. You have to enlarge them every time. You might prefer to not have to constantly move or enlarge such windows. Depending on the application, these steps might solve the problem once and for all.

1. Use ResEdit to open a copy of your application, then open the 'WIND' resource type.

2. Find the 'WIND' you want to alter, and open it.

3. The 'WIND' editor opens, displaying the resource you selected. Make sure the editor's MiniScreen matches your screen. Pull down the MiniScreen menu and choose your screen size, if it isn't already checked.

4. Now you can drag the image of the window to where you'd like it to appear. If you want to change the size, drag the size handle in the lower right corner to reshape the window until it suits you. You can also make adjustments by typing directly into the size and location fields below the MiniScreen.

5. Quit ResEdit, saving your changes.

6. Launch the copy of your application and test the new window size and location. If it's not quite right, or if you'd like to customize another window, simply repeat these steps. (You don't have to repeat Step 3. ResEdit remembers your MiniScreen selection.)

Dialogs

When you see the 'DLOG' editor, you'll probably have a vague feeling that you've seen it before, and actually you have. As you can see in Figure 10-8, this editor looks almost exactly like the 'WIND' editor. Add a field in which to specify the ID of an associated 'DITL' resource, and essentially you've got yourself a 'DLOG' editor, which makes sense, because a 'DLOG' is basically a 'WIND' plus a 'DITL'.

Virtually everything you just learned for 'WIND' resources applies to 'DLOG' resources, too. Changing the window type for a dialog (using the window-type buttons across the top of the editor) usually doesn't do you any good. You *can* change the colors. (See Chapter 18 if you're interested.) You shouldn't change the check boxes in the lower-right corner of this editor, either. The MiniScreen menu is the same, and the 'DLOG' menu is completely analogous to the 'WIND' menu.

> **Hint** If you change a dialog's location but the new position doesn't seem to "stick," it might be because the application employs special procedures for moving or centering its dialogs. In fact, ResEdit does this, so don't bother trying to reposition its dialogs. Any time you open a 'WIND', 'DLOG', or 'ALRT' and find it jammed up in the top-left corner of the MiniScreen, you can bet that the application has its own procedures for positioning the window. You can go ahead and customize its contents, if appropriate, but don't bother trying to tweak its position.

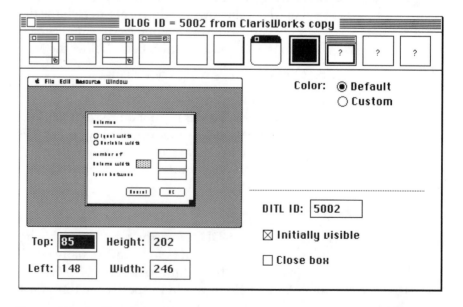

Figure 10-8. The 'DLOG' editor closely resembles the 'WIND' editor. (Compare with Figure 10-1.)

One important way the 'DLOG' editor differs in appearance from the 'WIND' editor is that the rectangle appearing on the MiniScreen usually shows some items inside. Everything in a 'DLOG' is stored in an intimately associated resource called a dialog item list, or 'DITL'. In other words, the 'DITL' is the business part of the dialog, and the 'DLOG' is the box in which the 'DITL' is packaged. The main inference you can draw from this apt analogy is that, unless you significantly change the size of the product (the 'DITL'), you don't have to worry about changing the package (the 'DLOG').

Translating software for foreign markets gives an example of this relationship. When you want to change the text in a dialog, you do that in the associated 'DITL'. Often text translated from English occupies more space, however, so the text item has to become larger. To make room for the translated text, you have to enlarge the text item in the 'DITL'. Then, to make room for the bigger text item in the 'DITL', you have to enlarge the dialog's rectangle, which you can do either in the 'DLOG' editor or in the 'DITL' editor. To understand how all this works, you have to understand how to edit the meat of a dialog, its 'DITL'. We cover that next.

Dialog Item Lists

Manipulating dialog items in a 'DITL' is almost as easy as manipulating files in the Finder or objects in a program like MacDraw. Before you can do anything to an item, you have to click it to select it. Once an item is selected, you can drag it to reposition it. You can also select groups of items by dragging out a rectangle that encloses the items you want to select. (Any item even partly inside the selection rectangle becomes selected.) Most kinds of items have size handles in their bottom-right corners that you can drag to resize the item. You see the size handle only when a single item is selected because you can resize only one item at a time.

Hint When an item, or group of items, is selected, each touch of one of the arrow keys moves the selection by one pixel in the chosen direction.

Dialog item lists are made up of collections of ten different kinds of items that can be arranged any number of ways within the 'DLOG' or 'ALRT' window they're associated with. Table 10-1 summarizes what you can and can't do when customizing dialog item lists (without changing the application's code). The next section describes the 'DITL' editor and gives more details.

Table 10-1. What You Can and Can't Do Safely When Customizing 'DITL's

Safe

- You can reposition items in a 'DITL'.
- You can change the size of items in a 'DITL'.
- You can add or change static items (static text, icons, pictures).
- You can make some items invisible (by dragging them out of the window).
- You can change the text in any item: buttons, radio buttons, static text, and so on.

Dangerous

- Do not change item numbers in a 'DITL'.
- Do not remove items from a 'DITL'.
- Do not change item types; for instance, don't change a button to a check box.
- Do not change pairs of characters such as ^0 or ^1, or other strange-looking clumps of punctuation and numerals resembling cartoon cursing. These markers tell the application where to insert text, such as file names, error numbers, or text from string resources ('STR ' or 'STR#').

The 'DITL' Editor

You can open the 'DITL' editor in a few different ways. If you know the ID of the 'DITL' you want to edit, you can open it from the 'DITL' picker. By convention, a 'DITL' resource should have the same ID number as the 'DLOG' or 'ALRT' it's associated with. You can also open the 'DITL' editor three ways from the 'DLOG' editor. You can choose Open 'DITL' Editor from the Resource menu, you can double-click the picture of the dialog on the MiniScreen, or you can press the Return or Enter key.

What you see when the 'DITL' editor opens depends on the 'DITL' you're editing. The size of the 'DLOG' or 'ALRT' rectangle determines the window size of the associated 'DITL'. Figure 10-9 shows the 'DITL' associated with the 'DLOG' you saw in Figure 10-8. No matter what 'DITL' you edit, you should understand the additional menus, item palette, and item editor.

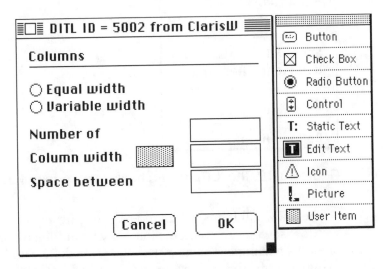

Figure 10-9. The 'DITL' editor shows all the items in a dialog.

The 'DITL' Menu

The 'DITL' menu, shown in Figure 10-10, offers extensive options for manipulating dialog items. Many of the commands are useful only to programmers, however, so they're not described here. (For more details, see Chapter 19.) For instance, the first group of commands, (down to the first separator line) are all concerned with item numbers. Since you should never change item numbers when customizing a 'DITL', you have no use for any of these commands.

The next two commands can help tidy up the appearance of a dialog you're customizing by letting you align items to an invisible grid. Align To Grid causes the upper-left corners of items to snap to the grid corners when you move the items. Grid Settings displays a simple dialog that allows you to set the size (in pixels) of the grid. (Remember, screens vary, but there are roughly 72 pixels per inch.)

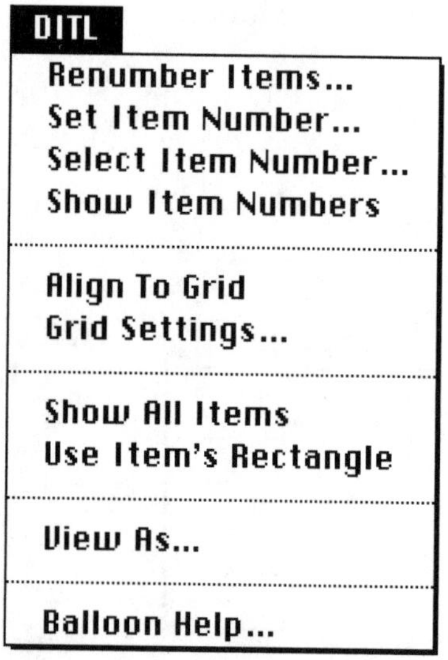

DITL

Renumber Items...
Set Item Number...
Select Item Number...
Show Item Numbers

Align To Grid
Grid Settings...

Show All Items
Use Item's Rectangle

View As...

Balloon Help...

Figure 10-10. The 'DITL' menu helps you manipulate dialog items.

The Show All Items command temporarily expands the 'DITL' window so you can see items that may be hidden outside the dialog's or alert's rectangle. The next item, Use Item's Rectangle, applies only to dialog items that are resources: icons, controls, and pictures ('ICON's, 'CNTL's, and 'PICT's). This command causes the 'DITL' to use the resource's rectangle instead of the rectangle set in the 'DITL'. This command comes in handy if you change pictures, streamlining the rectangle for an automatic fit.

The View As command lets you see how the 'DITL' would look in a different font or font size. Control Panel dialogs, for instance, use 9-point Geneva, so you might want to use that font when you edit the 'DITL' for a Control Panel dialog. (This command could also come in handy if you change your System font, as described in Chapter 15.)

The Balloon Help command is useful only to programmers developing applications to run under System 7.

The Alignment Menu

Making dialogs look nice is the whole point of the Alignment menu, shown in Figure 10-11. All but the last two commands on this menu apply to selections of two or more items, and the menu icons give

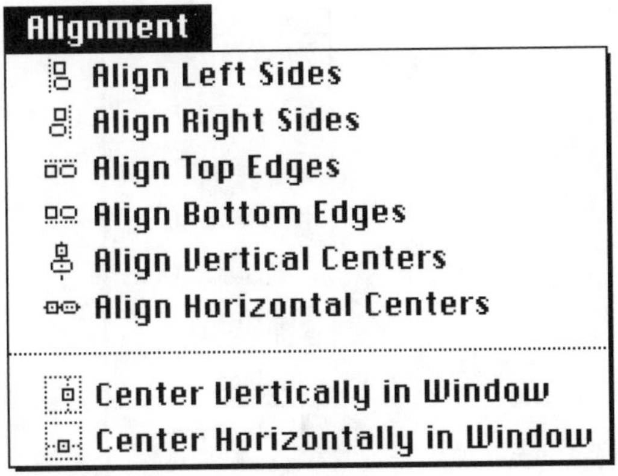

Figure 10-11. The Alignment menu helps line up dialog items.

you good visual clues about what the commands do. (This menu demonstrates a good use of menu icons, discussed in Chapter 8.)

The first four commands align items relative to each other. Choosing Align Left Sides lines up the left sides of all selected items to the position of the leftmost item. Similarly, Align Top Edges aligns the tops of all selected items so that they line up with the highest of the selected items. The other commands work analogously.

The next command, Align Vertical Centers, shifts the selected items horizontally so that their centers line up. ResEdit lines them up halfway between the center of the leftmost item and the center of the rightmost item. Align Horizontal Centers works analogously.

The last two commands work on single or multiple-item selections, aligning the items relative to the window rather than to each other.

The Item Palette

The item palette, shown in Figure 10-12, is a floating window that you can drag anywhere on your screen. To add a new item to a dialog, click the appropriate item in the palette and drag it into position in the 'DITL'. When you're customizing an existing 'DITL', however, you can only add three kinds of items: icons, pictures, and static text. For information about the other items, see Chapter 19.

The Mac uses lots of kinds of icons, but if you're thinking about adding one to a 'DITL', you have to find (or create) an 'ICON' resource in the same file. Adding pictures is similar, but the resource

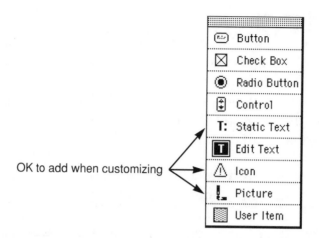

OK to add when customizing

Figure 10-12. You can drag items into a 'DITL' from the floating item palette.

type is 'PICT' and it's not limited to a certain size, as icons are. Static text items, as the name suggests, are the text items that you see but can't change when the dialog is in use. (The name distinguishes them from edit text items, which are fields that you can type into when the dialog is in use.)

> **Hint** If you're copying a picture from a paint or draw program, paste it into the file's 'PICT' picker. Remember that when you send a selection of bits to the Clipboard, it's handled as a 'PICT'. If the file doesn't have any 'PICT's (and therefore doesn't have a 'PICT' picker), paste into the type picker.

Dragging an item into the 'DITL' from the item palette reserves a spot for it, but you still need to set its individual characteristics. To set an item's characteristics, double-click it to open the item editor. (You can also select an item, then choose Open as Dialog Item from the Resource menu.) The item editor is where you fill in the unique text of a static text item, or the ID of the particular 'ICON' or 'PICT' you want to use.

The Item Editor

The item editor, shown in Figure 10-13, is a pretty simple editor. The current selection on the pop-up menu indicates the type of item you're editing. The four fields in the lower right probably look familiar to you because they're similar to the ones in the 'WIND', 'DLOG', and 'ALRT' editors. These fields allow you to set the size and location of the dialog item, but note that the origin for these measurements is the upper-left corner of the dialog (or alert) window, not the screen. You can choose between showing the height and width or bottom and right of the item, just as you've seen for other editors, using the two commands on the Item menu. The Enabled check box is a Programmers Only item.

The Text field is where you get to customize the dialog's message. If you run across things like "^0," remember not to change them. These are the placeholders applications use to figure out where to insert text that varies. The Text field scrolls to accommodate more

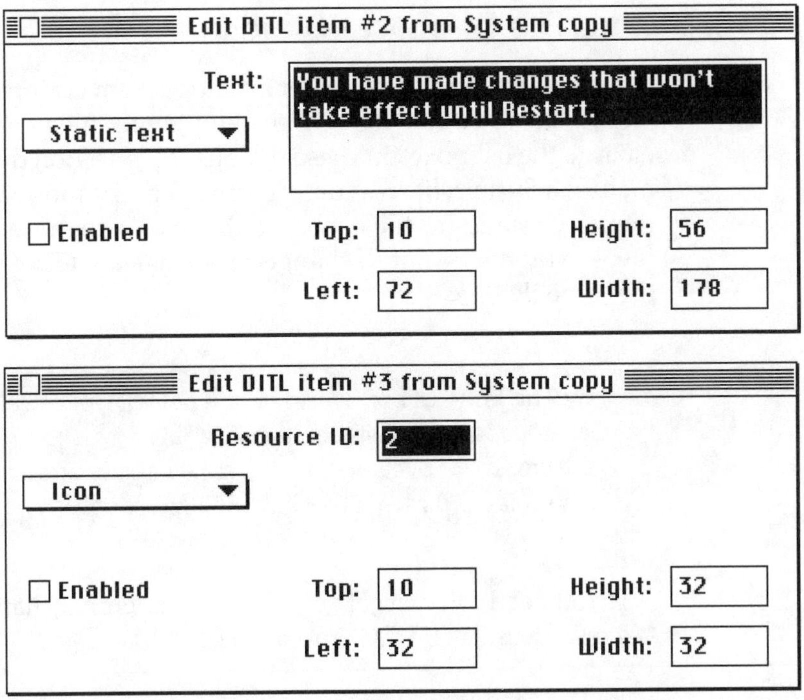

Figure 10-13. Two views of the item editor showing different kinds of items.

lines of text (in fact, it can hold 255 characters), but generally, if you have to scroll you're probably entering too much text. Remember, if your text item grows, you can always enlarge and reposition the static text item in the 'DITL'. If necessary, you can also enlarge the 'DLOG' or 'ALRT', too. Finally, the Resource ID field is where you enter the ID of the 'ICON' or 'PICT' you want to see in the dialog.

Hint Sometimes when you try to open a 'DITL' you see a dialog stating that you can't use the custom editor, but you can use the 'DITL' template. The 'DITL' editor wants any help items present to be at the end of the list and won't work unless they are. Fortunately, you can work around this problem. The next project explains how.

Enlarging the List Box in a Standard File Directory Dialog

Do some standard file directory dialogs seem cramped to you? If you would like to be able to see more and longer file names, you can enlarge the list boxes in these dialogs. This section describes how to modify a System file resource. Many, perhaps most, applications have their own standard file list boxes that override those in the System file, so you may want to change those instead. (They'll usually have the same ID.)

By The Way Under System 6, the default Open 'DLOG' was ID -4000, and the default Save As 'DLOG' was ID -3999. They're still present in System 7, for the sake of older applications, but the new default IDs are -6042 and -6043, respectively.

If you need to revert at some point, remember that you're changing *two* resources—a 'DLOG' and a 'DITL'.

1. Use ResEdit to open a copy of your System file, then double-click the 'DLOG' resource type.

2. Find ID -6042 in the 'DLOG' picker and double-click it. You see the Open dialog, which should look something like the window shown in Figure 10-14.

3. Make sure the editor's MiniScreen matches your screen. Pull down the MiniScreen menu and choose your screen size, if it isn't already checked.

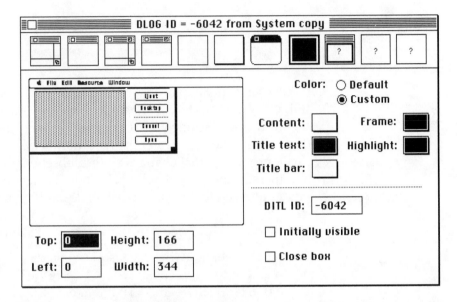

Figure 10-14. Some applications use this Open dialog from the System file (shown in the 'DLOG' editor).

4. Double-click the dialog on the MiniScreen to open the 'DITL' editor. ResEdit displays a dialog that says, "This resource cannot be edited with the custom DITL editor because one or more help items are not at the end of the list. You may open this resource using the DITL template." That's what you're about to do, so click OK. (Yeah, we could have skipped showing you this dialog, but if you're going to have to work around something, we thought you might as well see what it is.)

5. From the Resource menu choose Open Using Template. You'll get the alert telling you the resource is compressed. Click Yes, and you'll see the Select Template dialog. The 'DITL' type should already be selected, so click OK.

6. The 'DITL' appears in template form, which is like a long, complex dialog. (You can learn more about templates in Chapter 14.) The item you want to move to the end is the third one. Click the 3 that's followed by five asterisks. A box appears around the 3 and its asterisks, letting you know it's selected. Copy it with Command-C.

Hint Items whose kind is 1 or 81 are the ones you want to move to the end.

7. Scroll to the very end of the list, and click the last item, a 9 followed by five asterisks. Paste with Command-V. Go back to the third item (the one you just copied). Change the Item Type to 0 and delete the contents of the Item Info field. (You can't delete the item because that changes all the subsequent item numbers and messes things up royally. So you leave the item as a place holder and change it to an invisible, do-nothing item.) Now you can close the template window, and when you double-click the dialog on the MiniScreen, the 'DITL' editor will open.

8. Drag the size handle (the black square) on the 'DITL' window down and to the right, as shown in Figure 10-15. (You'll have to move the item palette first.) That makes the associated 'DLOG' rectangle bigger so it can accommodate a longer and wider list box.

9. Now you can move and enlarge dialog items to take advantage of the extra space you added on the bottom and right. Click the smallest gray rectangle (this horizontal user item is where the disk name goes) and drag it to the right (or use the right-arrow key). Select the four buttons and the separator line and drag them to the right, under the item you just moved, and down a bit. (The easiest way to select these items is to drag the mouse pointer in a rectangle that encloses all of them.) Exact placement doesn't matter just yet.

10. You're ready to enlarge the list box. Click the large gray rectangle. When it's selected, you'll notice a darker spot in the lower-right corner. Drag this size handle down and to the right, but don't crowd the other items. Your 'DITL' should now look something like Figure 10-16.

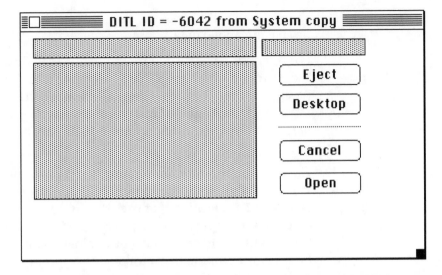

Figure 10-15. Dragging the 'DITL' editor's size handle down and to the right makes the associated 'DLOG' rectangle bigger.

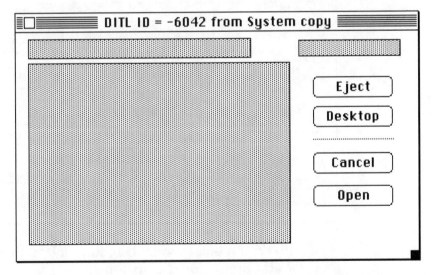

Figure 10-16. Drag peripheral dialog items into the space you added.

11. Once you've got the list box sized and positioned, you can resize the user item on top. Make the long, skinny rectangle the same width as the list box, but don't change its height. You can

change its size the same way you did for the list box. Preserve its spacing above the list box.

12. For cosmetic reasons, you might want to consider spreading out the buttons a little. Simply click each one and drag it into position, or use the arrow keys. Remember, the Alignment menu and the Align To Grid command on the 'DITL' menu can help you tidy up the items. Figure 10-17 shows one possible new look.

13. Close all the windows, save your work, and quit ResEdit. When you reinstall your System file, you'll see your new enlarged list box in any application that uses this System resource for its Open dialog. If you want to reposition something in the dialog, (or if you want to customize the analogous dialogs in your favorite applications), just follow the appropriate steps.

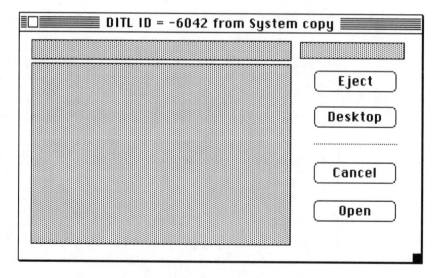

Figure 10-17. An enlarged list box surrounded by appropriately rearranged companion dialog items.

Alerts

Alerts are a special subset of dialogs, so after reading the preceding sections you know a lot about them already. The same guidelines apply for moving or changing the size of an alert's window and for editing the 'DITL's in which alerts store their contents. As you search through your applications for the alerts you want to customize, you should be aware that alerts aren't always stored in 'ALRT' resources. Dialogs can easily masquerade as alerts, and often do. Just because 'ALRT's offer a convenient way of showing a modal dialog window doesn't mean applications have to use them. Something else to be aware of is that many applications make their 'ALRT's do extra duty by substituting different text strings, depending on the situation. For instance, Figure 10-18 shows a 'DITL' from an alert that the Finder can use as it pleases, and there's not much you can do to change it.

Numerous other alerts offer greater customization potential than this one does, however, and you can make several useful changes to them.

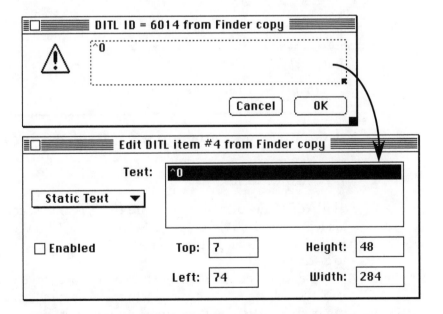

Figure 10-18. This 'DITL' from an 'ALRT' gives the Finder great flexibility but offers users little possibility for customization.

The 'ALRT' Editor

The 'ALRT' editor, shown in Figure 10-19, resembles a streamlined 'DLOG' editor. The most conspicuous difference is the absence of the window-type buttons across the top of the editor window because alerts automatically and unchangeably have modal windows. The MiniScreen menu works just as in the 'WIND' and 'DLOG' editors. You can edit associated 'DITL' resources just as you would for any dialog. To make changes unique to alerts, you have to go to the 'ALRT' menu.

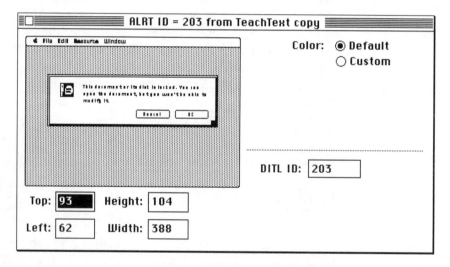

Figure 10-19. The 'ALRT' editor resembles the 'DLOG' editor.

The 'ALRT' Menu

The 'ALRT' menu, shown in Figure 10-20, is almost completely analogous to the 'WIND' and 'DLOG' menus. Choosing the first menu item, Set 'ALRT' Stage Info, causes the dialog shown in Figure 10-21 to be displayed.

A glance at the 'ALRT' Stage Info dialog may give you ideas for a variety of changes you can make to alerts. As you can see, an alert can beep from zero to three times, and the alert box doesn't have to be visible. This dialog is also where you set an alert's default button, the dark-bordered button you can activate by pressing Return or Enter.

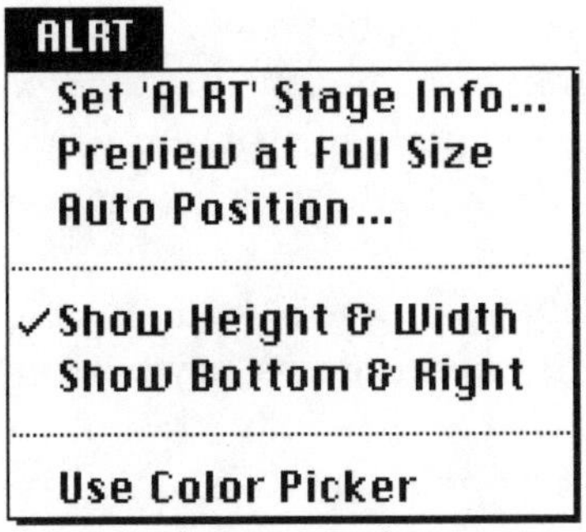

ALRT

Set 'ALRT' Stage Info...
Preview at Full Size
Auto Position...

✓ Show Height & Width
  Show Bottom & Right

Use Color Picker

Figure 10-20. The 'ALRT' menu.

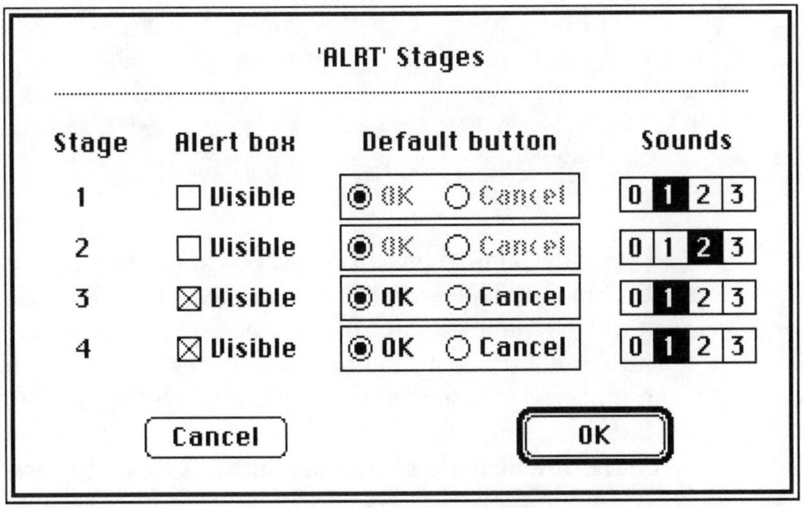

'ALRT' Stages

Stage	Alert box	Default button	Sounds
1	☐ Visible	◉ OK ○ Cancel	0 **1** 2 3
2	☐ Visible	◉ OK ○ Cancel	0 1 **2** 3
3	☒ Visible	◉ OK ○ Cancel	0 **1** 2 3
4	☒ Visible	◉ OK ○ Cancel	0 **1** 2 3

[Cancel]   [**OK**]

Figure 10-21. The 'ALRT' Stage Info dialog contains several useful settings.

You may be wondering what an alert stage is. Actually, you probably already know, because anyone who has used a Macintosh for a while knows on some level what alert stages are. Let's say you type a letter in a field that can only accept numeric characters. The application assumes you've simply made a mistake, so it beeps. Stage 1 settings are used for the first occurrence of a problem. If you do it again, the application still gives you the benefit of the doubt, and beeps again, using Stage 2 settings. If you try this three times, the

Stage 3 settings assume you probably really don't understand the situation, so it's time to make an alert visible that explains the problem. The Stage column in the dialog lists the four possible Macintosh alert stages. An alert can do something different at each stage, but it doesn't have to.

To make an alert invisible, simply click the Visible check box to uncheck it. However, if an alert contains any buttons besides an OK button, do not make it invisible! The only kind of alert that should be invisible is one that contains only an OK button. You can't get into too much trouble changing sounds. Simply click the number that represents the number of beeps you want to hear.

Hint If the beeping of a certain alert annoys you, you can decrease the number of beeps, or even turn the beep off. Open the offending 'ALRT' resource and choose Set 'ALRT' Stage Info from the 'ALRT' menu. In the Sounds part of the dialog, click the number of beeps you want to hear.

An alert has to have a default button, but you can change which button it is. The radio buttons in the Default button section of the dialog are labeled OK and Cancel, which follows Apple's suggested human interface guidelines for buttons in an alert. However, you might find it easier to think about OK as Button 1 and Cancel as Button 2, since obviously the text in alert buttons can say anything. To find out which alert button is Button 1, open the associated 'DITL' and press the Option key (or choose Show Item Numbers from the 'DITL' menu) to see the item numbers, as shown in Figure 10-22.

By The Way You may have noticed that all buttons in a 'DITL' look the same, causing you to wonder at what point the default button in an alert acquires its dark outline. The Dialog Manager, one of the Macintosh's user interface middlemen, takes care of it using the information set in the 'ALRT' Stage Info dialog. Because no such setting exists for regular dialogs, applications have to resort to other means for marking the default button. This means you can change the default button in an 'ALRT' but not in a 'DLOG'.

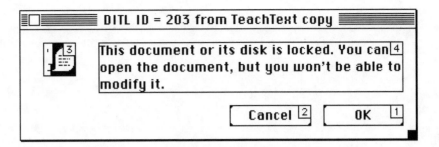

Figure 10-22. Press the Option key to see the item numbers in the 'DITL'.

Summary

This chapter covers four types of interrelated resources and how to edit them: 'WIND's, 'DLOG's, 'ALRT's, and 'DITL's. Windows ('WIND's) define a rectangle having a specified size and location on the screen. Their window frames can vary, and they can have an optional title. Dialogs ('DLOG's) and alerts ('ALRT's), which are a special subset of dialogs, store their contents in dialog item lists ('DITL's). Generally the bulk of dialog customization takes place in the 'DITL' editor, where you can add or change icons, pictures, and certain text items. You can also reposition and resize dialog items. This chapter shows how to change the size and location of a 'WIND' and how to enlarge the list box in standard file directory dialogs by changing the appropriate 'DLOG' and 'DITL'. The chapter concludes with 'ALRT' resources and some of the changes you can make to alerts.

Chapter 11

 Changing Time, Date, and Number Formats

Your Macintosh comes with resources that set the standard date, time, and number formats for your country. Every application that displays a date, time, or number should use these in the System file. Otherwise, getting the application to work in different countries becomes much more difficult. (Each country has its own version of these resources.) In general, you can expect most major applications and many smaller ones to follow the rules and use the 'itl0' and 'itl1' resources.

System 7 added two Control Panels (Date & Time, and Numbers) that let you adjust the standard formats for your country. These Control Panels work with the 'itl0' and 'itl1' resources in your System file, and they have simplified the most common changes. But they don't give you access to all of the possible changes, and they let you keep only one custom setting. What if you do business with several countries and frequently switch formats? With ResEdit you can add new versions of these resources and select them from the pop-up menus in the Control Panels.

The 'itl0' resource contains the defaults for the format of numbers, short dates, and time. Figure 11-1 shows the U.S. 'itl0' resource. The numbers and times shown in a different font on the left side of the window are examples of the current settings. As you make changes, the examples change to show you what the new settings will look like. You should not change the Country Code field unless you are actually creating a resource for a new country, but looking at the list is

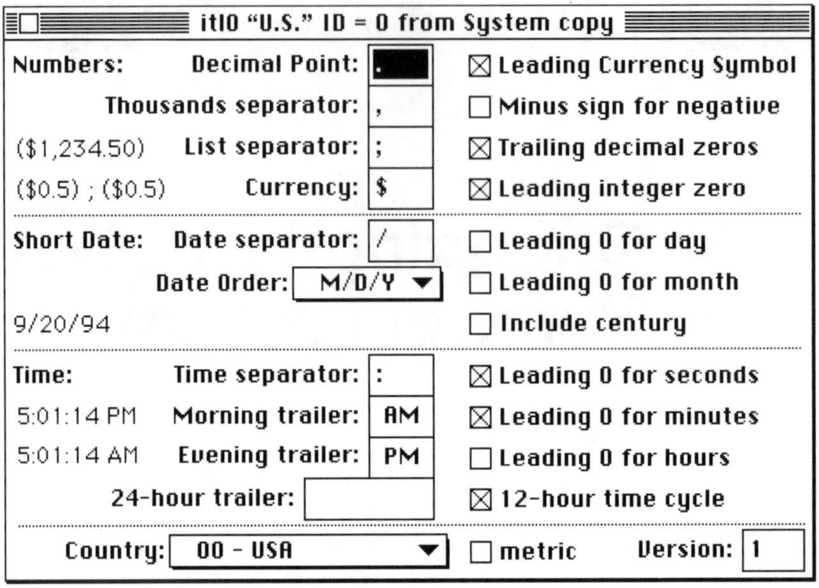

Figure 11-1. The U.S. 'itl0' resource.

interesting. You can type any character you want into the editable fields (for example, you could make your decimal point be shown as "x" instead of ".").

Manipulating this resource is as easy as filling in a dialog box. For example, changing to 24-hour time is a simple matter of clicking the 12-hour time cycle check box to turn it off. You may wonder how your changes take effect. For example, will the AM and PM indicators go away when you switch to 24-hour time? The examples on the left side of the window show exactly what the new format will look like.

The 'itl1' resource shown in Figure 11-2 contains the defaults for the long date format, including the names of the months and days and the order of the month, day, and year. The date in the lower-left corner in a different font shows an example of the abbreviated and long date formats. These examples change as you enter new values. As with 'itl0', you should not change the Country Code field unless you're making a new resource. The fields lined up across the middle of the window represent the order of the parts of the date, and the separators that should be used. The date has four parts (day, month,

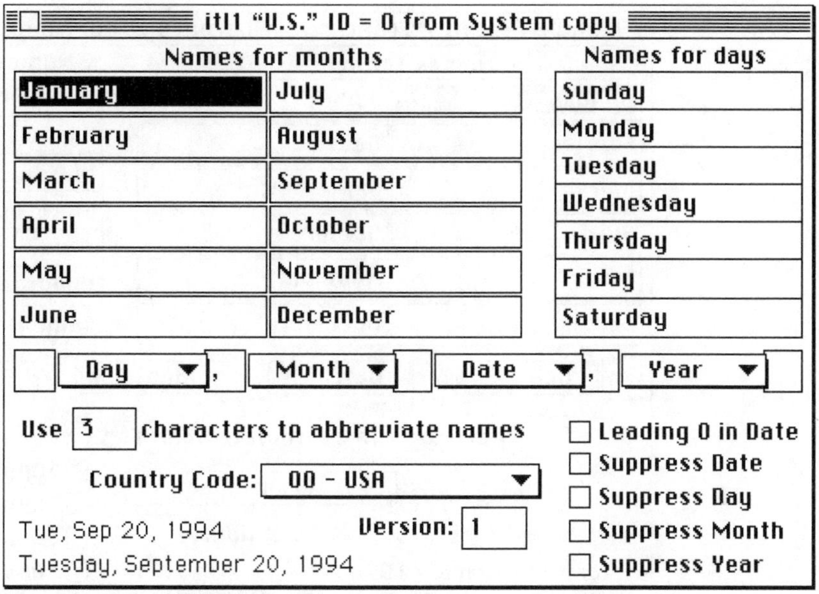

Figure 11-2. The U.S. 'itl1' resource.

date, and year), and they can appear in any order. Simply reset them using the pop-up menus. You can also have any separator you want (up to three or four characters, depending on the field), including spaces. For example, the separator between Day and Month in Figure 11-2 is a comma and a space character.

Again, as with the 'itl0' resource, making changes is simply a matter of filling in a dialog box. For example, to show only the month, day, and year and not the day of the week, simply click the Suppress Day check box in the lower-right corner of the window. You can substitute anything you want in the Names for Months and Names for Days fields. For example, if you type "banana" in place of Wednesday, every time you would normally see the word Wednesday, you'll see "banana" instead. Substituting for foreign languages is just as easy. Figure 11-3 shows the French 'itl1' resource.

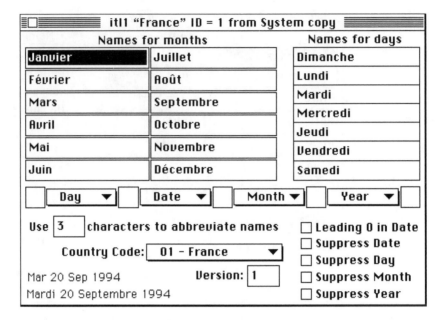

Figure 11-3. The French 'itl1' resource.

Saving a Couple of Different Formats

If you need to change your Mac's date and time or numbers format, you can create alternate versions of the 'itl0' and 'itl1' resources that you keep in your System file. When you want to switch, simply choose your alternate resource from the pop-up menu in the appropriate control panel.

1. Use ResEdit to open a copy of your System file.

2. Open the 'itl0' or 'itl1' picker.

3. Use the Duplicate command (Command-D) on the Edit menu to get a spare version of the resource.

4. Open your new spare resource and make whatever changes you will want to use. Use Command-I to give it a new name.

5. When you're through, close and save the file. Install the modified file and restart.

Hint You can try a different approach if you want to use your special format only in certain applications. Make a copy of the application and use ResEdit to install your custom 'itl0' and 'itl1' resources with ID 0 right into the application. In many applications (including HyperCard, Microsoft Excel, and MacProject II), the new formatting will be used the next time you use the copy of the application. This allows you, for example, to keep your Macintosh in French but use a U.S. copy of Microsoft Excel.

Summary

In this chapter we show you the resources responsible for your Mac's time, date, and number formats. The Date & Time and Numbers control panels use these resources, and you can add new versions of the resources to create new "standard" settings to choose from. The 'itl0' resource lets you change your number, short date, and time format. The 'itl1' resource lets you change your long date format. These resources are intended to allow the Macintosh to be localized for other countries, but you can use them to make sure your times, dates, and numbers are formatted just the way you want them.

Chapter 12

 Fiddling with Fonts

The variety of fonts and text styles available on the Macintosh has certainly contributed to its popularity. Despite this embarrassment of riches, at times you may have wished you could change some letters in your favorite fonts, or add a few special characters or symbols. Maybe you'd like to add a fraction or a mini-icon, or put a slash through the zero in a certain font so you can distinguish it from an uppercase *O*.

Whole books have been written about fonts and typography, so obviously a thorough treatment of the topic goes beyond the scope of this chapter. That's why we skip the terminology distinctions between typefaces and fonts, and don't mention kerning, proportional fonts, or fractional character widths. (Well, OK, we just mentioned them, but that was *it*.)

In all honesty, ResEdit's 'FONT' editor isn't up to speed with the changes System 7 brought about and doesn't always work right. Turning off 32-bit addressing helps, but some glitches still remain. In fact, if you're interested in heavy-duty font projects, you should look into the various font-editing software packages available. But ResEdit can help you adjust some fonts, and it is as good as ever at modifying associated font resources such as the 'FOND'.

There are two general categories of Mac fonts, and you need to understand the difference before you can figure out which fonts you can attempt to restyle with ResEdit. Knowing a few basics about fonts will not only help you figure out which fonts you can modify, it will also help you understand ResEdit's 'FONT' editor. Our goal here is simply to give you a basic understanding you can apply when tinkering with your fonts.

Two Ways to Draw Text

It may sound strange, but the Mac can do so much with text partly because it doesn't have what's called a text mode on more primitive computers. The Mac treats everything, including text, as graphics. QuickDraw, the graphics wizard residing in ROM, controls what your Mac draws on the screen, as well as what some printers, such as the ImageWriter, print. When QuickDraw sends a character to a screen or a printer, it sends a bitmap of the character. Such fonts are often called *bitmap fonts* or *screen fonts*.

There's another way to draw fonts. Some fonts are made up of mathematical descriptions of characters rather than bitmaps. Such fonts are often called *outline fonts* or *scalable fonts*. (The misleading term *laser font* probably arose partly because PostScript, a standard page description language for drawing outline fonts, is included in the ROM in some laser printers.) For our purposes in this chapter, all you need to know about outline fonts is that you *cannot* edit them with ResEdit. You may be able to edit their corresponding screen fonts, however, which are bitmap fonts. Just remember that such changes won't affect the printer's output.

In fact, if you have Adobe Type Manager or Apple's TrueType, you can probably skip most of this chapter. Both of these products solve the schizophrenia of screen *versus* printer fonts because they use outline fonts to create both. As a result, you can't do any useful editing with ResEdit. Many people, however, still have a few old picture fonts such as Mobile that they use occasionally, and ResEdit will work just fine with them.

By The Way If you need to edit outline fonts, look for applications specifically developed to do just that. Fontographer (Altsys Corporation) is one such program.

Bitmap Fonts

Having dispensed with outline fonts, let's focus on bitmap fonts. There are two types of bitmap font resources: 'FONT' and 'NFNT' (New FoNT), which came along with the 128K ROM (not so new anymore!). This resource type has the same format as the 'FONT' type but can accommodate many more fonts. (You can find out about 'NFNT' resources in the "Font Manager" chapters of *Inside Macintosh*.) Although you can open 'NFNT' resources in ResEdit's 'FONT' editor and browse through them, you can't seriously edit them. You can alter the characters somewhat, but you can't change their sizes at all. Commercial 'NFNT' editors are available if you have a serious editing project in mind.

Under System 7, many of the old familiar fonts changed from 'FONT' resources to 'NFNT' and 'sfnt' or TrueType resources. Lest you should feel you're left with typographical dregs, rest assured that there are still some useful things you can do with your fonts. After a few more font basics, the rest of this chapter is devoted to various font resources and what you can do with them.

> **Warning** Never edit active font files or suitcases, especially under System 7.1. Always make a copy of the suitcase and drag it out of the Fonts Folder before working on it. Not only is it safer, it's less confusing. As discussed in Chapter 4, the resource over-rides in System 7.1 can make resources appear in files where they aren't really present. There's no point in even browsing your active font suitcases with ResEdit—it's just too confusing and dangerous. Work only on copies.

Font Basics

When you're deciding how to display text, you choose the font by its name, such as New York or Chicago, and you choose a size. The *font size*, as shown in Figure 12-1, is the distance between the *ascent line* (the height of the tallest characters) and the *descent line* (the lowest point that the "tails" of letters like *g* and *y* touch). Depending on the font, individual characters may vary in width.

Font size ↕   Ascent line ----
Baseline ----
Descent line ----

Figure 12-1. The size of a font is the distance between the tops of the tallest characters (the ascent line) and the bottoms of the lowest characters (the descent line).

By The Way Font size is measured in *points*, a typographer's term that roughly equals 1/72 of an inch. (That's why many screens display 72 dots per inch.) But two fonts with the same font size may not actually be the same size on the screen or when printed. Font sizes tend to be most useful for distinguishing between sizes within the same font.

Although you keep track of fonts by their names, your Mac keeps track of font numbers. All the different sizes of a 'FONT' belong to the same *font family*, which has a unique font number. The resource ID for a font family is calculated from its font number. (We'll explain more about font numbering later.) Each size of a font is stored as a separate resource, as you can see in Figure 12-2, which shows a 'FONT' picker. Because every size of a font is a separate resource, you have to remember to modify each size you use.

ID	Size	Name
393	2594	Geneva 9
396	3176	Geneva 12
521	2468	Monaco 9

FONTs from System copy

Figure 12-2. The 'FONT' picker shows that each size of a font is a separate resource.

You may also choose a style, such as italic or bold, when you're deciding how to display text. You can get styled text two ways. Font families may include styled fonts as separate resources, such as an italic Athens. If styled fonts aren't available, your Mac can apply the style, achieving italics, for instance, by slanting the characters. The important thing to remember is that you can't edit styled text unless it's a separate font resource.

> **Hint** Remember that to get the best results with your ImageWriter, you need an installed font twice as large as the size you want. That is because the ImageWriter prints 144 dots per inch, which is twice the typical screen resolution of 72 pixels per inch. Other printers may have similar requirements. For example, if you want 9-point text to look as good as possible in Best mode, you should have an 18-point font installed. So if you edit the 9-point resource, you should also edit the 18-point resource if you want to see your results on both the printer and the screen.

A font can contain 255 unique characters, but every character need not be defined. (All the font sizes in a font family don't have to contain exactly the same set of characters, either.) The standard Macintosh characters and their ASCII (American Standard Code for Information Interchange) numbers are shown in Figure 12-3. As you might expect, certain fonts made up of symbols or pictures correspond only minimally with the ASCII chart. Every font contains a missing symbol (an empty rectangle character) in addition to the maximum 255 distinct characters. The Mac draws the missing symbol if you type a character that's missing from the font.

Another thing to remember is that, depending on which Mac you have, some fonts may reside in ROM. Although some fonts and some sizes may be duplicated in the System file (for the sake of older, smaller ROMs), ROM fonts override them.

	0	16	32	48	64	80	96	112	128	144	160	176	192	208	224	240
0		⌘	space	0	@	P	`	p	Ä	ê	†	∞	¿	–	‡	
1		⌘	!	1	A	Q	a	q	Å	ë	°	±	¡	—	·	Ò
2		✓	"	2	B	R	b	r	Ç	í	¢	≤	¬	"	‚	Ú
3		◆	#	3	C	S	c	s	É	ì	£	≥	√	"	„	Û
4			$	4	D	T	d	t	Ñ	î	§	¥	ƒ	'	‰	Ù
5			%	5	E	U	e	u	Ö	ï	•	µ	≈	'	Â	ı
6			&	6	F	V	f	v	Ü	ñ	¶	∂	Δ	÷	Ê	^
7			'	7	G	W	g	w	á	ó	ß	Σ	«	◊	Á	ˉ
8			(	8	H	X	h	x	à	ò	®	∏	»	ÿ	Ë	˘
9			)	9	I	Y	i	y	â	ô	©	π	…	Ÿ	È	ˇ
10			*	:	J	Z	j	z	ä	ö	™	∫		/	Í	˙
11			+	;	K	[	k	{	ã	õ	´	ª	À	¤	Î	˚
12			,	<	L	\	l	|	å	ú	¨	º	Ã	‹	Ï	¸
13			-	=	M	]	m	}	ç	ù	≠	Ω	Õ	›	Ì	˝
14			.	>	N	^	n	~	é	û	Æ	æ	Œ	fi	Ó	˛
15			/	?	O	_	o		è	ü	Ø	ø	œ	fl	Ô	ˇ

Figure 12-3. **To find the ASCII number of a character in the standard Macintosh character set, add the character's column number to its row number. (For example: R = 80 + 2 = 82.)**

The 'FONT' Editor

As you can see in Figure 12-4, the 'FONT' editor has three panels and a fairly standard tool palette. The sample text panel displays text in the font and size you're editing. If the character you're working on isn't represented in the sample, simply click the panel and type some new text. The text sample gets updated as you edit, so you can always see your changes in the context of surrounding characters— as long as your monitor is set to show just black and white. ResEdit alerts you if your monitor is set to display more than two colors, explaining that you won't get to see the results of your changes.

The character selection panel shows a three-character section of the list of characters in a font. (They're listed in ASCII order.) The selected character occupies the middle position and has a box around it. The box is drawn with solid lines to indicate when this panel is active; otherwise the box is dotted. When this is the active panel, you can

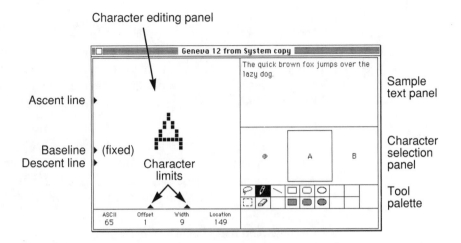

Figure 12-4. The 'FONT' editor has three panels and a standard tool palette.

select a character simply by typing it, using whatever key combination is necessary. You can also scroll through the character list by clicking the end characters. To scroll quickly, click in the panel and drag the pointer left or right outside the selection panel.

The character editing panel shows a fatbits enlargement of the selected character. The three black triangles along the left edge of the window mark the ascent line, the baseline, and the descent line, as described in Figure 12-1. You can move the ascent or descent lines by dragging them, but doing so alters the font size for the entire font, not just for the character you're editing. Any bits you click outside these limits are ignored, which can be a little confusing since the bits do appear. The two black triangles along the bottom mark the left and right limits of the character, and the distance between them is the character width. We recommend that you avoid changing character widths, because doing so affects how the characters look when flanked by other characters. If you want to see how a character is spaced relative to one of these five limit lines, click and hold the appropriate triangle marker to make a dotted limit line appear across the editing panel.

Hint This editor doesn't have all the features of the other fatbits editors, and some things work a bit differently. The differences are minor, so you might not notice at all, but then again you might have an unsettling, slightly confused feeling. Since knowledge is the best weapon to fight confusion, here's a list of a few of the differences.

- In the other fatbits editors, the eraser can knock out up to four bits at a time. The 'FONT' editor's eraser can erase only one bit at a time. (You'll quickly figure out which corner is the important one.) When in use it looks different, too, so you have a visual reminder.
- There's no hand pointer. You move selections with the arrow pointer.
- The 'FONT' editor doesn't have the tool palette mouse shortcuts described for the other editors in Chapter 5 (such as double-clicking the eraser to clear the editing panel).
- You can't use the arrow keys to nudge a selection.

Information about the current character is listed across the bottom of the panel. Its ASCII number is on the left, followed by the offset, which is the distance (in pixels) from the left limit to the first pixel of the character. The character width and its location in the font data are also listed. As you edit, your changes are reflected in the sample text and the character selection panel.

Now you're ready to start improving your fonts.

By The Way Just an advisory. As of this writing, the 'FONT' editor doesn't seem to work very well with System 7.1. Sometimes you don't see the correct font in the sample text panel or character selection panel. And the ascent, descent, and character limit controls don't work unless you turn off 32-bit addressing (in the Memory Control Panel).

Editing a Character

There are a number of changes you may want to make to the bitmap fonts you have. Maybe you'd like to turn the solid black cat character in Mobile into a tabby, or transform the dog character into a Moof, as shown in Figure 12-5. Of course, you can fix other fonts, too, and the steps are the same. Remember, you can modify 'NFNT's, as long as you don't change the size. (And the sample text and character selection panels may not show your changes.)

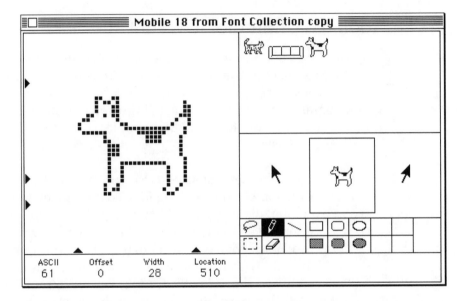

Figure 12-5. You can change the cat to a tabby and the dog to a Moof.

Whether the font you want to edit is in a font suitcase or your System file, make a copy first.

1. Use ResEdit to open a copy of the file containing your font. Open the 'FONT' type to get to the 'FONT' picker.

2. Open the 'FONT' resource you want to edit.

3. The font resource opens in the 'FONT' editor, with the letter *A* (or ASCII character 65) selected. To move to the character you want to change, scroll or just type it.

4. Make whatever changes you want. If you want to try out your new character, click the sample text panel and type in something appropriate.

5. Save your changes and quit ResEdit.

When you drag your font suitcase back into the fonts folder, or swap System files and restart, you'll see your changes. If you work on a font that has multiple sizes, remember that you have to individually edit each size.

Adding a Character to a Font

Adding a special character to a font can be almost as easy as editing an existing one. You can create the character right in the font, or you can copy the bits from another font or even from a paint or draw program. You just have to do a little preparation first to figure out where in the font to add it. Make copies of the font file(s) involved before you start.

1. Open the Key Caps desk accessory and look at the font you want to change. You're looking for easy-to-remember key combinations that aren't already taken. Control or Option-Shift often have lots of openings. Make a mental or written note of the available spot(s) you want to use. (The Control key is usually available because it's reserved for terminal emulation and other software. If you use the Control key for terminal emulation or any other purposes, maybe you should stick with Option-Shift. Also, if you have a Mac Plus, your keyboard doesn't have a Control key, so you should definitely stick with Option-Shift.) If you're copying a character from another font, you may also want to verify that you know the location of the character you want to copy. If you're going to draw an original character, you can skip the steps about copying and go directly to Step 5.

By The Way You can also look for likely key combinations using the 'KCHR' editor, if you're familiar with it. Just be sure to switch to the particular font you're interested in. For more information, see Chapter 9.

2. If you're copying a character from a font, use ResEdit to open your copy of the file containing that font. Open the 'FONT' type, then the particular resource.

3. When the 'FONT' resource opens in the 'FONT' editor, select the appropriate character by dragging the box in the character selection panel, or simply by typing it.

4. Click the selection tool, drag the marquee around the character, and copy it. Close the 'FONT' resource.

5. Now open a copy of the font you want to add to. Type the key combination you're adding the character to.

6. Draw a new character or paste the one you copied. If necessary, position it by dragging.

7. The new character has a character width of 0, which means it will appear right on top of the surrounding characters. (You can test this by typing some sample text.) The left and right character limits (indicated by the black triangles) are stacked on top of each other in the bottom center of the editing panel. To give the character width, just drag one triangle to the left and the other to the right. Leaving an extra one-bit space on each side is nice, but that's up to you.

8. If you want to do any final positioning, simply drag the selection marquee around the character, then drag the selection where you want it, keeping an eye on the sample text.

9. When you're satisfied with your work, save the file and quit ResEdit.

You can add the symbol to other sizes of the font following this same procedure. You may need to redraw the symbol slightly so it will look right with surrounding characters. (You could scale the character by pasting it into a larger or smaller selection rectangle, but you'll probably have to touch it up anyway.) You can also try adding fractions, scientific or mathematical symbols, mini-icons, or your monogram. You're limited only by your imagination and the space within the font.

Hint Many fonts have unusual characters that you can type by pressing Option-Shift-tilde (~). Robots, hearts, flowers, Macs, apples, borders, and various animals are just some of what you'll find. Different sizes of the font may contain different characters, but Key Caps shows you only one font size. You can find all these "hidden" characters, and copy them if you wish, using the 'FONT' editor.

Creating New 'FONT's

We don't encourage you to try to create a whole new font using ResEdit. At best it's a long, tedious process, and as we mentioned early in this chapter, other software packages are better suited to the task. Still, you may want to keep a small collection of characters or symbols handy all in one place. If you gather them together into a 'FONT' resource, you'll be able to use the Key Caps desk accessory to jog your memory about which characters are available and where. Before you can do that, though, you need to know about another resource type.

Hint Remember, the font you create will eventually be listed in your Font menu, so the name matters a little. Normally, the menu font is Chicago, but with some utilities the fonts write their own names. For cosmetic reasons, you might make a point of creating the characters that allow the font to spell its own name. That way you won't see the missing symbol rectangles on your font menu!

The 'FOND' Resource

For most of what you'll do with the 'FONT' editor, the only resource type you need to know about is the 'FONT'. But if you add a new font resource to a font family or create a new font (both potentially major undertakings!), you need to update or create an associated 'FOND', which is sort of a font bookkeeping resource.

One 'FOND' resource is associated with each font family, and it can store a great deal of information about the 'FONT' (or 'NFNT') resources it "owns." You can edit this information in a 'FOND' template. (For more information about using templates, see Chapter 14.) Each 'FOND' has a unique ID, which is the same as the font number your Mac uses to keep track of fonts. Table 12-1 shows the standard font numbers for some common 'FONT's. (The 'NFNT'

Table 12-1. Standard Font Numbers for Some Common 'FONT's

Font number	'FONT' Name
0	System font (Chicago)
1	Default application font (usually Geneva)
2	New York
3	Geneva
4	Monaco
5	Venice
6	London
7	Athens
8	San Francisco
9	Toronto
11	Cairo
12	Los Angeles
13	Zapf Dingbats
14	Bookman
15	N Helvetica Narrow
16	Palatino
18	Zapf Chancery
20	Times
21	Helvetica
22	Courier
23	Symbol
33	Avant Garde
34	New Century Schlbk

versions may be numbered differently.) The resource IDs of 'FONT' and 'FOND' resources in a family are related. The ID of the parent 'FOND' multiplied by 128 gives you the Font Family resource ID; add the point size of a 'FONT' to determine that 'FONT' resource's ID. (Font number x 128 + point size = 'FONT' resource ID. For Geneva 10: 3 x 128 + 10 = 394.)

Because 'FONT' resource IDs are calculated this way, 'FOND' resources can have IDs only from 0 (Chicago, the default System font) through 255. Only half of those numbers are available for third-party font families, however, because Apple reserves IDs 0 through 127. Numbering conflicts are unavoidable because the number of existing bitmap fonts exceeds the number of IDs available. 'NFNT' resources avoid this problem. The IDs of 'NFNT's are not calculated from the resource IDs of their parent 'FOND's, so more IDs are available for both 'NFNT's and 'FOND's.

Creating or Updating a 'FONT' and Its 'FOND'

We'll touch on only a few of the fields in the 'FOND' template. Many of the fields are optional. For more information, see the "Font Manager" chapters of *Inside Macintosh*.

1. As always, the first step is to make a copy of the file to which you'll add your new 'FONT'. Then open the copy with ResEdit.

Hint You can put your new font in its own font suitcase. Here's how. Open ResEdit, choose New from the File menu, then give the file an appropriate name in the dialog that appears. Now choose Get Info for <filename> from the File menu. In the info window that appears, change the Type to "FFIL" and the Creator to "DMOV"—all caps. Close the info window, save, and continue with Step 2. When you're done, your new font will show up in its own suitcase, complete with the familiar icon.

2. Create a new 'FONT' resource. (Choose Create New Resource from the Resource menu.) Remember, you can do this from the type picker or from the 'FONT' picker. You see the alert shown in Figure 12-6. Click OK.

3. Next you see the dialog shown in Figure 12-7. Fill in the new name and point size, then click OK. ResEdit then opens the 'FONT' editor.

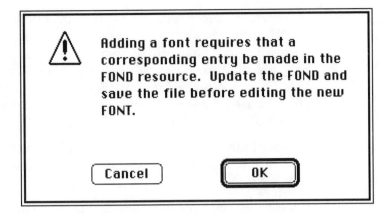

Figure 12-6. If you create a 'FONT', you have to update (or create) the associated 'FOND' resource, as this alert box reminds you.

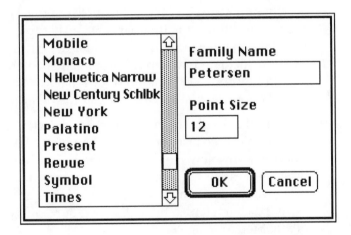

Figure 12-7. You name your new font family in this dialog.

4. You can create and edit your new characters now or later, or you can divide the work into several sessions. Before you can experiment with your new font outside the editor, you've got to create a new 'FOND' resource. Close the 'FONT' editor and go back to the 'FONT' picker.

5. In the 'FONT' picker you can see that, in addition to your new 'FONT' resource, ResEdit automatically created the Font Family resource, which has a size of 0 and is required for a font to be recognized. Make a note of both ID numbers. You have to enter the 'FONT' resource ID into the 'FOND' you're about to create, and you need the Font Family resource ID to calculate what the ID of the 'FOND' should be.

6. Go back to the type picker, or the 'FOND' picker and create a new 'FOND' resource. (Choose Create New Resource from the Resource menu.)

7. Choose Get Resource Info from the Resource menu. Type the name of your new font in the Name field. (If you need a refresher, see the end of Chapter 3.) Divide the Font Family resource ID (you made a note of it in Step 5) by 128 and enter the result in the ID field. Close the Resource Info window.

8. Now you're ready to fill in a few fields in the 'FOND' template. Figure 12-8 shows the first part of a fairly typical 'FOND' template. In the Family ID field, enter the resource ID of the 'FOND' calculated in Step 7. You can enter $4000 (for a mono-spaced font) or $6000 (for a proportional font) in the Flag word field, or you can just leave these and the other fields blank.

9. Scroll to the bottom of the template and click the row of five asterisks you see just above the field called "The Tables." Choose Insert New Field(s) from the Resource menu, and the three fields shown in Figure 12-9 are inserted. Fill in the appropriate values for Font Size, Font Style (generally 0 for plain, unstyled characters), and 'FONT' Resource ID (you made a note of it in Step 5).

10. Save your changes, quit ResEdit, and install the font file you've altered. After you drag the font suitcase into your Fonts Folder, or swap System files and restart, you should see your new font on the Font menu.

If you add a new 'FONT' resource to an existing font family, you have to update the associated 'FOND' to make sure your Mac can find your new 'FONT'. Just open the existing 'FOND' and follow Steps 9 and 10.

```
┌──────────────────────────────────────────────┐
│ ▤□▤▤▤ FOND "New York" ID = 2 from New York copy ▤▤▤ │△│
│                                                │ │
│  Flag word      │$7000        │                │ │
│                                                │▓│
│  Family ID      │2            │                │▓│
│                                                │▓│
│  First Char     │$0000        │                │▓│
│                                                │▓│
│  Last Char      │$00FF        │                │▓│
│                                                │ │
│  Ascent         │4096         │                │ │
│                                                │ │
│  Descent        │-1024        │                │ │
│                                                │ │
│  Leading        │342          │                │ │
│                                                │ │
│  WidMax         │5244         │                │ │
│                                                │▽│
│  Offset to      │$00000000         │           │▽│
│  width tables                                  │⌷│
└──────────────────────────────────────────────┘
```

Figure 12-8. The first few fields of a typical 'FOND' resource.

```
┌──────────────────────────────────────────────┐
│ ▤□▤▤▤ FOND "Petersen" ID = 25 from Examples ▤▤▤ │△│
│                                                │ │
│  # of Font       0                             │▓│
│  entries                                       │▓│
│                                                │▓│
│     1) *****                                   │▓│
│                                                │▓│
│     Font Size   │12          │                 │ │
│                                                │ │
│     Font Style  │0           │                 │ │
│                                                │ │
│     Res ID      │3212        │                 │ │
│                                                │ │
│     2) *****                                   │▽│
│                                                │▽│
│  The Tables   $ │                       │     │⌷│
└──────────────────────────────────────────────┘
```

Figure 12-9. You have to add this set of three fields (Font Size, Font Style, and Resource ID) to the corresponding 'FOND' any time you create a new 'FONT'.

Changing the Names of Fonts

You might want to change the names of some of your screen fonts for several reasons. You might want to group your fonts so that you can easily find the particular font you're looking for. For example, you might want all your text fonts at the top of the menu, followed by your display fonts. Or you might not want to list the bold and italic versions of the fonts in your Font menu. Or maybe you just don't like the name the manufacturer gave the font. Whatever the reason, it's easy to change the name of any font. If you use PostScript fonts with a LaserWriter printer, you don't need to worry about confusing the LaserWriter. No matter what name the screen font has, the LaserWriter still knows it by its original name.

> **Warning** Before you dive in, you should know that you'll have to set the fonts again in all your documents because applications keep track of fonts by their names. For example, if you change the Los Angeles font to "Siberia," you'll have to change every document that used Los Angeles to use Siberia instead. Also, if you change the names of your fonts, your document won't look the way you expect when you take it to someone else's Macintosh. We recommend that you don't change the names of standard fonts.

Here are the steps to follow to change the name of a 'FONT'.

1. Use ResEdit to open the System copy or the suitcase copy containing the font you want to change.

2. Open the 'FONT' picker (double-click the 'FONT' type).

3. Select the item in the list that starts with "Font Family:" followed by the name of the font you want to change. If you don't find a Font Family resource, skip to Step 6. If you do, choose Get Resource Info from the Resource menu.

4. In the Resource Info window, change the name to anything you like.

5. Close the Resource Info window and the 'FONT' window.

6. Open the 'FOND' picker (double-click the 'FOND' type).

7. Select the 'FOND' resource with the name of the 'FONT' you want to change, and then choose Get Resource Info from the Resource menu.

8. Change the name of the 'FOND' to be exactly the same as the new name you specified for the 'FONT' in Step 4.

9. Close and save the file, and reinstall it. The next time you pull down an application's Font menu, you should see your new font name.

Not all fonts have a Font Family resource, and the steps vary a little depending on the type of font resource you're renaming:

- For a TrueType font ('sfnt'), change the name of the 'sfnt' resource and the 'FOND' resource.

- For an 'NFNT', just change the name of the 'FOND'.

Once you've done this, you'll probably want to change the suitcase name, too.

Summary

This chapter describes some basic information about fonts to give you enough background to successfully tinker with your fonts with ResEdit. You can edit only bitmap fonts with ResEdit, and because each size of a font is stored in a separate resource, you have to edit each size individually. We describe how to edit an existing character, how to add a character or symbol to a font, and how to create a new font. Creating new 'FONT' resources requires that you create or update the corresponding 'FOND', so we explain how to do that, too. We also describe how to change the names of fonts. Now you're ready to have fun fixing fonts.

Chapter 13

Tips and Tricks

This chapter contains a collection of mostly unrelated projects involving an assortment of resource types and various aspects of ResEdit. Other chapters also contain projects related to their topics, so be sure to scan the Table of Contents for the tips that interest you.

Using the Fonts Folder for More Than Fonts

When is a Font suitcase not a Font suitcase? When you pack it with other resources—like sounds and Fkeys. That's right. Get ready to pack, because resources you've been installing directly into your System file can be collected into font suitcases instead. Plus, you'll never have to reinstall these resources when new System software comes out, which is the point of the Fonts Folder. (Of course this only works with System 7.1, because System 7.0 doesn't have a Fonts Folder.) The Fonts Folder doesn't understand sound and Fkey suitcases, so you'll have to repack them into font suitcases. Once you've used ResEdit to create the suitcases of your dreams, you'll be able to install and remove resources at the Finder level—without needing ResEdit again or even having to restart! To fool the Fonts Folder, you start with an empty suitcase.

1. Start ResEdit, choose New from the File menu, then give the file an appropriate name in the dialog that appears. Choose Get Info for <filename> from the File menu. In the info window that

appears, change the Type to "FFIL" and change the Creator to "DMOV"—all caps. Close the info window. Your new file is now a font suitcase.

Hint You can also start by emptying a copy of an existing font suitcase. Copy any font suitcase (Option-drag it out of the Fonts Folder), open it with ResEdit, and remove all the resources by choosing Clear or Cut from the Edit menu. You can rename the file before you open it with ResEdit, or after you're done.

2. Now you can use ResEdit to copy 'snd ' or 'FKEY' resources from elsewhere and paste them into your new, bogus "fonts" suitcase. When you're done, quit ResEdit and save your work.

Hint Some Fkeys are really mini applications that contain more resources than just 'FKEY's. You'll need to copy all the resources—not just the 'FKEY's—in the file.

3. After you drag your new suitcase into the Fonts Folder, the System will be able to find all the sounds and Fkeys you've added. Sounds will appear in the Sounds Control Panel, and Fkeys will be immediately available for use.

Reading Screen Shots into Your Paint Program

If you ever make screen shots to include in your documents, you've probably been frustrated by the fact that you can't just double-click the screen shot file to start your paint program. Double-clicking launches TeachText, which doesn't help much. Of course, System 7's drag-and-drop feature may work, but sometimes leaving icons lying around where you can drag and drop them may not be convenient. Here's how to change the System resource that controls what kind of a file Command-Shift-3 creates.

1. Start ResEdit and choose Get File/Folder Info from the File menu.

2. In the standard file directory dialog that appears, select your paint program (the one you want to open when you double-click a screen shot).

3. Write down the four characters shown in the Creator field on the right side of the window. For example, as shown in Figure 13-1, SuperPaint's creator is "SPNT". Copy the characters (uppercase or lowercase) and spacing exactly. Close the info window.

4. Use ResEdit to open a copy of your System file.

5. Open the 'FKEY' resource with ID 3, which is the Command-Shift-3 screen shot 'FKEY'. (Click Yes in the alert asking if you want to edit the compressed resource.) The 'FKEY' resource opens in the hexadecimal editor. Appendix C explains how to use the hex editor, but we'll tell you what you need to know here.

6. Choose Find ASCII from the Find menu.

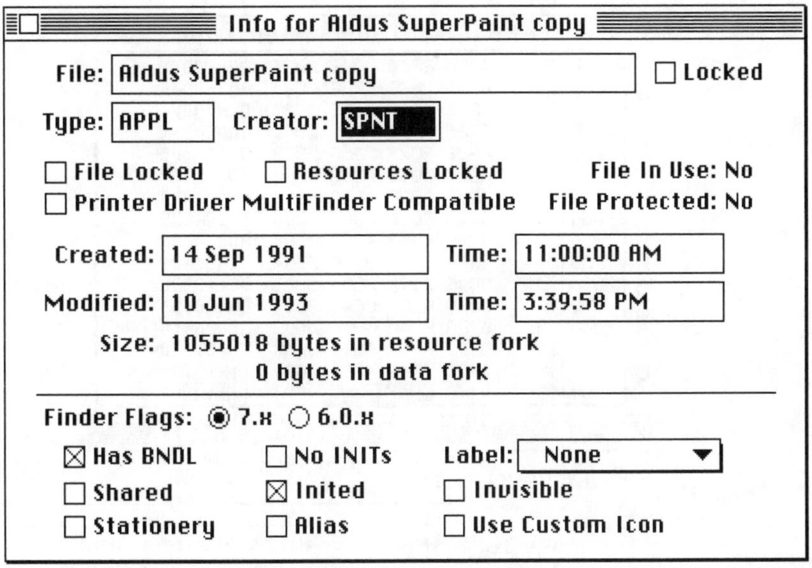

Figure 13-1. Make a note of the characters in the Creator field of your paint program.

7. Enter "ttxt" which is TeachText's Creator. Be sure to type it in lowercase letters. Click the Find Next button. You'll see "ttxt" highlighted near the bottom of the window, as shown in Figure 13-2. (You may have to move the Change ASCII window.)

8. Change "ttxt" to the four characters you found in the Creator field of your paint program ("SPNT" for SuperPaint). You can do this using the Change features of the Change ASCII window, or by typing your new characters over the selected characters (ttxt) in the right part of the window. Be sure not to make any other changes in this window. (If you accidentally change something else, choose Revert This Resource from the Resource menu and try again.)

9. Close and save the file.

10. Install your modified System file and restart.

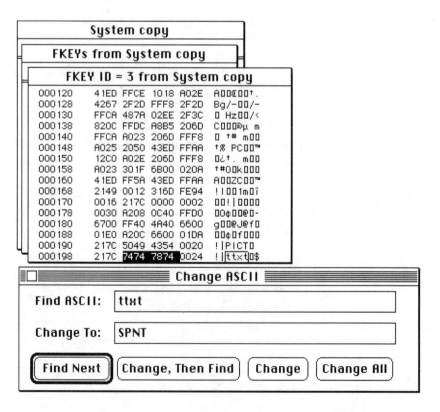

Figure 13-2. Use the Find ASCII command to change "ttxt."

Now when you use Command-Shift-3 to take a screen shot, double-clicking the resulting file will launch your paint application. In fact, the Finder will use your paint program's icons for the files produced.

Remapping Which Programs Open Certain Files

TeachText is a handy little program, but sometimes it's annoying to see the alert in Figure 13-3. It would be much nicer to open graphic files in your preferred graphics program and to open text files in your word processing program. Here's how to get the Finder to do just that.

1. Start ResEdit and choose Get File/Folder Info from the File menu.

2. In the standard file directory dialog that appears, select your paint program.

3. Write down the four characters shown in the Creator field on the right side of the window. As you saw in Figure 13-1, "SPNT" is SuperPaint's creator. Copy the characters (uppercase or lowercase) and spacing exactly. Close the info window.

4. Repeat these steps to find the Creator for your word processing program. It's "MWPR" for MacWrite Pro.

Figure 13-3. Maybe you'd rather not open files in TeachText.

5. Now open a Finder copy with ResEdit, then open 'fmap' ID
    17010. The 'fmap' resource opens in the hexadecimal editor.
    Appendix C explains how to use the hex editor, but we'll tell
    you what you need to know here. You'll see a window like the
    one shown in Figure 13-4.

```
▤▢▤ fmap ID = 17010 from Finder copy ▤▤▤
000000    5445 5854 7474 7874    TEXTttxt       ⇧
000008    5049 4354 7474 7874    PICTttxt
000010    0000 0000 0000 0000    ᴾᴾᴾᴾᴾᴾᴾᴾ
000018                            |
000020
000028
000030
000038
000040
000048
000050
000058
000060                                           ⇩
000068                                           ⊡
```

**Figure 13-4. This 'fmap' resource tells the Finder to use
TeachText (Creator = ttxt) to open unknown TEXT and PICT files.**

6. You can think of the right side as saying, "If the file's Type is
    TEXT (or PICT), then open it with the application whose
    Creator is ttxt." Your job is to change the first "ttxt" (after TEXT)
    to match the creator of your word processor (MWPR in this
    example), and the second "ttxt" (after PICT) to match the
    creator of your paint program (SPNT in this example). Don't
    change anything else.

7. Close and save the Finder copy, reinstall, and restart. Now
    whenever you encounter a text or graphics file created by an
    application you don't have, you can just double-click it. You'll
    see a dialog like the one in Figure 13-3 but with your chosen
    program instead of TeachText.

You can take this mapping further if you wish. Let's say you frequently have text files from Program A that you need to open with
Program B. Start by using ResEdit to discover the Types and Creators
involved. Find the Type of a generic document that Program A
creates; let's say it's "abcd." Find the Creator of Program B; let's say
it's "EFGH." Open the fmap resource we just modified, and click at

the end of the line, right after "PICTttxt." Now type "abcdEFGH." Don't add any spaces or other characters and be sure that the last line is all zeroes. Then quit, save, swap files, and restart. Double-clicking one of Program A's files should now open Program B instead of Program A.

Changing Graphical Elements in HyperCard

HyperCard contains many special icons and pointers that you might want to fiddle with, but they aren't stored where you would expect. If you want to change, say, the paint bucket, in most applications you would look for a 'CURS' resource, but in HyperCard you must look in a font, or 'NFNT', resource. HyperCard keeps all its graphical elements in an 'NFNT' resource. Like Cairo and Zapf Dingbats, the characters in the HyperCard font display pictures instead of the usual alphabetic characters. For example, typing an *A* displays a picture of a padlock. The contents of the 'NFNT' for HyperCard version 2.1 are shown in Figure 13-5. As you may remember from Chapter 12, you can use the 'FONT' editor to modify the characters in an 'NFNT' resource, as long as you don't change their sizes.

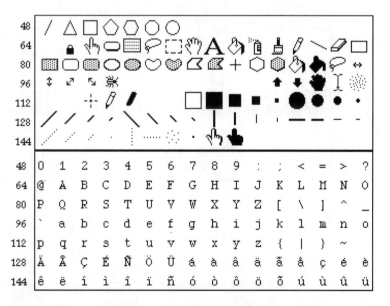

Figure 13-5. Graphics in the HyperCard font (top) and their corresponding normal characters (bottom).

Before we tell you how to find and change the item you're looking for, you need a bit more information about editing this particular font. From ResEdit's point of view, this is a very strange font. Not only is it not part of a normal font family, but it doesn't even have a font family record—the resource with a length of zero that contains the name of the font family. Because of this, when you open this font the 'FONT' editor won't show you any of the special characters on the right side of the window in the character selection list or sample text, as illustrated in Figure 13-6. Don't worry about this—the changes you make will still show up in the font.

Note that this section shows you only how to change HyperCard. If you want more details about how to modify fonts, please refer to Chapter 12.

Also note that by following these instructions, you'll be changing the pictures HyperCard uses. Except for the brush shapes, however, you can't change the actions HyperCard performs when it uses the pictures. Changing this font is really only useful if you want to

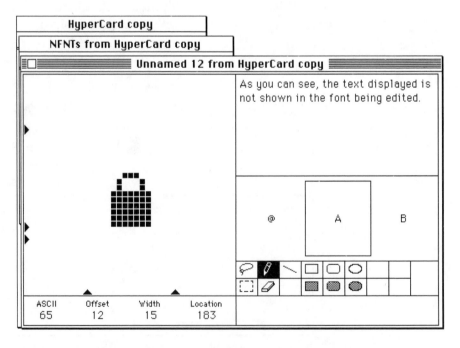

Figure 13-6. HyperCard's font contains graphics instead of characters.

change one or more of the available brush shapes, if one of the pointers doesn't suit you, or if you just like to fiddle with your applications.

First, let's open up a copy of HyperCard (or HyperCard Player) and look at what's in the font.

1. Use ResEdit to open a copy of HyperCard.

2. Open the 'NFNT' picker.

3. You should see one 'NFNT' resource with resource ID 32268. Open that font.

You can browse through the font to see which pictures it contains. Remember, to get a different character to appear in the fatbits area of the window, you can either click a different character in the list in the middle of the right part of the window or press the key whose corresponding symbol you want shown. If you press the Z key, for example, the picture that's in the spot normally occupied by Z appears. If you want to move quickly through the list, just click the right or left character in the list and, while still holding down the mouse button, drag the pointer out of the list rectangle.

The top of Figure 13-5 shows the pictures in the font, and the bottom part shows their corresponding normal characters. For example, to move to the spray can, find the spray can in the top part of Figure 13-5; notice that it's in the row labeled 64. Now look down the page to the row labeled 64 in the table of normal characters at the bottom of the figure, and you'll see that you should type a J. The numbers on the left side of Figure 13-5 are the ASCII numbers of the first picture in each row. The selected character's ASCII number appears in the lower-left corner of the 'FONT' editor window.

Changing the Font

Now let's look at an example of how to change one of the pictures in the font. If you want to change a different one, just follow these steps, substituting the picture you want to change. We'll look at how to change the paint bucket pointer.

1. Use ResEdit to open a copy of HyperCard.

2. Open the 'NFNT' resource, as described previously.

3. Type \ to move to the paint bucket.

4. Modify the cursor any way you like.

5. Click the next character in the list, the].

6. Change this mask to be a filled-in copy of your new pointer. You can do this by copying your new pointer, pasting it into the mask, and filling it in. (Selecting the entire editing area before you copy assures that the selection is aligned properly when you paste.)

7. Close and save the file.

From now on, when you use your new copy of HyperCard, you'll see your new pointer instead of the normal paint bucket. If you want to change the paint bucket in the Hypercard tool palette so that it matches, edit the picture in the *I* position in the 'NFNT'.

Displaying a Color Picture at Startup

If you have a Mac with Color QuickDraw in ROM (which means just about any Mac except Classics, SEs, and older machines), you can display just about any picture you want while your Mac is starting up—including one in full color. You see your picture instead of the "Welcome to Macintosh" message. All you have to do is create a file in your System Folder that contains a 'PICT' resource with ID 0. Of course, some extensions (startup documents that the System loads) clear the screen when they're loaded, so if you have any extensions that do this, you might have only a few seconds to enjoy your startup picture.

Even if an extension doesn't clear your picture, your normal desktop replaces it as soon as startup is completed. If you want to replace your desktop with a picture, try using an extension such as ColorDesk. But, if you don't have ColorDesk and you'd like to see your company logo or your spouse's face when you start your Mac, you can follow these instructions.

1. Start your favorite paint program and copy the picture (or part of a picture) that you want to use for your startup screen.

2. Start ResEdit and create a file in your System Folder called "StartupScreen."

3. Paste in the 'PICT' resource that you copied in your paint program.

4. Double-click the 'PICT' resource type to open the 'PICT' picker and select the resource you just pasted.

5. Select Get Resource Info from the Resource menu.

6. Change the resource's ID to 0.

7. Close and save the file.

Next time you restart your Mac you'll see your picture during the startup process.

By The Way Even if you have a Classic or an SE, you can still have a startup screen displayed when you start your Mac. Unfortunately, you can't use ResEdit to create the startup screen because the picture isn't stored in a resource. (It's stored in the data fork.) All is not lost, however, because many paint programs (including MacPaint and SuperPaint) let you save a picture as a startup screen. Just make sure you save the picture in a file called StartupScreen in your System Folder.

Changing Your Printer's Default Number of Copies

When you ask an application to print, you always see the same print dialog, with the number of copies set to 1. But if you routinely print duplicates, or some other number of copies, you may want to change this default. If you have an Apple printer, here's how you can change your printer's default number of copies.

1. Use ResEdit to open a copy of the printer file (LaserWriter, for example) in the Extensions Folder in your System Folder. Open the 'DITL' resource type, and then open resource ID -8191. You'll see a window that looks almost exactly like your print dialog. (See Chapter 10 if you'd like to know more about 'DITL' resources.)

2. Double-click the field to the right of the word "copies." Another window opens in which the default copy number is already selected. Simply type the number you want to change it to.

3. Close ResEdit's windows, save your changes, and quit ResEdit.

You can throw away the original printer file, but you might want to leave both versions in your Extensions Folder. They'll both show up in the Chooser, so if you know you'll be doing a lot of printing requiring one of these preset numbers of copies, you can just choose the appropriate printer file. If you keep more than one version, rename alternates appropriately. It's a good idea to put the distinguishing feature early in the name, because the Chooser doesn't have room to show you more characters at the end.

Adding Version Information to Documents

It can be handy to keep information about a document in the comment area of the Finder's Get Info window. The problem with such comments is that they're lost when you rebuild your Desktop—which your Mac user's guide suggests that you do once a month or so. Fortunately, there's a better way. Applications have 'vers' resources that contain, among other things, text strings that the Finder displays in the Get Info window. You can use ResEdit to add 'vers' resources to your documents to keep track of a version number or just to record some information about the file. You can add two 'vers' resources for every file. Figure 13-7 shows where your comments will appear. (For more information about 'vers' resources, see Chapter 21.)

Here's how to add 'vers' resources—permanent comments—to documents.

1. Use ResEdit to open your document.

Hint Many document files don't have a resource fork, so you'll need to add one to store a 'vers' resource. When you open a file without a resource fork, ResEdit displays a dialog asking if you want to create one. Just click OK and proceed with the steps outlined.

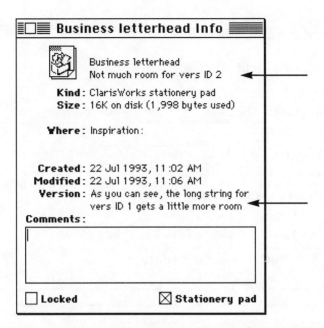

Figure 13-7. The Finder's Get Info window showing the location of the custom version strings.

2. Choose Create New Resource from the Resource menu.

3. A dialog appears to let you select the resource type for the resource you're creating. Type 'vers' or scroll to it, then click OK.

4. You should see a window like the one shown in Figure 13-8. The last field, labeled Long version string, is the one you're interested in; enter any text string you want. There's room for, at most, two lines of text. You can leave the rest of the fields blank.

5. After you've entered your string, close the editor window. In the resource picker, select the resource you just created, and choose Get Resource Info from the Resource menu. In the Resource Info window, change the resource ID to 1. While you're there, check the Purgeable check box so the resource will be removed from memory when the Finder's done with it.

6. If you want to create another 'vers' resource for a second, shorter, comment, repeat these steps, but set the ID to 2.

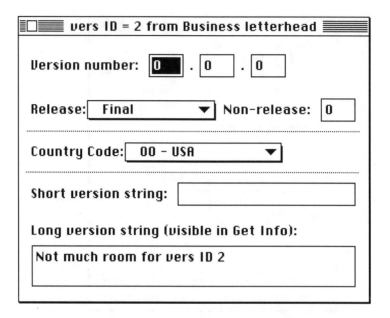

Figure 13-8. The editor window for a 'vers' resource.

7. Close and save the file. From the Finder, select the file and
    choose Get Info from the File menu. You should see your
    comments in a window like the one you saw in Figure 13-7.

If you don't see your comments, you've got to make the Finder
update itself. At the Finder level, press Command-Option-Escape,
then click the Force Quit button in the dialog that appears. The Finder
will know about your changes after it relaunches.

Creating a Debugger 'FKEY'

If you're a programmer or you just like poking around inside your
Macintosh, you've probably spent some time using MacsBug, Apple's
low-level debugger. This tip shows you how to add an 'FKEY' to your
System file that causes you to enter MacsBug. An 'FKEY' is more convenient than trying to find the programmer's switch on your Mac—
especially if you accidentally press the wrong button as often as most
people do.

As you probably know, the Macintosh treats Command-Shift-0 through Command-Shift-9 in a special way. When you press one of these key combinations, the Mac looks for an 'FKEY' resource in the System file with the same ID as the number you pressed. Your Mac comes with one or more 'FKEY' resources built in that you're probably familiar with. For example, Command-Shift-3 takes a snapshot of your screen and saves it to a file. If you look in your System file, you see an 'FKEY' resource with ID 3 that corresponds to the Save Screen command. (Command-Shift-1 and Command-Shift-2 eject disks from floppy disk drive one or two, but they don't use 'FKEY' resources.) You can follow these steps to make Command-Shift-6 break into MacsBug.

1. Use ResEdit to open a copy of your System file.

2. Open the 'FKEY' picker (double-click the 'FKEY' type).

3. Choose Create New Resource from the Resource menu.

4. You should see a window similar to the one shown in Figure 13-9. Type "A9FF4E75". Don't press Return or put in any spaces. (This is just a Debugger trap followed by an RTS instruction.)

5. Choose Get Resource Info from the Resource menu. Change the resource ID of your new 'FKEY' to 6 (or any other unused num-

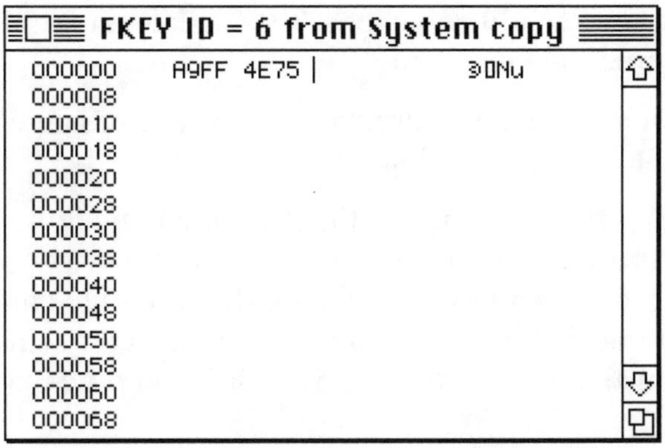

Figure 13-9. Fill in an 'FKEY' resource with these values to break into MacsBug.

ber between 0 and 9). Also check the Purgeable check box to help with the System's memory management.

6. Close and save the System copy, swap files, and restart. Now, when you press Command-Shift-6, you will immediately enter MacsBug (or see a bomb displayed if you don't have MacsBug installed).

For the nonprogrammers who try this and then wonder how to get *out* of MacsBug, type G-Return or Command-G. From a crashed application, type ES.

Changing the Creation Date and Time of Files

Have you ever been really annoyed to discover that your Mac has been set to the year 1999 for the last three months? You cringe, realizing you have dozens of files with weird creation and modified dates. Or maybe you wish your files could help create the impression that you work longer hours than you really do. With ResEdit you can change the creation date and last modified date of files to anything you want. Of course, you may have other reasons for changing the dates. For example, Apple sets the time part of both the creation date and the last modified date to exactly 12:00 PM on the day a product is released. Whatever your reason, here's what to do.

1. Start ResEdit and choose the Get File/Folder Info command from the File menu.

2. Select the file whose date you want to change from the standard file directory dialog that appears.

3. A window similar to the one shown in Figure 13-10 should appear. You can enter any dates or times you want in the Created and Modified fields. Be careful to enter the dates and times following the format you see in the window. You can find further details about the File Info window in Chapter 22.

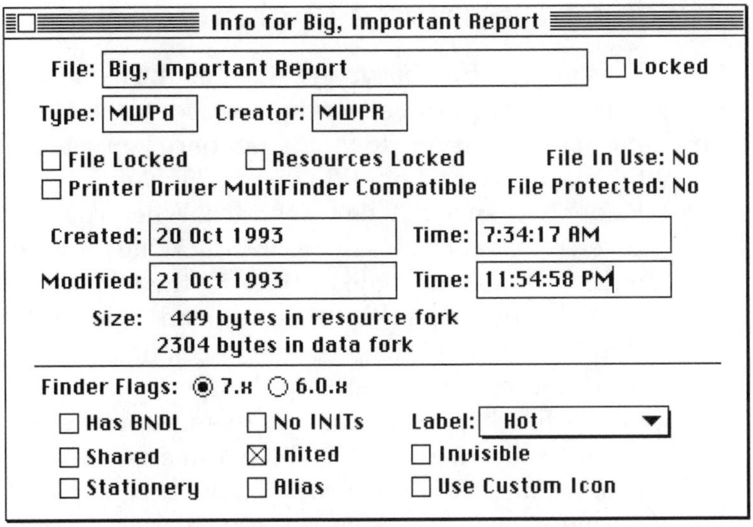

Figure 13-10. Change the Created and Modified dates and times to anything you want.

Making Your Own Read-Only TeachText Files

If you need to protect your files from tampering (accidental or otherwise), you have several options. Here's how you can make your own read-only TeachText files.

1. Create the file in TeachText and save it as usual.

2. Start ResEdit and choose Get File/Folder Info from the File menu.

3. Select your file in the dialog that appears and click the Get Info button. You'll see a window similar to the one you saw in Figure 13-10 (and Figure 13-1). Change the letters in the Type field from "TEXT" to "ttro". Don't change the Creator.

4. Save the file and quit ResEdit.

Once you change the file type with ResEdit, your file will have the familiar newspaperlike icon used for the Read Me files. You'll be able to open, read, and print the file—and even change its name or throw it out—but no one will be able to modify the data it contains. The next tip outlines another option.

Making a File's Name Unchangeable

Let's say an office busybody changed the name of that important document you've been slaving over for weeks. Not only did you lose precious time trying to find it, but once you set to work, you realized the macros you set up didn't work. Now you've got to go back to the Finder to change the file name back. When you got home, you discovered that your kids thought "MacWrite" was boring, so they renamed it something like "Blotzo" (they think?), then buried it several folders deep. Not even the Find command can help you now! Why not prevent such problems? Locking files using the Finder's Get Info window may thwart your kids, but you have to remember to unlock files before you can edit them. And determined name changers like the office busybody can easily unlock the file. There's another, more foolproof way. Follow these steps to take advantage of the mechanism that protects the System file's name.

1. As long as you have a backup (in case there's a power failure or other disaster), you don't have to make a copy of the file you want to protect. Just follow these instructions exactly and don't do anything else to the file.

2. Make sure the file you want to change is in a folder, not on the desktop.

3. Start ResEdit and choose Get File/Folder Info from the File menu.

4. Find your file in the standard file directory dialog that appears, and click the Get Info button. You see a File Info window similar to the one you saw in Figure 13-10.

5. Click the first check box in the top right, labeled Locked. This tells the Finder not to let the file's name change.

6. Quit ResEdit, saving your changes.

7. Close and open the folder containing the file to make your change take effect.

By The Way You can't change the icon of locked files and folders. If you're having trouble getting a custom icon to stick to a file, it may be locked. Unlock it with ResEdit's File Info window. After pasting the new icon, you can set the Locked bit again. During this process, you may need to get the Finder to update itself, as described previously, by pressing Command-Option-Escape.

You can follow these steps for any file whose name you want to protect. Note that if you copy the file with the Finder's Duplicate command, the copy won't have the Locked bit set. Also, even though people can't change the file's name, they can still throw it out. With the next tip, you can go one step further to protect your files.

Making Files or Folders Invisible

The previous tip showed you how to stop people from changing the names of your files. But if your kids or co-workers have ever deleted important files, maybe you'd like more advanced file protection. Why not make your important files and folders invisible so they can't be deleted?

One of the most useful changes you can make to protect your Mac from kids is to make the entire System folder invisible. You can always make it visible again if you need to work with it. Files are invisible only in the Finder, so you can make programs invisible and still launch them by double-clicking their documents. And if you're concerned about people sneaking in and giving themselves access privileges, make your Sharing Setup control panel invisible.

One caveat: If you've got the original for an alias in a folder that you later decide to make invisible, the alias won't work anymore.

Just follow the steps outlined in the preceding tip, but check the Invisible check box rather than the Locked check box. If the file or folder is in an open Finder window, you may have to close and reopen the folder to get invisibility to work. If the file or folder is on the desktop, you may need to update the Finder before the file will disappear. (Use Command-Option-Escape to force quit from the Finder, as described previously.) Now all you have to do is keep this trick a secret from your co-workers and kids!

This Little Piggy Says "Oink!"

Here's a trick that's good for a laugh. Hold down the Command, Option, and Shift keys while choosing About ResEdit from your Apple menu. You'll see the first alert shown in Figure 13-11 and you'll also be treated to a humorous snorting sound. That's it. You can click Cancel and go on about your business. For our purposes here, the only reason to turn on pig-mode is so you can turn it off (the same way you turned it on) and hear the pig again. Which leads us to the next section.

By The Way Pig-mode actually has a purpose. It's useful for programmers who need to test custom editors, but it makes ResEdit run very slowly because memory is repeatedly compacted and purged.

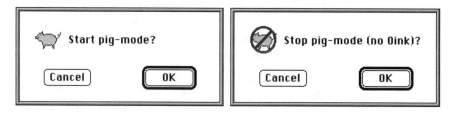

Figure 13-11. These alerts are accompanied by an appropriate sound.

By The Way To see the names of the people who created ResEdit, hold down Command-Option while choosing About ResEdit from the Apple menu.

Sounding Off

As the piggy in the previous trick demonstrates, sounds are one of the most fun aspects of the Mac. You've undoubtedly run across them—one example is the beep you set in the Sound Control Panel. You may have also encountered sounds in HyperCard and many other applications, games, and accessories.

Playing Sounds

Apple has defined the 'snd ' resource to contain all kinds of sound information, but some applications use their own sound resource formats. ResEdit's 'snd ' picker has an 'snd ' menu that lets you try out a sound in three different ways. The first command, Try Sound, just plays the 'snd ' resource. The second command, Try as HyperCard Sound, adjusts the sound to middle C before it's played. This is what HyperCard does if a specific note isn't specified in the PLAY command. You'll notice that some 'snd 's sound the same when played normally and as a HyperCard sound. Sounds aren't adjusted if they were recorded with a base note of middle C. You may also notice that some HyperCard sounds end up played too fast; that depends on how the sound was recorded. The next command, Try Scale With Sound, plays the sound adjusted to the notes of a major scale. This command can produce some pretty silly results when a sampled sound (such as a grunt or a dog barking) is played with a scale. The last command, Record New 'snd ', works just like recording in the Sound Control Panel.

By The Way Some sampled sounds (sounds that have been digitally recorded for use with the Mac) won't work with the Try Scale With Sound command. If you don't hear anything when you try a sound with the scale, the sound can't be adjusted to be played with different notes.

Where to Look for Sounds

You've no doubt got sounds tucked away in all sorts of places on your Mac. Use ResEdit to open copies of all the commercial and shareware games and HyperCard stacks you have. They're some of the best places to look for sounds. Here are a few more places to look.

- After testing out the pig-mode oink in the previous section, you know that ResEdit has an 'snd ' resource you can copy.
- You never have to actually solve the Puzzle DA to hear it's congratulatory "Ta-da!"
- The scrapbook contains a raspy cricket sound.

- The camera shutter you hear when you take a screen shot with Command-Shift-3 is in your System file, along with some more familiar beep sounds. The next project tells you how to add beep sounds to your system.

Hint Why not create a new file with ResEdit and use it to collect the sounds you rustle up? Simply copy the 'snd ' resources you like and paste them into your sound collection. Also, if you're using System 7.1, check the first tip in this chapter, "Using the Fonts Folder for More Than Fonts," for another idea.

Adding Beep Sounds to Your System

It's easy to add sounds to the list that appears in the Sound Control Panel—just add the sound resources to your System file. The hardest part is finding good sounds to use. If you aren't set up to record your own sounds, you'll need to find a file that contains some fun sounds. Bulletin boards and user groups often have files of sounds available for free. Once you've got some sounds, follow these steps to make them available in the list in the Sound Control Panel.

Hint Sound resources can be very large, so you have to be careful not to run out of memory in ResEdit. If you're going to be copying lots of 'snd' resources and have enough memory in your Macintosh, the first thing to do is increase the memory available to ResEdit. You can do this from the Finder by selecting ResEdit and then selecting the Get Info command from the File menu. Put a larger number into the Application Memory Size field at the bottom of the Get Info window. Changing the size to 750K should be enough, but no matter how much memory you give ResEdit, it might still run out if you copy a lot of large resources. Resources you paste into a file remain in memory until you save the file, so if you paste lots of big 'snd 's, they'll take up lots of room in memory. The solution to this problem is easy, though. Just save the file occasionally.

1. Use ResEdit to open the file containing the sounds.

2. Open the 'snd ' picker.

3. Use ResEdit to open a copy of the System file.

4. Select and copy the sounds from the first file. You can play them first using the 'snd ' menu to hear which ones you want to copy.

5. Paste them into the System copy.

6. Close and save the System copy.

7. Install your modified System copy and restart.

8. Open the Control Panel desk accessory and select the Sound Control Panel. Your new sounds should be in the list of sounds you find there.

Adding Sounds to HyperCard

If you want to use a new sound in HyperCard, all you have to do is copy the 'snd ' resource into HyperCard or a stack. If you want to use the sound only in one stack, just add it to the stack itself. If, on the other hand, you want to be able to play the sound from any stack, you might want to add it to the Home stack. Either way, you can follow the steps outlined in the previous tip, substituting Home or your stack for the System file.

Hint When you use ResEdit to open a HyperCard stack, you might see an alert warning you that the file doesn't contain a resource fork. This simply means that you haven't added any special functionality to your stack yet. It's OK to let ResEdit add a resource fork.

File Verification's Hidden Diagnostic Window

If you press the Option key while choosing Verify File from the File menu or while opening a file (if you have file verification turned on in ResEdit's Preferences dialog), a diagnostic window appears that shows the details of the resource verification operation. Although this feature probably won't help most users, some technical support engineers and developers might find it useful. Progress through the verification procedure is indicated by a series of status and error messages. A diagnostic window for a damaged file is shown in Figure 13-12.

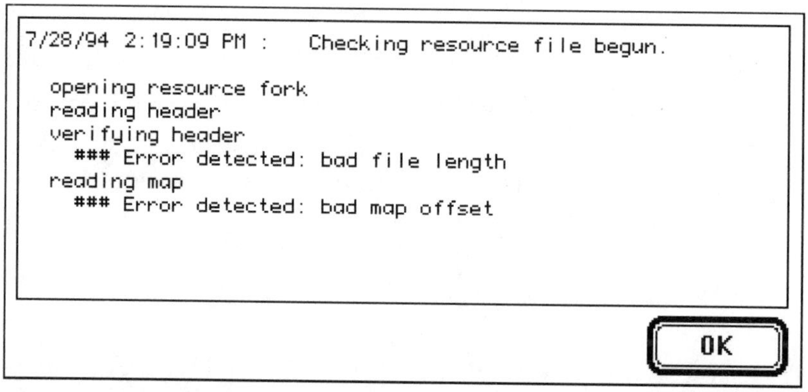

```
7/28/94 2:19:09 PM :    Checking resource file begun.

 opening resource fork
 reading header
 verifying header
   ### Error detected: bad file length
 reading map
   ### Error detected: bad map offset



                                              ┌─────────────┐
                                              │     OK      │
                                              └─────────────┘
```

Figure 13-12. A hidden window that gives you details about the health of your files.

Stopping Finder Window Zooming

Some people just love the zoomy rectangles the Finder draws as it opens and closes windows, but these special effects actually slow things down a bit. Maybe you'd like to turn off these "ZoomRects," as they're sometimes called. On faster machines the change is negligible, but on slower machines you'll notice the difference.

1. Open a copy of the Finder with ResEdit, then open 'CODE' resource ID 4. (Click Yes to decompress it.)

2. The resource opens in ResEdit's Hex editor and looks something like the top window in Figure 13-13. Choose Find Hex from the Find menu (or type Command-F), and type in the text exactly as you see it in the bottom window in Figure 13-13. Those are all zeroes, not the letter *O*. Click Find, then click Change.

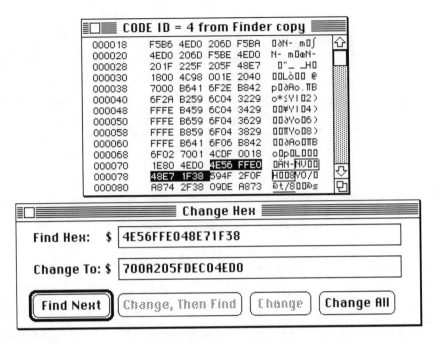

Figure 13-13. Use ResEdit to find and change the hex string.

3. Quit ResEdit, save your changes, swap Finders, and restart.

This trick overrides the procedure the Finder uses to draw ZoomRects, so you won't see them any more.

Taking Drag and Drop to the Limit

You're aware that dragging and dropping any file on ResEdit launches the program and opens the file. But drag and drop doesn't always work with other applications if the document isn't a certain type. Let's say you work with a variety of word processor files, but you prefer one program. Wouldn't it be nice if you could drop any of those files on the application? Here's a way.

Warning You'll be able to drop any file onto your application. Most applications are not designed to open all file kinds, and a well-designed application will ignore a file that it doesn't understand. But there are no guarantees that the file won't be corrupted. Microsoft Word, for example, lets you open any file—even another application—which is pretty scary! To be safe, drop only files that you know the application could read from a Standard File dialog.

1. Be sure your application is backed up on a separate disk.

2. Open the application (*not* a copy) with ResEdit.

3. Open the 'BNDL' resource. (There's only one. For more information on 'BNDL' resources, see Chapter 21.)

4. Choose Create New File Type from the Resource menu (or type Command-K). Figure 13-14 shows how this looks for TeachText.

5. In the Type column of the row you just added, change the four question marks to four asterisks.

6. Close and save the file.

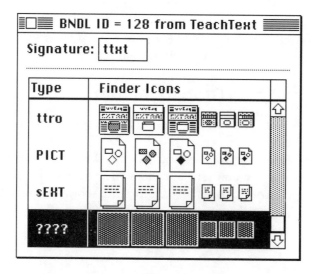

Figure 13-14. Change ???? to **** in the 'BNDL' editor.

7. You've got to make the Finder rebuild its Desktop before your changes can take effect. That's why you want only one copy of the application—the one you're changing—on your disk when you do this. Now restart and hold down the Command and Option keys to rebuild the desktop.

Summary

In this chapter we show you a variety of tips and tricks to personalize your Mac. On the silly side, you saw how to customize the graphical elements HyperCard uses, how to display a color picture when your Mac starts up, and how to play and collect sound resources. On a more serious note, we describe how to protect or hide files and folders, how to record permanent comments, and how to direct screen shots to your paint program. There are other tips, both silly and serious, so scan the Table of Contents for ones that interest you. This chapter contains just a few examples of the zillion customizations you can make with ResEdit. You'll find more projects in Chapter 16, and you'll discover even more as you use ResEdit to explore your Macintosh.

Part Three

Templates: Keys to Dozens of Resources

Chapter 14

 Using Templates

Although ResEdit has built-in special editors for many resource types, there are numerous others you might want to edit. ResEdit allows you to edit a variety of resource types in dialog-box-like windows called *templates*. ResEdit comes with over 70 templates, each allowing you to edit a different resource type. Some of these resource types are obscure, and you'll probably never need to edit them. Others, however, affect a variety of fun or useful Macintosh characteristics. For example, Chapter 6 has already shown you how to use the 'acur' resource to change animated cursors. Other resources edited with templates include 'PREC' resources, which define the defaults for your print dialogs; 'FOND' resources, which contain information about your fonts; and 'STR ' and 'STR#' resources, which contain text strings that can be fun to change. The template editor uses the templates stored within ResEdit to set up the window differently for each resource type. These windows can contain a variety of editable fields and radio buttons. Even though you can modify numerous resource types with the template editor, you use the same editing techniques for all of them.

This chapter begins with an overview of what templates are and a list of the resource types that you can edit with templates, and it finishes up with details of how the various template fields work. If you're interested in creating your own templates, Chapter 23 leads you through the necessary steps.

What Is a Template?

Let's start with an example using a hypothetical desk resource type ('DESK'). A simple 'DESK' template would contain fields for defining four legs, a top, and some drawers—the parts that define a desk. The templates for other furniture resource types would contain different fields. But a 'DESK' template isn't a desk. Only when the fields contain valid values is a 'DESK' resource specified ('DESK' ID 128, for example). The same 'DESK' template allows you to see or enter values that specify other desk resources, too.

More realistically, a template stores a list of instructions that define what fields a window should contain to edit a particular resource type. As illustrated in Figure 14-1, the template editor resembles a special decoder that employs a variety of templates to let you see and edit existing resources or create new ones.

A template displays the contents of a resource as a list of fields. Each field is identified by a label on the left and has a way of changing the field's contents on the right, perhaps an editable field or a pair of radio buttons. For example, the window shown in Figure 14-2 contains a resource displayed using a simple template made up of fields called Value and Title.

To edit this resource, you could enter a number into the Value field and a string of characters into the Title field. Fields that contain different kinds of data are described later in this chapter. The kind of data you're expected to enter is usually obvious, but even if you enter the wrong kind of data (for example, text where a number is required), ResEdit tells you what you've done wrong when you try to close the window.

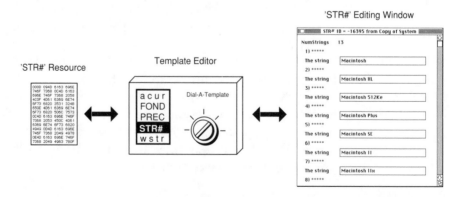

Figure 14-1. The template editor is like a special decoder that uses templates to let you edit resources.

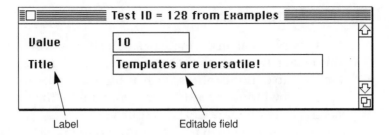

Label   Editable field

Figure 14-2. A window showing a resource displayed using a simple template.

Available Templates

ResEdit comes with built-in templates for editing many different resource types, as shown in Table 14-1. Appendix B contains a short explanation of these and other resource types.

Table 14-1. ResEdit's Built-In Templates

actb	FRSV	PICK
acur	FWID	PICT
ALRT	GNRL	pltt
APPL	hwin	POST
BNDL	icmt	ppat
cctb	inbb	ppcc
clut	indm	PRC0
CMDK	infa	PRC3
CMNU	infs	PSAP
cmnu	inpk	qrsc
CNTL	inra	resf
CTY#	insc	RMAP
dctb	ITL1	ROv#
DITL	itlb	RVEW
DLOG	itlc	scrn
DRVR	itlk	sect
errs	KBDN	SIGN
FBTN	LAYO	SIZE
FCMT	MACS	STR
fctb	MBAR	STR#
FDIR	mcky	TEXT
finf	mctb	TMPL
fld#	MENU	TOOL
FOND	minf	vers
FONT	nrct	wctb
FREF	PAPA	WIND
		wstr

Filling in Templates

First, let's look at an example of a 'CNTL' resource. The template for this resource type is one of the simplest you'll find. 'CNTL' resources are used to define controls, such as buttons and scroll bars, that can appear in windows. The template contains all the information necessary to define a 'CNTL' resource.

The window shown in Figure 14-3 contains a template that looks and acts like a normal dialog box, except for a couple of differences. Unlike many dialog boxes, template windows aren't modal, so you can switch to other windows and use the menus while the template window is open. Also, notice that there's a scroll bar and a size box on the right side of the window. Because many (in fact, most) templates are much larger than the window in which they're displayed, you'll need to scroll to see all the information contained in the resource.

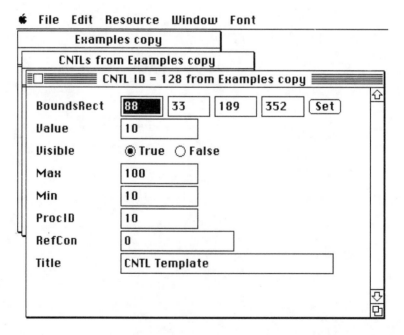

Figure 14-3. A 'CNTL' resource displayed by the template editor.

Moving from Field to Field

The Tab key allows you to move between editable fields while skipping other field types, such as radio buttons. Shift-Tab performs a similar function in reverse, moving to the previous field. (From the first field it'll move to the last field.)

Number Fields

You can enter either decimal or hexadecimal values (see Appendix C for details about hexadecimal numbers) into a numeric field. To enter a number in hexadecimal, simply precede it with a $ character. The length of the field tells you how big a number you can enter. Figure 14-4 shows the different field lengths and the maximum numbers they can contain. The smallest field can contain numbers between 0 and 255, the middle-size field between –32,768 and 32,767, and the biggest field between –2,147,483,648 and 2,147,483,647.

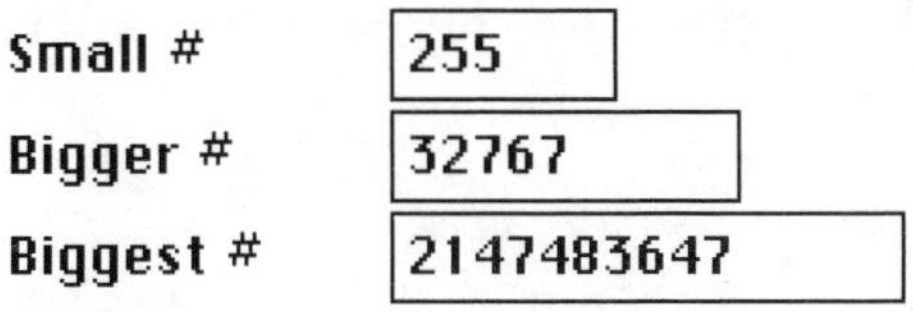

Small #   255

Bigger #   32767

Biggest #   2147483647

Figure 14-4. Number fields and the biggest numbers they can contain.

String Fields

String fields contain simple strings of characters or numbers, as shown in Figure 14-5. They're often used for titles or text that might change when the application is translated to a different language. Strings can have different maximum lengths: Some strings are limited to 255 characters, while others allow up to 32,767. You usually need to type only a few characters, but when you need to enter a long string, the field grows, adding lines as necessary.

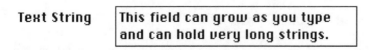

Text String   This field can grow as you type and can hold very long strings.

Figure 14-5. A typical string field.

True/False Fields

A true/false field consists of a pair of radio buttons, as shown in Figure 14-6. Click the one you want to set.

This is fun. ◉ True ○ False

Figure 14-6. A true/false field.

Bit Fields

Bit fields—which always come in multiples of eight—allow you to set a series of on or off values. As shown in Figure 14-7, for each bit there's a pair of radio buttons that can be set to either 0 (off) or 1 (on). Since all eight bits must always be defined in the template but aren't always needed by the resource, you'll often see labels like "Undefined 1" or "Reserved 1" for some of the bits. It's usually safest to leave these undefined bits set to 0 for compatibility with future versions of the resource.

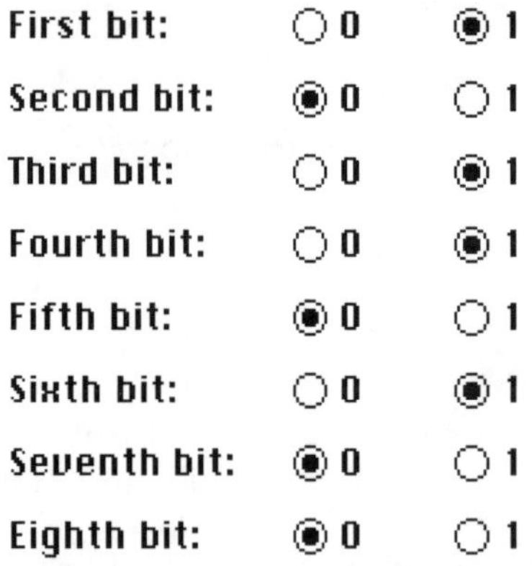

First bit: ○ 0   ◉ 1

Second bit: ◉ 0   ○ 1

Third bit: ○ 0   ◉ 1

Fourth bit: ○ 0   ◉ 1

Fifth bit: ◉ 0   ○ 1

Sixth bit: ○ 0   ◉ 1

Seventh bit: ◉ 0   ○ 1

Eighth bit: ◉ 0   ○ 1

Figure 14-7. Each pair of radio buttons represents one bit of a byte.

Resource Type Fields

In many cases a resource needs to know the resource type of another resource so they can work together. This information is stored in a resource type field, as shown in Figure 14-8. For example, the 'ROv#' (ROM override) resource contains the resource type of the resource being overridden. (Remember, resource types are always four characters long.)

Type name | ICON |

Figure 14-8. A resource type field.

Rectangle Fields

The rectangle is a special field in a template usually used to define the size and location (in pixels) of screen elements, such as dialogs and their contents. It consists of four small, editable fields containing the coordinates of the rectangle. (For example, in the 'CNTL' template in Figure 14-3, you can set the rectangle that defines the location of the control.) The first two fields contain the values for the top and left corners of the rectangle, and the last two fields contain the bottom and right values, as shown in Figure 14-9.

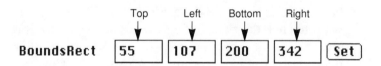

Figure 14-9. A rectangle field.

Using the Set Button with Rectangle Fields

The Set button lets you drag an outline of the rectangle you want to define. When you click the Set button, it becomes highlighted until you're done defining the new rectangle. Clicking the Set button again cancels the operation. After you click the Set button you can click and drag anywhere on the screen to draw a gray outline rectangle, and the values in the fields are updated, as shown in Figure 14-10. Since the rectangle you drag is relative to the entire screen, not to the window containing the template, the (0,0) location is in the upper-left corner of the screen.

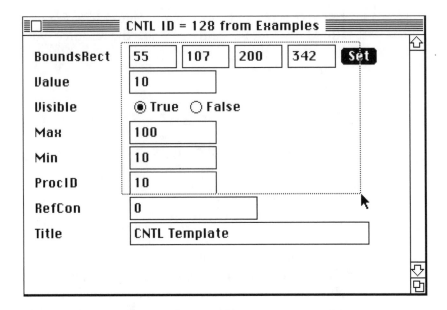

Figure 14-10. Using the Set button to define a rectangle.

When you want to use the Set button to define a rectangle, all you have to do is click and drag. Simple, right? But what if the place you want to click happens to be over a window of another application? You guessed it: The Finder switches you to that other application instead of letting you define your rectangle. The only way around this is to move the template window so that it covers the location where you want to start your rectangle.

Hexadecimal Fields

There are two kinds of hexadecimal (or hex) fields: fixed-length and variable-length. Both kinds have a $ character outside the field to indicate that data entered or displayed in the field is always in hex format. (Remember that hexadecimal is base 16. You can find more details in Appendix C.) The numbers are formatted in pairs, with a space between each pair. Each pair of numbers represents one byte in the resource (since FF hex is 255 decimal and is the largest number that fits in a byte). Since the numbers are formatted only when you open the window, things get pretty messy as you enter new numbers. No matter how you format the numbers you enter, ResEdit assumes that each pair of hex digits represents a byte and ignores all spaces. A fixed-length field like the one in Figure 14-11 can appear anywhere in a template and is truncated if you enter too many digits.

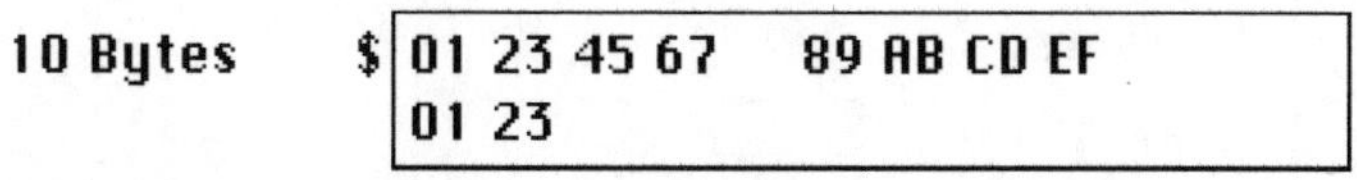

10 Bytes $| 01 23 45 67   89 AB CD EF
                   01 23

Figure 14-11. A fixed-length hex field.

Variable-length hex fields appear only at the ends of resources and contain all the rest of the data in the resource, as shown in Figure 14-12. In many cases, a resource contains some information at the beginning that you might want to modify and a lot of other information at the end that you should not modify. The data at the bottom is simply shown as a large hex field. If you do need to add to such a field, it grows as you enter more digits.

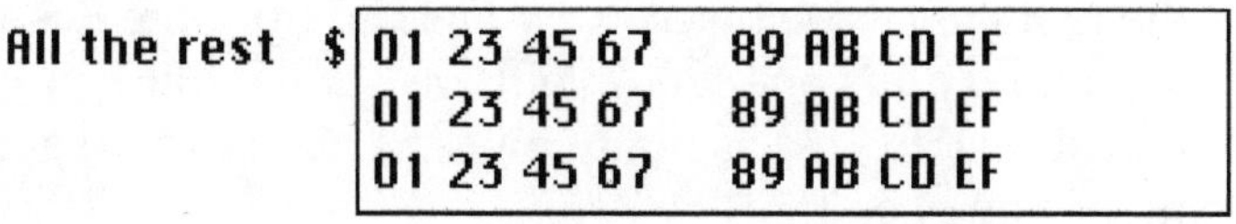

All the rest $| 01 23 45 67   89 AB CD EF
                  01 23 45 67   89 AB CD EF
                  01 23 45 67   89 AB CD EF

Figure 14-12. A variable-length hex field.

As you're modifying a hex field, it might look something like Figure 14-13, but after you close and reopen the window, ResEdit formats it, as shown in Figure 14-12.

All the rest $| 0123456789abcdef
                  0123456789abcdef
                  0123456789abcdef

Figure 14-13. A hex field that you just filled in.

Repeating Lists

Most resources contain a few general fields at the beginning followed by a variable-length list of information. For example, an animated cursor resource ('acur') contains two numeric fields followed by a list of cursor IDs. When a new 'acur' is created, it contains only the two numeric fields, as shown in Figure 14-14.

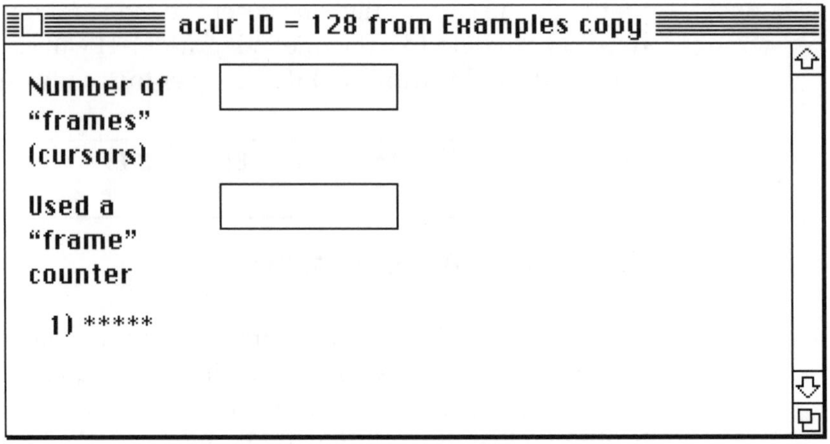

Figure 14-14. A new, empty 'acur' resource.

To add a cursor to the list, select the row of asterisks by clicking them, then choose Insert New Field(s) from the Resource menu. This command adds one set of fields, as shown in Figure 14-15. You can repeat this process as many times as necessary to get the number of fields you need.

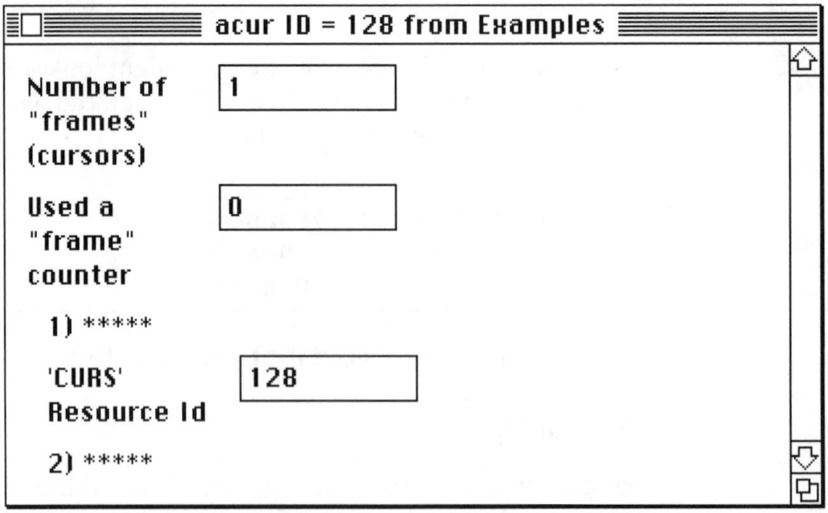

Figure 14-15. An 'acur' with one cursor ID.

By convention, the label used to indicate the start of a list is a row of five asterisks, but you might encounter other characters. Though lists may contain other lists, each nested list is indented, so you can see where it starts. For example, Figure 14-16 contains a list within a list: one identified by the ***** label and one identified by the ----- label.

```
┌──────────────────────────────────────────────────────────────┐
│ ▤□▤▤▤▤▤▤▤▤▤ LIST ID = 128 from Examples ▤▤▤▤▤▤ │ ⇧
├──────────────────────────────────────────────────────────────┤
│  A number       ┌─────────────────┐                            │
│                 │0                │                            │
│                 └─────────────────┘                            │
│  Count one       1                                             │
│    1) *****                                                    │
│    A field       ┌──────────────────────────────────────────┐ │
│                  │                                          │ │
│                  └──────────────────────────────────────────┘ │
│    Count two     2                                             │
│      1) -----                                                  │
│      Inner field ┌──────────────────┐                          │
│                  │10               │                          │
│                  └──────────────────┘                          │
│      2) -----                                                  │
│      Inner field ┌──────────────────┐                          │
│                  │0                │                          │
│                  └──────────────────┘                          │
│      3) -----                                                  │
│    2) *****                                                    │ ⇩
└──────────────────────────────────────────────────────────────┘ ▣
```

Figure 14-16. A template with two nested lists.

There's also usually a field just above a list that indicates how many sets of fields are contained in that list. Depending on the kind of list, this count can start at zero or one, or not be present at all. If the count is –1 before you add any fields to the resource, you'll know it starts with zero instead of one. You can always tell how many sets are in the list by looking at the number in front of the last list separator (usually a ***** label). The number of sets is one less than this last number. For example, the last number in the list in Figure 14-17 is nine, so the list repeats eight times.

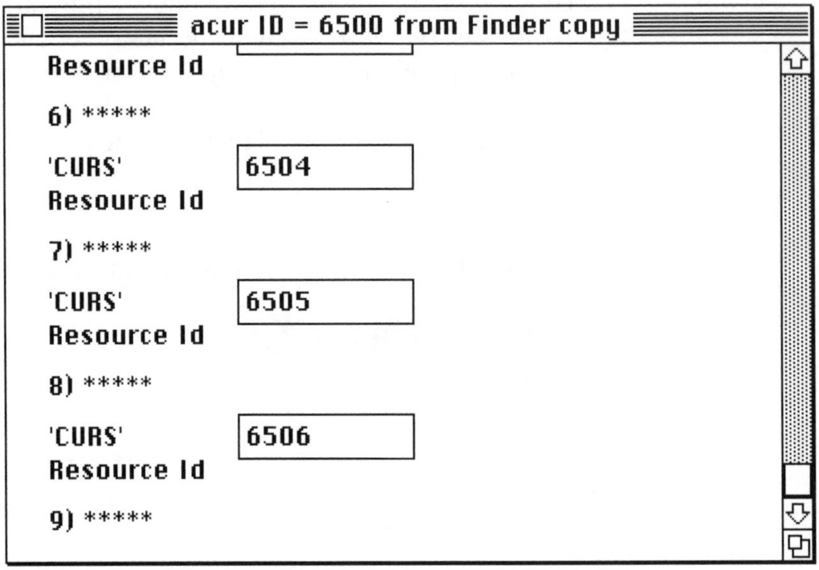

Figure 14-17. An 'acur' resource containing eight cursors.

Adding and Removing Fields

The Insert New Field(s) command on the Resource menu is used to insert a new set of fields before the selected list separator. Selecting a separator selects all the fields between that and the next separator. The Edit menu commands work on these selected fields. For example, you could move a set of fields within a list by selecting the separator just above the fields, cutting the fields, selecting the separator just above where you want them to be moved, and pasting. Removing a set of fields is as easy as selecting a list separator and choosing Cut from the Edit menu or pressing the Delete key.

Using Templates When There's a Custom Editor

There are a few cases where you'll want to use a template rather than the custom editor for a resource. For example, the 'PICT' editor simply shows the 'PICT' resource at full size, whereas the 'PICT' template lets you change the rectangle that defines the location and size of the 'PICT'. You can follow these steps to edit a 'PICT' resource with a template instead of with the custom editor.

1. Choose Open Using Template from the Resource menu or hold down both the Option and Command keys while you double-click the resource.

2. You see the dialog shown in Figure 14-18. Since 'PICT' is already filled in, just click the OK button. (If you want to use a different template, you can select it from the list or type it into the field.)

3. A window appears containing the 'PICT' resource in the specified template.

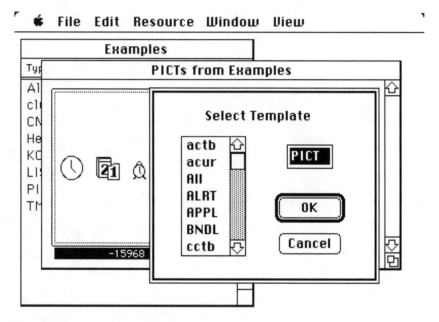

Figure 14-18. This dialog lets you select which template you want to use.

Summary

This chapter describes how ResEdit uses templates to let you edit over 70 different resource types. You use templates by filling in a scrollable list of editable fields and radio buttons. The window for each resource type presents a different set of fields. We describe each possible field type and show you how to add and remove sets of fields from variable-length field lists. In Chapter 23 we show you how to design your own templates.

Chapter 15

 Template Projects

This chapter contains a collection of both practical and fun changes you can make using ResEdit's template editor.

Customizing Finder Menus

OK, here's what you've been waiting for since Chapter 8. As you may recall, System 7 Finder menus are no longer stored in easy-to-edit 'MENU' resources. Editing the new Finder menu ('fmnu') resource is a pain if you have to do it in the Hex editor, so we've included an 'fmnu' template on the disk with this book. First we'll tell you how to install the template, then we'll show you how to add a Command-key shortcut.

Installing the Finder Menu Template

To install the template, simply copy it to ResEdit's Preferences file.

1. Double-click the Finder Menu Template file that's on the disk that came with this book. When the file opens in ResEdit, copy the 'TMPL' resource you see, then close the file.

2. Use ResEdit to open the ResEdit Preference file that's in the Preferences Folder within your System Folder. Paste, then close the file, saving your changes. ResEdit will be able to use the template immediately. You don't have to quit and relaunch.

Adding a Command-Key Shortcut

Aliases come in handy, and they become even more convenient when you add a Command-key shortcut for Make Alias on the File menu.

1. Open a copy of your Finder with ResEdit. Double-click the 'fmnu' resource type.

2. Open 'fmnu' ID 1252. You'll see a window that looks something like the one shown in Figure 15-1.

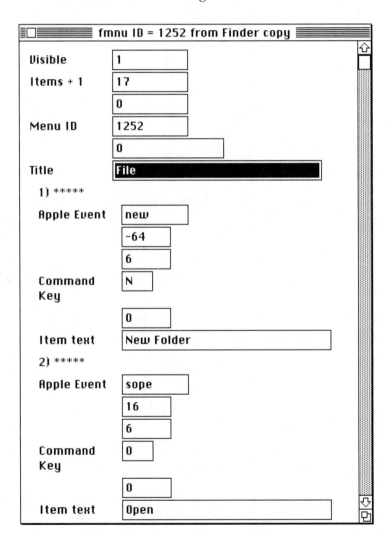

Figure 15-1. The template editor opens the File menu in the 'fmnu' template.

3. Scroll to item number nine. You should see the fields shown in Figure 15-2. In the "Command Key" field type an "=" or an "M" or whatever makes sense to you. Remember that the Command-key shortcut considerations discussed in Chapter 8 still apply. For example, you can't use Command-A, because that's already taken for Select All on the Edit menu.

4. Close and save the file, and quit ResEdit. Swap Finders as described in Chapter 4 and restart. You'll be able to use your new Command-key shortcut as soon as the Finder launches.

The procedure is similar for adding other Command-key shortcuts. If you want to use Command-T for the Empty Trash command, go to item 2 on the Special menu, ID 1255. There's nothing to do to the Apple menu (ID 1251) and the Labels Control Panel lets you customize the Label menu (ID 1256), but the Edit menu is ID 1253, and the View menu is ID 1254, in case you want to tweak those. We advise you not to fiddle with the other resources you see in the 'fmnu' type picker.

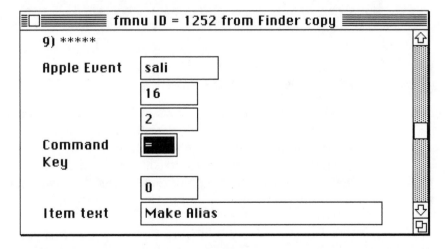

Figure 15-2. Type in the character you want to use for your Command-key shortcut.

Other Finder Menu Changes

You can make other changes to your Finder menus, but don't get carried away if you want your menus to still work when you're through. Specifically, don't change the contents of any fields other than the Command Key and Item text fields. To change the text of a menu item, you can simply type in your improvements in the Item text field. You should know, however, that changing menu item text within the 'fmnu' resource doesn't always work. Sometimes you have to change a string resource. We'll give you more details in the "Fun with Strings" section later in this chapter.

Finally, if the order of the menu items irks you, you can rearrange them, using the usual methods for cutting and pasting items in templates. You can even move items from one menu to another. If you do this, be sure to update the "Items + 1" field (near the top of the template) for both affected menus.

Hint Don't forget about the template editor's Font menu. If you'd like to see more of a resource you're working with, switch to a more compact font like Times.

More Efficient Mouse Clicks

Why waste time clicking your mouse any more than you have to? You probably have some applications that require one click to make a window active, then another click to actually *do* something in the window. Why not make one click accomplish both? The Finder already works this way, but most applications don't. It's an easy fix— simply turn on the Get Front Clicks bit in your application's 'SIZE' resources.

This doesn't seem to work for every application (for instance, Microsoft Word), but it *ought* to work for most. We know it works in ResEdit, and you can follow the same steps for your other applications.

1. It's hard to imagine how you could get into trouble with this one, but, as always, the safest approach is to work on a copy.

Use ResEdit to open a copy of ResEdit or the application you want to alter.

2. Open the 'SIZE' resource type. ResEdit has only one 'SIZE' resource, but other applications may have two or three, and you will have to follow the same steps for each one.

3. Open the 'SIZE' resource. You should see a window that resembles the one shown in Figure 15-3.

4. The seventh item in the list, which is shown at the bottom of Figure 15-3, is labeled Get front clicks. Change the setting from 0 to 1.

5. If the application has more than one 'SIZE' resource, open and change each one.

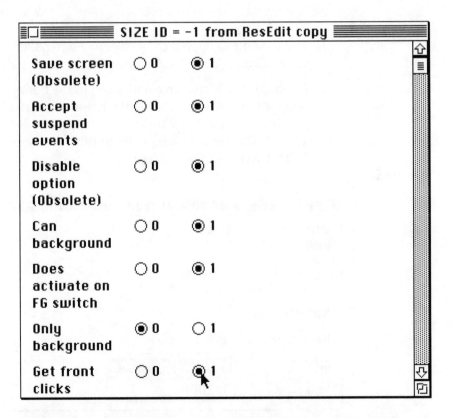

Figure 15-3. Turn on the Get front clicks bit in all the 'SIZE' resources in the file.

6. Close and save the file. Now when you run the application, one click will do the work of two. (If you used ResEdit on itself, rather than on a copy of itself, you'll have to quit and relaunch to see the effect of your changes.)

Giving the Finder More Memory

You may not run out of Finder memory very often, depending on your system, but when you do it's pretty annoying. Increasing the Finder's memory was easy under System 6, and with ResEdit, it's easy under System 7, too. You just make a simple change to the resource type discussed in the previous tip, the 'SIZE' resource. Of course, memory is finite and the more you give to the Finder the less is left for your applications. In most cases a boost of 50K ought to be plenty. (Add less if that seems like too much.) Here's how to go about it.

1. Use ResEdit to open a copy of your Finder. Open the 'SIZE' resource type. There should be one resource with ID -1.

2. Open the 'SIZE' resource and scroll to the bottom of the template window. You'll see the fields shown in Figure 15-4. Initially, the Size and Min size fields contain the same number. To add 50K, simply change the number in the Size field to 352080, as shown in the figure.

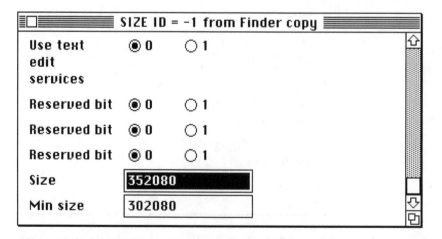

Figure 15-4. Increase the number in the Size field to give the Finder more memory.

3. Close and save the file, and quit ResEdit. Swap Finders as described in Chapter 4 and restart. The Finder will launch with more memory.

Speeding Up Your Mouse

Do you ever wish the Mouse Control Panel would let you set a speed in between two settings, or faster than the fastest setting? Relief is at hand! With a few quick changes to a template, you can change any of the speed settings for the Mouse Control Panel.

There are seven 'mcky' mouse resources in your System file corresponding to the seven possible mouse speeds in the control panel. The resource with ID 0 controls the speed of the Very Slow or Tablet setting, the resource with ID 6 controls the Fast setting, and the resources with IDs 1 to 5 control the speeds in between. Each resource contains eight threshold values that determine how far and how fast you have to move your mouse before it starts speeding up. By changing these threshold values you can tune your mouse to respond just the way you like.

Making a "Fast" Mouse into a "Very Fast" Mouse

1. Use ResEdit to open a copy of your System file.

2. Open the 'mcky' resource type.

3. Open 'mcky' ID 6. You'll see a window similar to the one shown in Figure 15-5.

4. Change the 8 Threshold fields to those shown in Figure 15-6.

5. Save your changes and quit ResEdit.

6. Swap System files and restart, as described in Chapter 4.

7. Open the Mouse Control Panel and make sure the Fast radio button is selected.

Move the mouse pointer about your screen. Is it moving too fast? Not fast enough? If it's moving too fast, you might try increasing some of the higher threshold values a little. If it's moving too slowly, lay off the coffee for a few hours and check it again. If it's still too slow, try reducing some of the numbers a little. Small changes can have a big effect on your mouse speed, so try subtracting 1 from each threshold value. Keep changing the numbers until you get a speed you like. It's generally a good idea to keep the smallest number in Threshold 1 and increase the numbers as you progress to Threshold 8. Remember that after each change you must reinstall the System and restart.

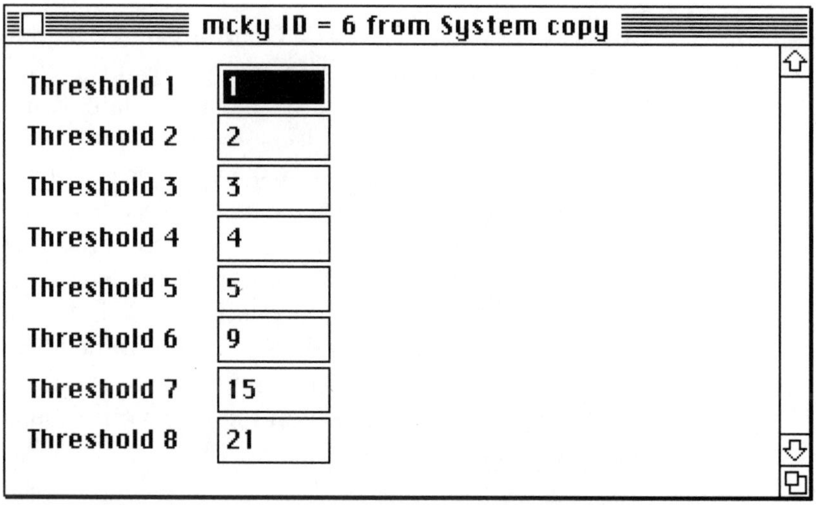

Figure 15-5. The 'mcky' resource controls the speed of your mouse.

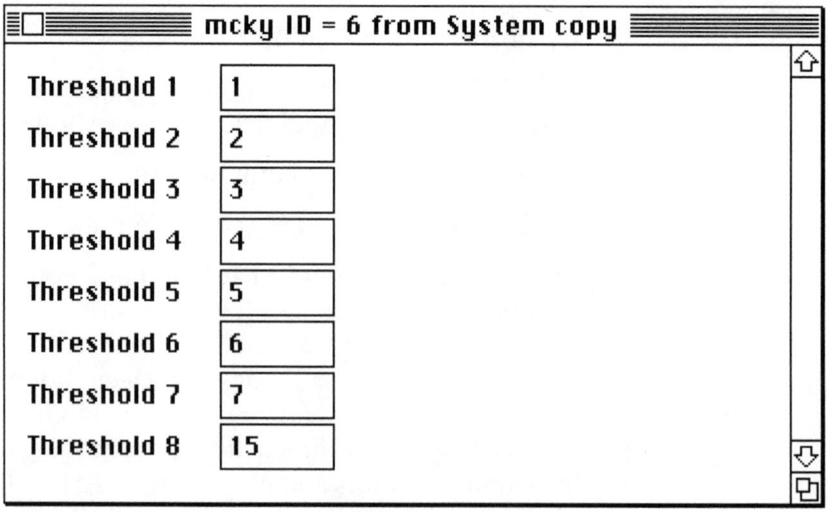

Figure 15-6. Threshold settings for a faster mouse.

Changing Your Printer's Paper Size

Most of the time, you probably use your printer's standard paper sizes, but wouldn't it be convenient to set up your own paper size? Maybe you'd like to print your own birthday card, use a preprinted form, an index card, or your own stationery. All of these options would require tedious adjustments each time you print, but with a little planning you can set up your own custom paper sizes. If you have any non-Postscript Apple printer (such as an ImageWriter, Personal LaserWriter SC, or StyleWriter), you can change the paper-size settings available in the Page Setup dialog.

Every printer driver contains a set of 'PREC' (Printer RECord) resources that control the behavior of the printer. The 'PREC' resource with ID 3 specifies the paper sizes displayed in the Page Setup dialog. You can specify up to six different paper sizes that correspond to the six possible radio buttons in the Page Setup dialog. Even better, you can override 'PREC' ID 3 by including a new 'PREC' resource with ID 4. That way you don't have to change your original resource, and you can easily restore it any time you want by deleting (or renumbering) your custom resource.

> **Hint** Some applications come with their own 'PREC' resource that contains what the manufacturer believes to be the best paper sizes for that application. If your changes don't show up in one of your applications, check to see if it contains a 'PREC' resource with an ID of 4. If so, you'll have to either change its resource ID (so that it doesn't get used) or add your custom changes to it, too.

How to Add Custom Paper Sizes

Here's how you can add custom paper sizes to your Page Setup dialog. Your printer driver should be in your Extensions Folder within your System Folder, and should have the same name as the printer you're using.

1. Make a copy of your printer driver file. Save this copy as a backup in case something goes wrong later on.

2. Use ResEdit to open your printer driver file (the file you just copied in Step 1).

3. Double-click the 'PREC' resource type to open the 'PREC' picker.

4. Select 'PREC' ID 3.

5. Choose the Duplicate command from the File menu.

6. Select the new resource (Duplicate probably gave it a resource ID of 128).

7. Choose the Get Resource Info command from the Resource menu.

8. Change the resource ID to 4 and close the Resource Info window.

9. Double-click the new resource to open an editing window like the one shown in Figure 15-7. Other printer drivers have different numbers of buttons, and they may have different names and dimensions.

10. The first field (Number of Btns) contains a number between 1 and 6 that indicates how many radio buttons should appear in the Page Setup dialog. If you're going to add a paper size, be sure to update this field.

11. The next twelve fields contain the height and width for each of the six possible paper sizes. The height and width are specified in $1/120$-inch increments. For example, if you want to add an 8-inch-wide paper size, put 8 times 120, or 960, into the width field.

12. The next six fields contain the names to be displayed with the radio buttons. Change the field corresponding to the sizes you added or changed in Step 11. Be careful not to change the contents of the Data field at the end of the resource.

13. That's it. Now close and save the file, and select Page Setup from the File menu to see your changes. (If you don't see the results of your changes, check the Chooser desk accessory to make sure the correct printer is selected.) Figure 15-8 shows the ImageWriter's Page Setup dialog with a few new paper sizes added.

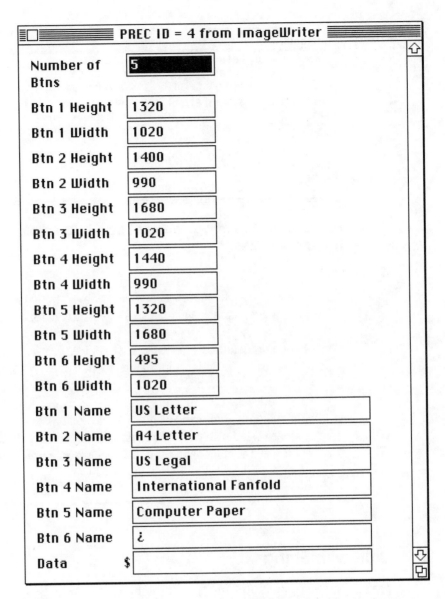

Figure 15-7. The 'PREC' resource from the ImageWriter file.

```
┌──────────────────────────────────────────────────────────────────────┐
│ ImageWriter                                    7.0.1      ┌─────────┐  │
│ Paper:     ⦿ US Letter         ○ A4 Letter              │   OK    │  │
│            ○ US Legal          ○ Greeting Card           └─────────┘  │
│            ○ Insurance Form    ○ Biz Envelope                         │
│                                                          ┌─────────┐  │
│ Orientation    Special Effects:  ☐ Tall Adjusted         │ Cancel  │  │
│  ┌──┐ ┌──┐                       ☐ 50 % Reduction         └─────────┘  │
│  │  │ │  │                       ☐ No Gaps Between Pages             │
│  └──┘ └──┘                                                            │
│                                                                        │
│ ┌───────────┐                                                          │
│ │ Document...│                                                          │
│ └───────────┘   ☐ Use As Default                                      │
└──────────────────────────────────────────────────────────────────────┘
```

Figure 15-8. The ImageWriter's Page Setup dialog with a few new paper sizes.

By The Way Some applications may have problems with custom paper sizes, especially small sizes like index cards. Applications are generally tested only with the standard paper sizes, so, although most major applications should work, it's possible you'll find a few that don't. Unfortunately, there's nothing you can do about this. Fortunately, you can still select the standard paper sizes from your customized Page Setup dialog, so you can use your custom paper sizes with other applications and use the standard sizes with these uncooperative applications. Microsoft Word has a slightly different problem. Custom paper sizes only affect Word if you add them to the 'PREC' resource with ID 3 in the printer driver file. Word ignores 'PREC' resources with ID 4.

Fun with Strings

Most applications, including the Finder and the System file, contain lots of text strings, which can be stored in either 'STR ' or 'STR#' (string list) resources. Unless you're localizing an application for another country, it's usually not important to change a string resource. You can't make your Mac behave in some neat new way by changing a word here and there. You can, however, buck convention and make the messages you see a lot more fun. We'll give you a few examples of strings to change, but we encourage you to explore. It's unlikely you could cause damage by changing a string, so just poke through your applications, the Finder, and the System file and see what you can find. Before you race off to customize what your applications have to say to you, here are a few tips.

- Don't make a string a lot longer than it was originally. If you do, it may no longer fit in the space provided for it. (If you really want a longer string in a dialog, you can find out how to change the size of a dialog item in Chapter 10).
- Be sure to save a copy of the file so you'll have the original strings to refer to later.
- Whatever you do, don't remove a string from an 'STR#' resource. Applications refer to strings by using an index into the list. If you delete the fourth string, thus making the fifth string the fourth, your messages will be very confused.
- If you find strings that contain things like ^0 or *0* or other combinations of characters that resemble cartoon cursing, that means the application is going to insert some text before it uses the string (a file's name, for example). You can change other contents of the string, but you should leave such characters alone.

Remember, applications should keep almost every piece of text you see on the screen in 'STR ' or 'STR#' resources, so just look around for interesting things to change.

Changing the Finder's Strings

Lots of strings in the Finder are fun to change. You'll find everything from error messages and Balloon Help text to menu items and the words the Finder tacks onto the end of file names. We'll start you off with some ideas, then you can explore further on your own—that's part of the fun! Here are the generic instructions, followed by specific suggestions for Finder version 7.1.

1. Make a copy of your Finder so you can restore the strings later if you want.

2. Use ResEdit to open the copy of the Finder.

3. Open the 'STR#' or 'STR ' picker, find the resource(s) you want to change, and edit them.

4. Close and save the Finder.

5. Swap Finders as described in Chapter 4, then restart to see all of your new strings. Be sure to keep your original Finder.

Now for some specific suggestions to plug into Step 3. You'll get your own ideas as you browse.

- If you changed your Trash icon into a toilet or something else in Chapter 7, now's your chance to carry the theme further. Open 'STR#' ID 11750. Part of the resource is shown in Figure 15-9, and as you can see, it contains numerous references to the Trash. The first string is the name that goes under the icon on the desktop; change it to "Slop," "Refuse," or a new theme. Scroll to the tenth string to change "Empty Trash" to "Flush," "Disgorge" or whatever fits. The other strings get used in various dialogs and alerts. If you want to be thorough, you can change every occurrence of the word "Trash." You'll find more Trash references in 'STR#' ID 8750 and 'STR#' ID 10250, and probably elsewhere. Also check your System file, 'STR#' ID -6046.

- The Finder's menu item text strings are spread over several resources, and we don't know what you might want to change, so you'll have to look around. You can start your search in 'STR#' ID 3000, 5000, and 10250.

- The third string in 'STR#' ID 11250 contains the name the Finder gives to new, empty folders. Try changing "untitled folder" to "new" or "empty" or just "untitled"—you already know it's a folder. This change is shown in Figure 15-10, along with the next two changes.

- You can make the Finder's Duplicate command create clones instead of copies. The fourth string in this same resource ('STR#' ID 11250) contains the text that's added to a file's name when it's duplicated. Change " copy" to " clone." Leave a space in front of the word you type in.

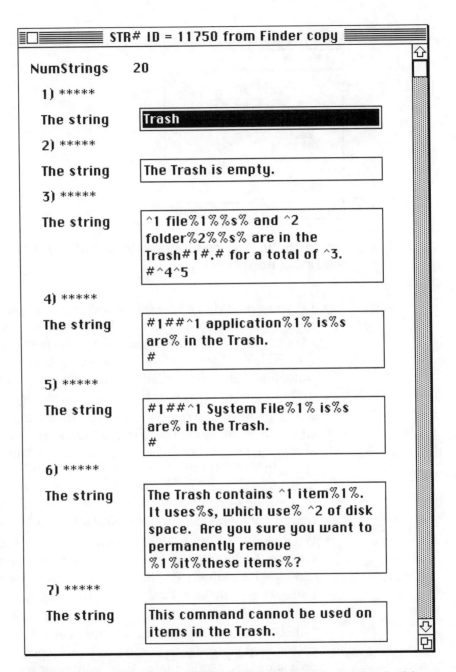

Figure 15-9. Some of the Finder's most prominent Trash strings are in this resource.

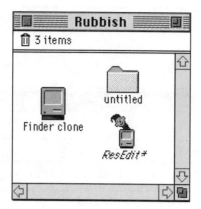

Figure 15-10. You can rename your Trash and change the way the Finder names things.

- Do you get tired of removing "alias" from the end of your alias names? It's easy to spot an alias by the italics, so why not remove "alias" once and for all? Go to the first string in 'STR#' ID 20500. You have to leave a space or an asterisk or something so that the alias name will differ from the original file.

- Seeing the hated string, "The application '^2' has unexpectedly quit, ^1," is usually pretty annoying. You could lighten up the situation by changing the string to "The application '^2' has abandoned ship..." or "...has wigged out..." Change the first string in 'STR#' ID 10000. And while you're at it, here's another target for editing: "An unexpected error occurred, ^1." Instead of stopping to ponder what an *expected* error might be, just remove "unexpected" from the fifth string in 'STR#' ID 1250.

- When you open fonts within your Fonts folder, you see this sentence in the selected font: "How razorback-jumping frogs can level six piqued gymnasts!" If you'd like to see something else, go to the first (and only) string in 'STR#' ID 14516.

- When you pull down the Apple menu, the first item reads "About This Macintosh..." How impersonal. You've probably customized your Mac in numerous way by now. It's really *yours*. So it should say so. Replace "this" with your name, as shown in Figure 15-11. You'll find the menu item text in string 56 of 'STR#' ID 5000. The window title is in 'STR ' ID 10000.

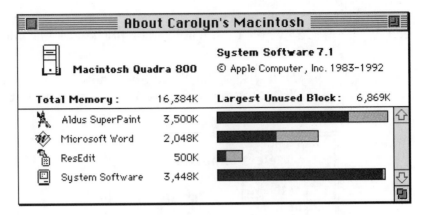

Figure 15-11. Add your name to the Finder's About box.

Other Strings

Check your applications for customizable strings—you're bound to find some. Your System file also has lots of strings to browse through. Even if you don't change anything, what you find can be amusing. Open the System's 'STR#' ID –16415 for an example.

Changing the Frame for a 'PICT'

When you open ResEdit's 'PICT' picker, you see all the 'PICT' resources in a file shrunk down to fit in equal-size cells. When you double-click a 'PICT', a window appears showing you the 'PICT' at its normal size. This is convenient if you want to see what 'PICT's are available in a file, but not so convenient if you want to make changes to the 'PICT'. If you want to change the contents of a 'PICT', you should use a graphics program like MacDraw Pro or SuperPaint. Use ResEdit if what you want to do is change the size or location of the 'PICT's frame. Here's how.

1. Use ResEdit to open the file containing the 'PICT' resource you want to change.

2. Open the 'PICT' picker.

3. Select the 'PICT' you want to change.

4. Select Open Using Template from the Resource menu (or hold down the Command and Option keys while you double-click the 'PICT').

5. You'll see a dialog like the one shown in Figure 15-12. Since the 'PICT' type is already selected, just click the OK button.

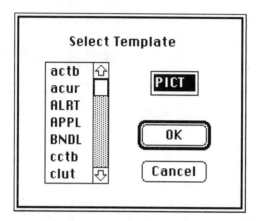

Figure 15-12. The template dialog defaults to 'PICT'.

6. Next you should see a 'PICT' template like the one shown in Figure 15-13. You can change the Rect field to anything you like. Don't change anything else in the template or you'll more than likely ruin your 'PICT'.

7. Close the template window. You can see the effect of your changes by opening the 'PICT' editor (double-click the 'PICT').

8. Once you're satisfied with your changes, close and save your file.

Hint Changing the frame of a 'PICT' doesn't affect its contents in any way. Changing the frame changes only which part of the contents you'll see when the 'PICT' is drawn. By making the frame smaller, you can effectively hide parts of the 'PICT'. By making it larger, you can add white space around the 'PICT' or control the positioning of the 'PICT' when it's drawn.

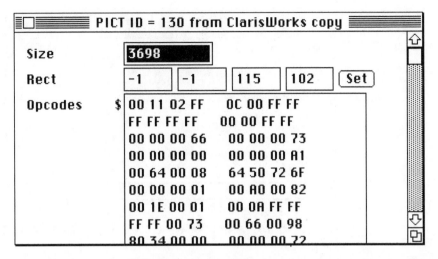

Figure 15-13. You can set the 'PICT' frame in the 'PICT' template.

Changing Your System Font

Tired of using Chicago 12 for your System font? You can use any font
you want, but you have to be careful. Once you've made this change,
you won't have access to Chicago 12 at all—it will be as if the font
doesn't exist anymore. (It still appears on your font menus but choosing it actually picks your new System font, not Chicago.) Since
Chicago contains some special characters (the check mark used in
menus and the apple used for the Apple menu, for example), you
may need to make a few changes to any other font you want to use as
the System font. Chapter 12 gives you details about how to edit a
font. Keep in mind that the font you substitute will show up in many
different places. The System font is used for menu titles and menu
items, window titles, dialog boxes, and the text in many applications'
windows. Because it's used in so many different places, you should
keep the font size approximately the same as the size of Chicago 12. If
you make the font bigger, the System will make the title bar of windows and the menu bar bigger to accommodate the new font, but
most applications' dialogs won't resize themselves to hold the bigger
characters. As you can see in Figure 15-14, a Finder window's title bar
looks fine with a larger font. Figure 15-15 illustrates the problems
you'll have with dialog boxes.

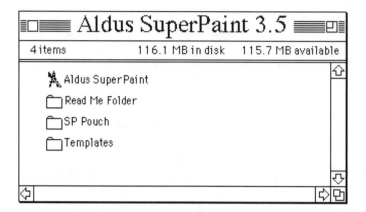

Figure 15-14. A Finder window using Times 24 for the System font.

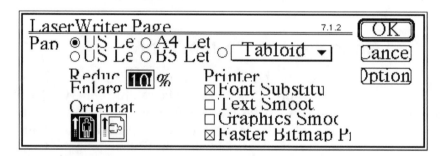

Figure 15-15. The Finder's Page Setup dialog doesn't look quite so good with Times 24.

Here's how to change your System font.

1. Using ResEdit, open a copy of your System file.

2a. **If you're using System 7.1 or later,** look through the fonts in the Fonts Folder in your System Folder and pick the one you want to use. Open a copy of the font suitcase with ResEdit. Open the 'FOND' for the font you want to use and scroll until you see a list of individual fonts. Find the font size you're interested in, make a note of its resource ID, and then close the file.

2b. If you're using System 7.0 or earlier, open the 'FONT' picker. Scan through the list of fonts until you find the 'FONT' you want to use for your System font. Make a note of its resource ID.

3. Switch to the type picker in the copy of your System file and open the 'FOND' picker.

4. Open the 'FOND' resource with ID 0.

5. Scroll to the bottom of the window (the Res ID field should be visible, as shown in Figure 15-16).

6. Change the Res ID field to the resource ID of the font you found in Step 2. For example, if you want to use Times 14, you can enter 11515 for the resource ID. (Times 14 works well as a substitute System font because it's approximately the same size as Chicago 12, although it's too thin to be readable when dimmed in menus.)

7. Close and save the file.

8. Install your modified System file and restart your Macintosh.

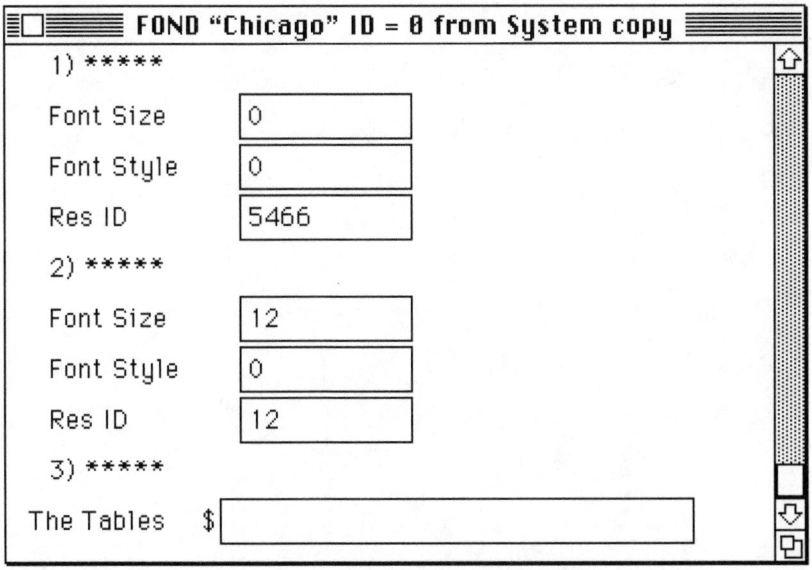

Figure 15-16. Change the Res ID field to the resource ID of any 'FONT' you want to use as your System font.

Summary

This chapter shows you a number of projects you can do with templates. Some examples show you how to customize specific resources. For instance, you can add Command-key shortcuts to Finder menus with the 'fmnu' template included on the disk with this book. You can speed up your mouse by customizing the 'mcky' resources in your System file. And with a simple change in the 'SIZE' resource, you can change most applications so that you no longer need that extra mouse click just to activate a window. We also explore general techniques for customizing string ('STR ' or 'STR#') resources found in almost every application and describe specific examples of changes you can make to the Finder's strings. This summary mentions only some of the projects in this chapter, and this chapter represents only a sampling of the many changes you can make with the more than 70 templates included with ResEdit.

Color, Color
Everywhere

Chapter 16

Color on the Mac

You've got a color Mac and you're just itching to customize with color. This chapter and the next two are for you. Those of you with monochrome monitors don't have to pout and flip to another chapter, because the grays your monitors display are "color," too. You don't need a color monitor to enjoy color resources. Whether you're working in color or gray-scales, you'll complete your customization projects more smoothly and enjoyably if you have an understanding of how your Macintosh handles color. This chapter gives a brief overview of Macintosh color principles and describes two important color resource types that come into play. We also introduce features common to several color editors. The discussion of color resource editors assumes you're already familiar with ResEdit's fatbits editors (see Chapter 5 if you need a refresher). Similarly, the treatment of specific color resources assumes you're already familiar with the original black-and-white ones discussed in Part 2.

Color Basics

The particular colors you see on your screen at a given moment result from complex interactions between software and hardware. Prior to the Macintosh II, you had no choice of displays. Mac screens were all black and white, built in, and the same size. But now Macs support a variety of built-in and stand-alone color monitors. The number of possible colors a monitor can display is related to the amount of memory available to store screen images. So, the color capability of your Mac depends not just on the monitor, but also on the amount of memory devoted to video—VRAM—whether it's built in or on a video card.

To appreciate why memory is so important to color, you have to understand the difference between bits and pixels. On an SE or a Classic, or on a color Mac set to the black-and-white mode, each dot on the screen, called a *pixel* (for picture element), requires one bit of memory. So when you're talking about black-and-white displays, bits and pixels amount to the same thing. Allocating more bits per pixel provides more information, allowing for shades of gray or various colors. The number of colors or grays a pixel can display is limited by the number of bits of memory dedicated to that pixel. The more bits per pixel an image or monitor has, the *deeper* it is said to be.

By The Way You've heard people tossing around terms like *two-bit color* and although you're not so naive as to assume they're referring to a monetary value, sometimes you wonder what they really mean. Here's the scoop. *Two-bit color* means you have enough memory to accommodate two bits per pixel. Because there are 2^2 or 4 ways to arrange those two bits per pixel (0,0; 0,1; 1,0; and 1,1), you can have four colors or grays. Here are the standard arrangements:

- 1 bit per pixel allows only white (0) or black (1)
- 2 bits per pixel (2-bit color) allows 2^2 or 4 colors or grays
- 4 bits per pixel (4-bit color) allows 2^4 or 16 colors or grays
- 8 bits per pixel (8-bit color) allows 2^8 or 256 colors or grays

You might also have 24-bit color, which works a little differently. ResEdit works just fine on 24-bit systems, but none of the resources we discuss take full advantage of all the colors.

Colors by Numbers

You rarely get very far into a discussion about color on the Mac before people start throwing numbers around, and some of those numbers are impressively huge. You don't have to memorize the numbers, but knowing where they come from and how they're related will help you understand what your Mac is doing when you see colors or grays shifting on your screen as you switch between windows. This understanding will also help you create and edit color resources intelligently. (As a side benefit, you can spout off some numbers yourself next time the conversation turns to color on the Mac.) Capsulized, the problem your Mac must solve is as follows: At any given moment it can display only a tiny fraction of a tremendous rainbow of possible colors (unless it's a 24-bit system, which can display them all). How does it determine that subset of colors?

Let's start with the monitor. Apple's RGB (red-green-blue) monitors are capable of showing 2^8 colors for each of the three color beams—or more than 16 million colors! (For math fans, that's $(2^8)^3$ or 2^{24}, which is 16,777,216.) Somehow your Mac has to tell the monitor exactly which 256 colors to display.

Looking at the software side of the situation doesn't immediately solve the problem. On the Macintosh, the red, green, and blue components of a color are each specified by 16 bits, so each of the three components can have values between 0 and 65,535. (That number may look familiar to you if you've experimented with the Macintosh Color Picker.) The number of possible RGB settings is humongous: Color QuickDraw could theoretically support the definition of as many as 2^{48} colors (that's $(2^{16})^3$ or $65,535^3$)—more than 281 trillion! So, your Mac has a problem. Out of the 281 trillion possible Color QuickDraw colors, and the 16 million possible monitor colors, how does the Mac determine which 256 colors you're going to get?

Hardware and software work together to decide which 256 colors to display. A streamlined description of the interaction follows. You don't have to remember the names of all the players, just the end result. The application asks one of the Toolbox Managers or Color QuickDraw for the colors it wants to use, choosing from the 281 trillion possible Color QuickDraw colors. Color QuickDraw then asks the operating system's Color Manager for the colors that are actually available on the monitor. For example, on a 16-color system, only 16 colors from the monitor's possible 16 million are available. The Color Manager figures out how to translate what Color QuickDraw wants into what the monitor can actually provide, making the best match possible based on the monitor, VRAM, and Control Panel settings. This matching process is called *mapping*. The Color Manager then communicates with the monitor and the screen dots get turned on.

> **By The Way** The frontmost window determines which specific colors are available on a monitor.

So if you try to draw in 256 colors or grays when your system is capable of displaying only 16, Color QuickDraw and the Color Manager map each of the 256 requested colors to one of the 16 colors available. Exactly what's involved in color mapping is a complicated part of the Macintosh magic. For most purposes, you don't have to worry about it. But it won't hurt to know something about two important resources that function as color collections your Mac can refer to when juggling colors.

Color Collections

When your Mac is figuring out how to map one color to another it needs a frame of reference; it needs to know exactly what colors are currently available. Similarly, when you create or edit a color resource, ResEdit needs to know which colors to make available. Color collections are stored in two types of resources. A 'clut' (Color Look-Up Table) is a collection of specific colors, or RGB values. This color roster resembles a list of recipes that tell the Mac exactly how to mix the red, green, and blue color beams. Mac ROMs contain default 'clut's that provide a standard set of colors for each of the three standard pixel depths (4, 16, and 256 colors). ResEdit lets you choose these or other color collections, including your own custom collection. We'll talk more about this later in the chapter when we discuss the Color menu.

If necessary, a 'clut' can easily be converted into the second type of color collection, the 'pltt' (PaLeTTe). A 'pltt' is similar to a 'clut', but it includes additional color usage information that tells the system how to handle color conflicts. Another difference is that a 'pltt' can be associated with a window, to make sure that the window always has a certain specific set of colors available whenever it's active. In fact, that's why 'pltt's were invented. Windows without palettes are drawn by mapping the requested colors to whatever colors are currently available. But if a 'pltt' is associated with a window, the colors in the 'pltt' take top priority whenever the window is active. Using information in the 'pltt', your Mac changes the color environment in whatever way necessary to ensure that the specified set of colors is available to that window.

By The Way You may sometimes notice a screen flash and colors or grays shifting as you switch between windows while you're editing various color resources. Your Mac is simply switching from one subset of colors to another among the many it can display. Let's say you create a color icon using the standard 256 colors, and a color pattern using 256 grays. To make sure you see your resource in the colors you used to paint it, ResEdit associates a 'pltt' containing those colors with the editor window. Your Mac has no choice but to switch the color environment as you go from one window to the other because it can display only one set of 256 colors at a time.

Most users won't have much reason to edit 'clut's or 'pltt's, but programmers can find out how to edit these resources at the end of this chapter.

Color Resources

ResEdit contains editors for numerous color resources, and several of its black-and-white resource editors allow you to colorize resource components. Table 16-1 lists the resource types that have their own editors. We've already introduced the first two resource types, 'clut' and 'pltt'. You edit the remaining resource types in fatbits (or more correctly, fatpixels) editors. We discuss color icons in Chapter 17 and color patterns in Chapter 18.

Table 16-1. Color Resource Types That Have Their Own Editors

Resource Type	Description
'clut'	Color look-up table
'pltt'	Palette
'ppat'	Pixel pattern
'ppt#'	Pixel pattern list
'crsr'	Color cursor
'cicn'	Color icon
'icl4'	Icon large (32-by-32 pixels), 4-bit (16 colors)
'icl8'	Icon large (32-by-32 pixels), 8-bit (256 colors)
'ics4'	Icon small (16-by-16 pixels), 4-bit (16 colors)
'ics8'	Icon small (16-by-16 pixels), 8-bit (256 colors)

Table 16-2 lists color resources that are created when you colorize a black-and-white resource. You edit these color table resources via the editor for the resource with which they're associated. In other words, the 'MENU' editor creates an 'mctb' when you add color to a 'MENU' resource, and you also edit those colors via the 'MENU' editor. (You can also edit them in templates.) In Chapter 18, we talk more about editing these types of resources.

Table 16-2. Color Resource Types Edited via Associated Editors

Resource Type	Description	Editor
'actb'	Alert color table	'ALRT'
'dctb'	Dialog color table	'DLOG'
'wctb'	Window color table	'WIND'
'mctb'	Menu color table	'MENU'
'cctb'	Control color table	'cctb' template

By The Way There are two additional color resource types. We mention them solely for the sake of completeness, because ResEdit doesn't have editors for them: 'ictb' (color dialog item list) and 'fctb' (font color table).

Using the Fatpixels Editors

ResEdit's color resource editors aren't mysterious. They work just like comparable black-and-white editors, except that they also have the ability to handle color. Figure 16-1 shows one of the fatpixels editors. Because color resources have common characteristics, the color resource editors share several features. For instance, three types of color resources ('ppat', 'ppt#', and 'cicn') differ from their original black-and-white counterparts in that they are not limited to a certain number of pixels; individual resources of these types can have different sizes. Consequently, these editors provide a way to let you adjust the size of the resources. Most of the fatpixels editors have a provision to include a black-and-white version of the resource. You can create this optional black-and-white version as easily as you can

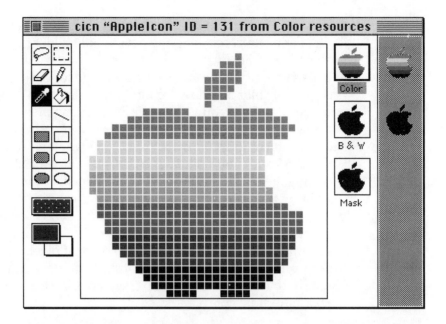

Figure 16-1. The 'cicn' editor is a prototypical fatpixels editor.

create a mask for an icon or pointer—simply drag the image to the appropriate part of the editor.

The fatpixels editors behave similarly to the black-and-white fatbits editors introduced in Chapter 5, and they use the same Transform menu. You click the swatch under the tool palette to see a tear-off pattern palette, just as in the black-and-white editors. But now you can change the colors of those patterns. Beneath the pattern swatch are two new swatches that show the current colors.

Foreground and Background Colors

In the pair of color swatches, the swatch that's above and to the left, or on top, shows the foreground color. The partially covered swatch shows the background color. You set these colors independently. Click either swatch and ResEdit displays the pop-up color palette filled with the color collection chosen from the Colors menu. (More on that in a moment.) Like the pattern palette, you can tear off the color palette, but only from the foreground color swatch. Working with the foreground color is exactly like working with black bits in a black-and-white fatbits editor, and the background color acts just like white. For instance, clicking the pencil tool toggles pixels back and forth between the foreground and background colors.

Let's say your foreground color is orange (or dark gray) and your background color is yellow (or light gray). The first thing you might notice, especially if you've torn off the pattern palette, is that some patterns are now orange on yellow. (If you set your foreground and background colors to the same thing, you won't be able to see some patterns because you no longer have any contrast.) Most tools work with only the foreground color. But the pencil, eraser, and selection tools bring the background color into the picture. If you click the pencil once, you place an orange pixel, but if you click it again in the same place, you remove the orange pixel and expose a yellow background pixel. The eraser removes all colors of pixels and uncovers the background color—effectively painting in the background color. Similarly, if you make a selection then move or delete it, you reveal the background color.

The Eyedropper

The tool palette has an additional tool just below the eraser—the eyedropper—that's indispensable for manipulating color. When you position it over a fatpixel and click, it "sucks up" a color from your resource and automatically sets that color in the foreground color swatch. Imagine trying to match a particular shade in a 256-color palette without the aid of the eyedropper!

Hint You can sometimes save yourself a trip to the tool and color palettes when you're working with the drawing tools. Simply press the Option key and the current tool (unless it's the eraser or one of the selection tools) transmogrifies into the eyedropper. While still pressing the Option key, use the eyedropper to click a pixel in your resource that's the color you want to switch to. When you release the Option key, the eyedropper changes back into the drawing tool that's now ready to draw in the new color.

Hint Here's another trick that can save you a lot of work—you can change every occurrence of one color to another color. Let's say you change your mind about a color you used in your resource. All the other colors are fine, but you're having second thoughts about chartreuse. You know that the paint bucket can change all the contiguous occurrences of a color, but because you used the chartreuse in a pattern, the paint bucket is no more useful than the pencil. Here's how to change every pixel of chartreuse to hot pink. Option-click a pixel of chartreuse to get the eyedropper to set that color in the color swatch. Now press the Command key as you click hot pink in the color palette. The color swatch momentarily shows both colors, but as soon as you release the mouse button, every pixel of chartreuse changes to hot pink.

The Color Menu

All the color resource editors have a Color menu, shown in Figure 16-2. This menu allows you to control the color palette you see when you click the color swatches.

The first item, Apple Icon Colors, displays the 34 colors Apple recommends for desktop icons. This color collection, which is a subset of the standard 256 and contains close matches to most of the standard 16 colors, is stored in ResEdit. These are the colors used in designing Apple's System 7 Finder icons.

The next item, Recent Colors, shows only the subset of colors used in the resource plus the ones you've selected while editing. As you select your favorite colors from one of the available color collections, ResEdit adds them to the color table that's part of the resource. Choosing Recent Colors tells ResEdit to display those colors. When you close the editor window after creating your color masterpiece, ResEdit deletes any colors you didn't actually use from the resource's color table. Thus, when you open an existing resource, the Recent Colors command displays only the actual colors used in the resource. (Black and white are always shown as recent colors even if you didn't use them. They're saved in the resource only if actually used.)

```
┌─────────────────────────────────┐
│ Color                           │
├─────────────────────────────────┤
│   Apple Icon Colors             │
│   Recent Colors                 │
│ ✓ Standard 256 Colors           │
│   Standard 16 Colors            │
│   Standard 16 Grays             │
│   Standard 4 Grays              │
│   Color Picker                  │
├─────────────────────────────────┤
│   Foreground <-> Background      │
├─────────────────────────────────┤
│   Recolor Using Palette          │
└─────────────────────────────────┘
```

Figure 16-2. The Color menu helps you manipulate the colors you use in color resources.

The next four items on the Color menu allow you to choose standard color collections. Three come from ROM and one is stored in ResEdit. There's at least one collection for each of the three standard pixel depths, and they all include black and white. The standard four grays make up the 2-bit collection, the standard 16 colors make up the 4-bit collection, and the standard 256 make up the 8-bit collection. An important advantage of using these ROM standards is that every Mac has these colors. The standard 16 grays are stored in ResEdit.

Hint Each time you add a color to a resource, the resource's color table gets six bytes larger. So, to keep your color resources compact, use the eyedropper or choose from the Recent Colors palette when you want to use the same color in two places. That way you can make sure you use the same colors, instead of ones that are similar.

Also, keep in mind that any time adding a color causes your resource to cross one of the "pixel-depth boundaries," it doubles in size. For example, the pixels in a 32-by-32-pixel icon occupy 128 bytes in black and white, 256 bytes in 4 colors, 512 bytes in 16 colors, and 1024 bytes—1K—in 256 colors. Adding *one* color to a 4-color icon doubles its size to 512 bytes (plus six more bytes for the additional color table entry). Similarly, a 17-color icon takes up as much room as if it contained 256 colors.

The last item in this section of the menu, Color Picker, provides a way to add custom colors to a resource. When this item is selected, clicking one of the color swatches displays the Macintosh Color Picker instead of a color palette. However, you should generally stick with the standard colors because spending hours and hours to get your colors "just right" could be a waste of time. If you invest a lot of time chasing the perfect hue, you should have a very good reason, and a good understanding of how color works on the Macintosh. The problem is that you can pick any color you want while you're creating your resource, but if that color isn't available later in the window where the resource is displayed, your Mac maps it to the closest available color. Fussing over subtle shadings could be a waste of time because unless the window the resource is going to be displayed in has an associated 'pltt' containing the custom colors, they may all end up mapped to another color anyway. ('pltt' resources are covered at the end of this chapter.) If you can stick with the standard 4, 16, or 256 colors, they should always be available, unless an application specifically requests a different collection of colors.

Foreground <–> Background simply swaps the colors in the foreground and background color swatches. The last command, Recolor Using Palette, lets you easily replace colors in your resource with those in the selected palette. If you choose the palette you want to use, then choose this item; all the colors in the resource get mapped to the closest match in the selected palette.

Guidelines for Using Color

Apple's intent when adding color to the Desktop Interface is to add meaning, not just to jazz things up so they look spiffy. Of course, it's your Mac, and we're not saying you have to follow their advice. If you want your Mac to remind you of a carnival midway, that's your privilege. But Apple's Human Interface designers put a lot of effort into thinking about how to use color effectively, so it wouldn't hurt to at least be aware of some of the principles involved. The principles may very well apply differently if you have your own Mac, and you're customizing resources just for yourself. Still, you might gain some insight into why well-designed applications use color the way they do.

When handled properly, color can convey additional information, but if used carelessly, it can confuse and overwhelm. Generally, you should design your resource in black and white, making color supplementary. If you want to avoid a garish look, try to use as few colors as possible. A little bit of color goes a long way. Use light or subtle colors for large areas and reserve bright, distracting colors for small areas or accents. Keeping the outlines of color icons black can help prevent a fuzzy appearance and possible eyestrain when the icon blends into various backgrounds.

Remember that colors often have associated effects and meanings. For instance, bright colors, such as reds and oranges, are good at attracting attention, but reds also connote "warning" or "danger." This can be a tricky combination. For instance, if you color a "dangerous" menu item red, your eyes might be more attracted to it, and you might be more likely to select the item by mistake.

By The Way There are several general uses for color. You can use color to discriminate between areas on the screen, show functionally related items, emphasize relationships among things, and identify crucial features. However, most people can effectively follow only four to seven color assignments on a screen at once, so there's probably not much point in getting carried away with complicated color relationship schemes.

For more information, see Apple's *Macintosh Human Interface Guidelines* (Addison-Wesley, 1992).

The 'clut' and 'pltt' Editors

The 'clut' editor and the 'pltt' editor look and act exactly the same. The only difference is that the 'pltt' editor provides a menu command that lets you assign usage information to the colors. As the 'clut' editor in Figure 16-3 illustrates, these editors can hold up to 256 colors. To select a color, simply click it. To select more than one color, click the first color, press the Shift key, and click the second color. All the colors in between also become selected, and you can cut, copy, or perform other operations on them. (The editors don't allow discontinuous color selections.) If you want to add colors to color collections having less than 256 colors, just choose Insert New Color from the Resource menu. This command adds one new color right in front of the cur-

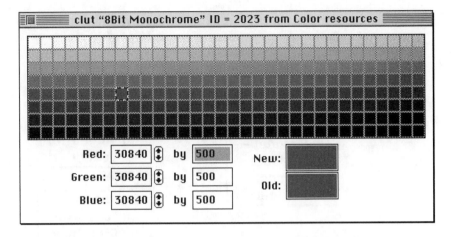

Figure 16-3. The 'clut' and 'pltt' editors, which are nearly identical, allow you to edit collections of 2 to 256 colors.

rently selected color (or at the end if nothing is selected). The new color is always black, but you can change it just as you can any color.

You can change an individual color by double-clicking, which causes the color picker to be displayed. You can also directly change the color values in the fields in the lower-left corner of the editor, just as you would in the color picker. The small arrow control buttons increment or decrement the color values by the amounts you specify in the fields to the right.

The New box in the lower-right corner of the editor shows you a larger swatch of the color you're experimenting with. The Old box shows you the original color. Clicking the old box restores the original color.

To fully appreciate what these editors can do with colors, you have to look at the menus.

The Menus

The 'clut' and 'pltt' editors add three menus to the menu bar. The first two menus are shown in Figure 16-4. The bottom half of the 'clut' or 'pltt' menu lists four standard color models, and the model you choose determines your options on the Sort menu. It also changes the color value fields in the lower-left corner of the editor window. (You're already familiar with two of the models. The color picker uses

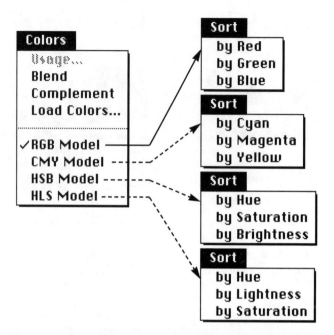

Figure 16-4. The 'clut' and 'pltt' editors give you a different Sort menu, depending on which color model you choose from the 'clut' (or 'pltt') menu.

RGB and HSB.) The third menu, the Background menu, lets you choose the background against which the colors are displayed. Your choices are white, gray, or black.

The Blend command works on a selection of three or more colors, blending them into a smooth color gradient. Obviously, the more colors you blend, the smoother the gradient you get. The Complement command changes the selected color into its complement, which is the color directly across the color wheel.

A good way to create new color collections is to load the standard colors from ROM (so you're using colors that are generally available), then remove any colors you don't need or want. The Load Colors command and dialog help you with the first part of that process. The Load Colors dialog, shown in Figure 16-5, displays a list of all the color collections ResEdit can find in any file that's open. You can choose between 'clut's and 'pltt's by clicking the radio buttons at the top of the window. The selected color collection is displayed to give you a chance to look it over. When you click OK, the color collection you just selected completely replaces the colors in the editor.

By The Way If you compare a few 'pltt's and 'clut's in the Load Colors dialog, you might notice that the first two colors in 'pltt's are always white and black. That's just as it should be—something to remember when you're creating your own 'pltt's. (In fact, ResEdit doesn't let you change the first two colors.) Similarly, the first 16 entries in a 'pltt' should generally be the colors you want used on 4-bit systems. That way, the same 'pltt' can be used on 2-, 4-, and 8-bit systems. If you create a 'pltt' with 16 shades of yellow at the beginning, you'll get only those colors on a 16-color monitor—not a very useful collection. The palette ResEdit uses for all its windows provides a good example. The first 2 colors are black and white, the first 4 are grays, the first 16 are the standard 16, and the remaining colors come from the standard 256 color palette. (To see for yourself, open a copy of ResEdit and open the 'pltt' with ID 0, named "ResEdit Standard Colors.")

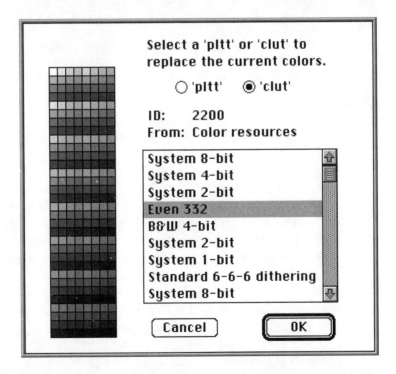

Figure 16-5. The Load Colors dialog lets you choose a color collection to replace the 'clut' or 'pltt' you're editing.

Hint If you have a color collection that you use frequently, you should add it to ResEdit's Preferences file so you can choose your own collection from the Color menu. Give your 'clut' a short, obvious name (with the Get Resource Info command) because that's how it will be listed in the Color menu.

As we've already mentioned, 'pltt's are associated with windows to provide color usage information to help the system deal with color conflicts. The 'pltt' editor's Usage command on the 'pltt' menu lets you determine usage parameters for selected colors, but setting color usage can be a pretty esoteric project. For more information about color usage, see the "Palette Manager" chapters of *Inside Macintosh*.

Hint If you're creating a resource that has to look good in either 16 or 256 colors, create it using the Standard 16. You get better color matches mapping from 16 to 256 colors than you do the other way around.

Summary

This chapter briefly describes how your Macintosh handles color. Your Mac can display only a limited number of colors at a time. How many colors it can show depends on the monitor, the amount of memory devoted to video, and the Control Panel settings. If an application asks the Mac for a color not available in the current color environment, the Mac maps the color to the nearest currently available color. Color collections are stored in two resource types: 'clut' (Color Look-Up Table) and 'pltt' (PaLeTTe). Several standard 'clut's are stored in ROM, and the advantage of using these standard colors is that they're usually available. If you need to guarantee that certain custom colors are available to a window, you can associate it with a 'pltt' containing the necessary colors.

ResEdit's fatpixels editors work like their fatbits counterparts, except that they can handle color. This chapter describes features common to all the fatpixels editors, such as the options on the Color menu, the foreground and background color swatches, and the eyedropper tool. Most users won't need to edit 'clut's or 'pltt's, but for programmers the chapter concludes with a brief description of the 'clut' and 'pltt' editors.

Chapter 17

 Editing Color Icons

If you have a color monitor, you can use ResEdit to colorize icons to brighten up your working environment. (Remember, "color" includes gray tones.) ResEdit has two color icon editors. One works on 'cicn' (Color ICoN) resources, the color equivalent of 'ICON' resources. The other, the Icon Family editor, handles System 7 icons, and we'll discuss it later in the chapter.

'cicn' Resources

Like 'ICON' resources, you can put 'cicn's in dialogs, alerts, and menus. Although 'cicn's can act as color stand-ins for 'ICON's, they differ in a few important ways.

- The size of a 'cicn' image is flexible. 'ICON' images are a defined size (32-by-32 bits), whereas 'cicn's can have almost any size. However, ResEdit only creates 'cicn's that vary from a lower limit of 8-by-8 pixels to an upper limit of 64-by-64 pixels. They don't have to be square, either.

- An 'ICON' resource always occupies the same amount of storage space. A 'cicn' resource can gobble a lot of space, depending on the size of the image and how many colors it uses. (Remember, in black and white, one pixel takes up one bit. But a color pixel can require 2, 4, or 8 bits, depending on whether you have 4, 16, or 256 colors.)

- A 'cicn' resource includes a mask and an optional black-and-white version of the icon; it's like a three-in-one package. An 'ICON' resource contains only one image.

Now that you have an idea what kind of creatures 'cicn's are, you're ready to learn how to create and edit them.

The 'cicn' Editor

With all the colors, tools, and patterns available, you can have a lot of fun in the 'cicn' editor, even if you never come up with an icon you like. Because so few applications have 'cicn's, you'll probably have to start by creating the new resource type in your file. (From the type picker, choose Create New Resource from the Resource menu. You have two choices in the dialog that appears: You can scroll until you can double-click 'cicn', or you can just type it.) ResEdit opens the 'cicn' picker, (which, of course, is empty), and then the 'cicn' editor, which should look something like Figure 17-1 (except empty, of course). By now, the tool palette, pattern swatch, and color swatches probably look familiar to you. (If not, you should review "Using the Fatbits Editors" in Chapter 5 and "Using the Fatpixels Editors" in Chapter 16.)

The right side of the window displays several actual-size views of the icon. The three next to the editing panel are labeled Color (the color version of the icon), B&W (the black-and-white version, if there is one), and Mask (more on the mask in a moment). To switch between views, simply click the one you want. A heavy box surrounds the selected view, and its label is highlighted. The two views on the far right show you the color and B&W icons combined with the mask and drawn on one of several possible backgrounds.

If you want to include a black-and-white version of your icon, it's easiest to let ResEdit create it for you. Simply drag the Color view straight down onto the B&W view. Depending on the colors or grays you used in your color icon, you may want to touch up the B&W version, because some parts of the image may disappear. When you drag the Color icon onto the B&W one, your Macintosh has to map every color to either black or white. Light colors may map to white and disappear.

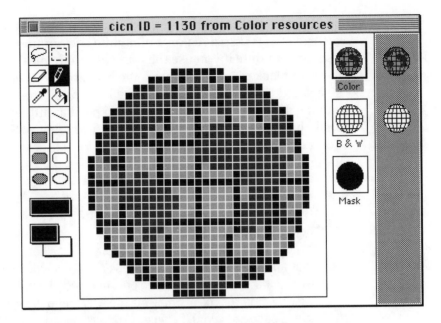

Figure 17-1. The 'cicn' editor is a full-featured editor.

Creating and Editing the Mask

As you may remember from the section on 'ICN#' resources in Chapter 7, a mask determines how an icon is drawn (and therefore how it looks) on various backgrounds. Although the general principle seems the same for color icons, the implementation is not. The mask for a 'cicn' works differently. (And you thought you could skip this section.) An 'ICN#' resource without a mask would be crippled, but you would be able to see the icon at least some of the time. A 'cicn' resource without a mask would give you an invisible icon, because you can't see any given pixel in a color icon unless there's a corresponding black pixel in the mask. The same general rule for creating a mask applies to both types of icon resources: The safest mask is a filled-in version of the icon.

When ResEdit creates a 'cicn' resource, it also creates a mask that completely fills the available area. You can keep that one if you want to, and for many icons that's the best mask. Sometimes, however, you'll need a more form-fitting mask so your icon can blend into the background. Let's say your icon consists of an exquisite arrangement of attractively patterned ovals, circles, and rounded rectangles. When such an icon is displayed on a nonwhite background, it will appear in a square of white if you use the original square mask. Wherever there's a black pixel in the mask, the background is erased. Anywhere no colored pixels are drawn in, the white shows through. That's fine if that's the effect you want; if not, you need a different mask. You can easily have ResEdit make a more form-fitting mask. Simply click the Color icon view, then drag it down onto the Mask view. *Voilà*—an instant, shapely mask!

Hint Creating the mask from the color icon is usually your best bet. You can also use the B&W icon to create the mask, but depending on the colors you've used, you may get a different mask. It all boils down to color mapping. When you drag the Color icon to the B&W icon, every color is mapped to either black or white. Some light colors may map to white, and those parts of the icon disappear. If you then use the B&W icon to make the mask, you won't see those light colors in the color icon either, because the mask won't allow for them. But when you drag the Color icon to the Mask, any nonwhite pixel is treated as black before the mask is filled in, so you get a better mask.

   If you create or edit a mask that doesn't work the way you want it to, and you want to go back to the filled-in square, do it the easy way. Click the Mask view and make sure you see solid black in the pattern swatch. Then use the filled rectangle tool or paint bucket to make a black rectangle the same size as the icon.

The 'cicn' Menu

The 'cicn' editor has a resource-specific menu with commands that help you work with color icons and the 'cicn' editor. The first four items let you choose the background upon which the editor displays the icon. You can choose white, gray, black, or your current desktop pattern. The next command, Icon Size, displays the dialog shown in Figure 17-2. ResEdit defaults to a 32-by-32 (pixel) size when it creates 'cicn's, but as we mentioned previously, they can range from 8 by 8 to 64 by 64. Here is where you change the size. ResEdit assumes you

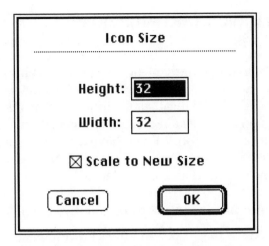

Figure 17-2. This dialog, which appears when you choose Icon Size from the 'cicn' menu, lets you change the icon's size.

would usually choose to scale an icon when changing its size, so the Scale to New Size check box is automatically checked. When scaling, ResEdit adds or removes pixels wherever necessary to stretch or shrink the icon image proportionally so it looks roughly the same in its new dimensions. If you shrink an icon without scaling, ResEdit simply truncates pixels from the bottom and right side. Similarly, if you enlarge an icon without scaling, ResEdit simply tacks on extra pixels, leaving them white. ResEdit also shrinks or enlarges the actual-size view and adjusts the editing area (in fact, the entire editor window) accordingly. Figuring out how you want to scale your icons may take some practice, so remember you can undo or revert any unsettling changes.

Deleting the black-and-white version of the icon from your 'cicn' resource saves space, so the Delete B&W Icon command lets you do just that. For example, if the application displaying the icon requires color, a black-and-white icon would never be used. This item only becomes available when the B&W icon is selected. If one doesn't exist, ResEdit fills the actual-size view of the black-and-white icon with a gray pattern so you'll know that it's nonexistent, not merely empty.

Now that you know how to create and edit 'cicn's, you're ready to start using them. You can substitute 'cicn's in most places where applications use 'ICON's.

Customizing Dialog and Alert Boxes with Color Icons

You can turn many of the same icons you altered in the 'ICON' section of Chapter 7 into color icons. Figure 17-3 shows one possibility. Your Macintosh automatically substitutes color icons if they're present, so you can have a red Stop alert icon, or a light gray or yellow Caution alert icon. All you have to do is create a 'cicn' with the same resource ID as the corresponding 'ICON', and you'll have colored icons in your dialogs and alerts.

1. Use ResEdit to open a copy of your System file.

2. Open the 'ICON' type, find the icon you want to colorize, and jot down its ID number. (The talking head's ID is 1.)

3. Copy the icon. Don't copy from the picker; open the icon and copy its bits from within the editor. (Double-clicking the selection rectangle automatically selects the whole image.)

4. Open the 'cicn' type picker. (If there aren't any 'cicn's in the file, use the Create Resource Type command on the Resource menu. ResEdit creates a new 'cicn' and opens it in the editor for you, so you can skip to Step 6.)

5. Create a new 'cicn' with the Create Resource command.

6. Paste to get a black-and-white start for your color icon.

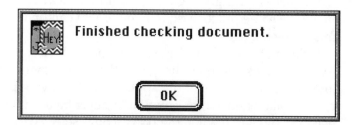

Figure 17-3. With a few shades of gray, it becomes obvious that the talking head in alerts is tall, dark, but still inarticulate.

7. Colorize, modify, and otherwise edit your icon. (If you click the paint bucket in the black pixels, you can change all contiguous pixels to the selected color.)

8. Choose Get Resource Info from the Resource menu, and set the resource ID to the number you noted in Step 2.

9. Close and save the file.

10. Reinstall your System file.

The next time a dialog or alert appears that uses your icon, it should appear in color.

Hint You can't necessarily stuff any size icon into dialogs and alert boxes, so you may be better off staying with a 32-by-32 'cicn'. Your Mac scales inappropriately sized icons, and the result might not be just what you'd like. If you want to use odd-size icons, you can change the size of the icon item in the associated dialog item list ('DITL') resource. See Chapter 10 for more details about resizing dialog items so you can work around potential size constraints. Remember, though, that alerts don't have icon items—the icons are inserted automatically. So for alerts, you're stuck with a 32-by-32 icon size.

Adding a Color Icon to a Menu

A 'cicn' can be substituted for an 'ICON' in a menu, too. In fact, you can't just add a 'cicn'; you have to add an 'ICON' first, then substitute a 'cicn' that has the same ID number. See Chapter 8 to find out how to add an 'ICON' to a menu. If you've already created the 'cicn' you want to use, you can just copy the bits from the B&W version and use them to create a new 'ICON'. Remember, icons in menus must have IDs between 257 and 511, so give both your 'ICON' and your 'cicn' the same appropriate ID.

You can substitute 'cicn's for 'SICN's, too, You still need to add a 32-by-32 pixel 'cicn', which your Mac shrinks to 16 by 16.

By The Way The System file has a 'cicn' you might want to play with. It's the abstract Macintosh you see when your Mac starts up.

Color Finder Icons

Part of the System 7 revolution was that it finally brought color icons to the desktop. To allow for standard screen depths, as well as large and small icon sizes, five new icon resource types were created:

- 'icl8'—(ICon Large, 8-bit) 32-by-32-pixel, 256-color icon
- 'ics8'—(ICon Small, 8-bit) 16-by-16-pixel, 256-color icon
- 'icl4'—(ICon Large, 4-bit) 32-by-32-pixel, 16-color icon
- 'ics4'—(ICon Small, 4-bit) 16-by-16-pixel, 16-color icon
- 'ics#'—(ICon Small, list) 16-by-16-bit, black-and-white icon, with mask

Along with the familiar 'ICN#' resource type, these five new resource types make up a Finder icon family. The 'ics#' resource is a small version of the black-and-white Finder icon ('ICN#') resource you learned about in Chapter 7. When an 'ics#' is present, the Finder doesn't have to shrink the 'ICN#' for a black-and-white small icon view, or for use on the Application Menu. (Shrunken 'ICN#'s often look clogged or clumpy or both.) The System 7 Finder chooses one of these six icons based on the number of colors available on the screen and the size of icon it needs. All six types of related icons are linked with the same resource ID, and are edited in the Icon Family editor.

The Icon Family Editor

The Icon Family editor, shown in Figure 17-4, lets you edit six related resources all in the same place, essentially at the same time. The tool palette, patterns swatch, and color swatches on the left side of the window and the fatpixels editing area behave exactly the same as in the 'cicn' editor. To the right of the fatpixel editing area you see the actual-size views of the related icon resource types and their masks.

Figure 17-4. The Icon Family editor lets you edit up to six related resources at the same time.

(All icons of the same size share the same mask.) Simply click the icon type you want to edit. Just as in the 'cicn' editor, the selected view has a dark outline around it, and the label underneath is highlighted.

On the right side of the window you see the icon you're editing as the Finder would draw it in several different states. As the labels indicate, the top views show the icon in its normal state (closed), the middle views show it open, and the bottom views show it offline (ejected but still mounted). In each case, the left side shows the icon unselected and the right side shows it selected. For large icons, you see the shrunken version of it underneath—even if the corresponding small resource type exists, you still see the reduced version of the selected large icon. (For small icons you see only the small icon.) You can change the background on which the samples are drawn with the aid of the Icon menu.

The Icon Menu

The Icon menu, shown in Figure 17-5, lets you do two things. You can change the background color used in the right side of the editor window between the four choices shown. (The fourth choice, Desktop

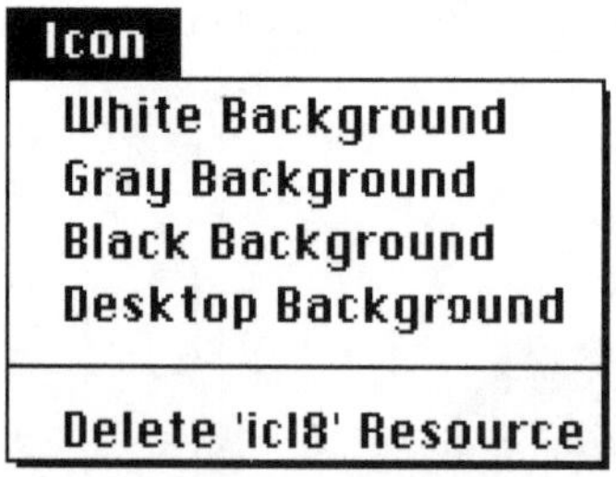

```
┌─────────────────────────────────┐
│ Icon                            │
├─────────────────────────────────┤
│ White Background                │
│ Gray Background                 │
│ Black Background                │
│ Desktop Background              │
├─────────────────────────────────┤
│ Delete 'icl8' Resource          │
└─────────────────────────────────┘
```

Figure 17-5. The Icons menu lets you change sample backgrounds and delete unwanted icon family members.

Background, uses your current desktop pattern or color.) The last item, Delete <type> Resource, lets you delete the currently selected icon type, saving you a trip to the corresponding picker. (Remember, selecting and deleting the pixels empties the resource but doesn't get rid of it. You have to use this command or go to the picker to delete.)

The Color Menu

We discussed the Color menu in the previous chapter, but we mention it again because the Icon Family editor uses a slightly different version. Your choice of color palettes is restricted to the standard 256 colors, or the Apple Icon Colors, which are the recommended colors for Finder icons.

Apple Icon Colors is the best color collection to use for desktop icons because the Finder knows how to work with them. For instance, when an icon is selected, it gets darkened—but only these 34 colors get darkened, so your icon won't look selected if you paint large parts of it with some other color. The story is the same for the Finder's color labeling mechanism. The label tints are applied properly only to these 34 colors.

By The Way Unlike 'cicn's, System 7 icons occupy a fixed amount of memory because they have fixed sizes and pixel depths. Even if you use only four colors in an 'icl8', it takes up as much space as if you used the full rainbow of 256 colors.

Creating New Icon Family Members

Creating new icon family members is as easy as creating a mask. Simply drag one of the existing icons onto the type you want to create, and ResEdit automatically scales the icon and maps its colors to the nearest colors in the appropriate pixel depth. Because of the level of detail you'll usually get better results if you make a small icon from a large one, rather than the other way around. Creating icons this way gives you the basic shape and a good start on the colors, but most likely you'll need or want to fine tune any icons you create by dragging. If you create black-and-white icons from color ones they can sometimes look odd or ghostly, so you pretty much have to touch them up. You're better off going the other direction, creating System 7 icons from existing 'ICN#' resources. We talk about that next.

By The Way Apple recommends creating the black-and-white icon first, the 8-bit icons next, and then the 4-bit icons. This is the top-to-bottom order shown in the editor. To aid creation of 4-bit icons from 8-bit icons, the color pattern palette contains a few dithered patterns you can use to approximate commonly used colors in the Apple Icon Colors palette (for example, fleshtone). Of course, you can create your own dithered colors with patterns that use the foreground and background colors. For example, if the foreground is red and the background is blue, an every-other-pixel pattern looks purple.

Updating an Application's Icons to System 7

If you use System 7 but your applications don't have the color icons you want or need, you might want to create some, starting with the 'ICN#' resources already present in the file. Remember, besides the application icon, there might be several document icons, so you need to repeat these steps for each kind of icon.

1. Use ResEdit to open a copy of the application, then open the 'ICN#' picker.

2. When the 'ICN#' picker opens, you'll see your application's black-and-white Finder icons. Double-click the one you want to update.

3. The 'ICN#' opens in the Icon Family editor, and you're ready to create other family members. Drag it to the 'icl4' or 'icl8' spot to give yourself a black-and-white start for your new icon. Now you can color and draw and fiddle to your heart's content.

4. If you think you're satisfied, go to the Icons menu and try out different backgrounds with your icon. You may want to make a new, more form-fitting mask. (See "Creating and Editing the Mask" in the 'cicn' section earlier in this chapter if you need more information.)

5. When you're happy with your work, you can use this new icon to create other new icon types. You might want to have an 'ics4' to go with an 'icl4'. Simply drag the 'icl4' to the 'ics4' spot, then touch up the new icon to suit yourself.

6. After you're finished, quit ResEdit, saving your changes. The Finder won't use your new icons unless it knows they exist, so you've got to update the Desktop database. (See Chapter 7 for a refresher on how the Finder keeps track of icons.)

7. You don't want to confuse the Finder with two copies of the same file; the easiest way to avoid that is to move the original version of the file to a floppy.

8. Restart your Mac while pressing the Command and Option keys. This makes the Finder automatically rebuild its Desktop database—which may take a while if your hard disk stores lots of files.

9. When the Finder is done, you should see your new System 7 icons.

Summary

The Macintosh uses several types of color icons, and this chapter describes them and the two editors that work on them. The 'cicn' (Color ICoN) resource type is the color equivalent of the 'ICON' resource type; it's used in dialogs, alert boxes, and menus. Unlike

'ICON's, 'cicn's can vary in the amount of space they occupy because they can vary in number of pixels, and in number of colors, or in pixel depth. More and more applications are taking advantage of the 'cicn' resource type, but you don't have to wait—you can create your own. In dialogs, alerts, and menus your Mac automatically substitutes a 'cicn' for an 'ICON' having the same resource ID.

Five new icon resource types came along with System 7, and together with the 'ICN#' type, they make up icon families. Icons in a family are linked by their common resource ID, and you can edit all six types in the Icon Family editor.

Chapter 18

Adding Color to the User Interface

Color icons may be what people think of first when they contemplate adding color to their work environment, but the Macintosh offers several other opportunities to brighten up the user interface. Why not add color to menus to help you find your way around? If you frequently forget Command keys, you can make them a bright color so you can quickly find them to remind yourself. Windows, dialogs, and alerts might also benefit from a touch of color. You decide. If you like color desktop patterns, you may find the Control Panel's limitations frustrating. You can create your own permanent repertoire of color desktop patterns once you know how to use ResEdit's color pattern editors.

Color Patterns

The two kinds of color pattern resources ('ppat' and 'ppt#') are analogous to the two black-and-white pattern resources ('PAT ' and 'PAT#') introduced in Chapter 5. (If you need a refresher, now would be a good time to flip back.) The editors, shown in Figure 18-1, are quite similar, too. In this section we focus mostly on the color aspects of the 'ppt#' editor, because if you understand it, you can understand the 'ppat' editor. You should already be familiar with the features shared with the black-and-white editors. (For instance, just as in the 'PAT#' editor, when the scrollable list part of the 'ppt#' editor is active, you can drag individual patterns to move them in the list, and the Edit menu commands work on selections of one or more patterns.)

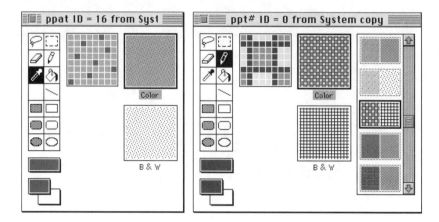

Figure 18-1. The color pattern editors: 'ppat' (left) and 'ppt#' (right).

Color patterns differ from their black-and-white counterparts in two ways, so the color editors have to support these differences. First, color patterns must include some sort of black-and-white version. They're really two-in-one resources. Second, whereas black-and-white patterns are defined as 8-by-8 bits, color patterns can vary in size (by powers of two), and they don't have to be square. However, ResEdit's pattern editors cannot work on patterns smaller than 8 by 8 nor larger than 64 by 64.

Hint Pressing the Option key when you create a color pattern (from the 'ppat' picker or the 'ppt#' editor) creates a *relative pattern*. Think of relative patterns, like the ones in ResEdit's pattern palette, as black-and-white patterns that can change color with the choice of foreground and background colors. The black pixels take on the foreground color, and the white pixels become the background color. Keep this in mind if you want to add patterns to ResEdit's pattern palette.

The black-and-white part of a color pattern exists even if you never click any bits in it; it's just all white. It doesn't have to correspond in any way to the color pattern, either. If you look at Figure 18-1 again, you'll notice that the patterns in the scrollable list box are split in half. The left half shows the color version, and the right half shows the black-and-white version. The bottom two patterns in the scrollable list have just the standard gray desktop pattern for their black-and-white half. The pattern above has a matching black-and-white version. To create a matching black-and-white pattern, click the sample of the pattern labeled Color and drag it straight down into the box labeled B&W. Any time you want to touch up the B&W pattern (some light colors or grays may drop out when you drag to create the B&W version), simply click it and it appears in the fatpixels editing panel.

If an 8-by-8 color pattern feels cramped, you can enlarge it. (The black-and-white version must remain 8 by 8, however.) To adjust a pattern's size, you have to go to the editor's pattern menu. (The 'ppat' and 'ppt#' menus are essentially the same.)

The 'ppat' and 'ppt#' Menus

The pattern editors' menus have only two items, and the first is the Pattern Size command, which displays the dialog shown in Figure 18-2. The dialog shows the possible sizes for a pattern; simply click your choice. ResEdit either repeats the pattern to make it larger or truncates it (from the bottom and/or right) to make it smaller. The pattern is not scaled.

Hint If you want to scale up a pattern (perhaps to add detail), it's easy. Double-click the selection rectangle to select all the pixels in the editing panel, then copy. Next, change the size in the Pattern Size dialog. Select all, just as before, and paste. The pattern is automatically scaled to the new size.

If you want to see your new pattern fill a larger expanse, choose the second and last item on the pattern editors' menus, Try Pattern. Just as in the black-and-white pattern editors, this command temporarily spreads your pattern over the entire desktop and updates it as you make changes.

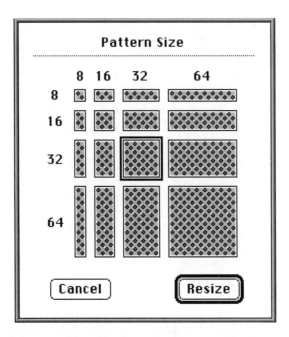

Figure 18-2. The Pattern Size dialog lets you adjust the dimensions of a pattern.

Customizing ResEdit's Pattern Palette

You might want to customize ResEdit's pattern palette for a variety of reasons. You can remove patterns you never use, add custom patterns you frequently use, or just change the ones already present. (If you increase the number of patterns, the tear-off palette window grows to accommodate them.) Before we list the steps, here are a few things to keep in mind. For consistency, your black-and-white patterns ('PAT#') should match your color ones ('ppt#'). Also, within your color patterns the black-and white version of the pattern should match the color version. (Remember, you can press the Option key if you want to create a relative pattern.)

1. Use ResEdit to open ResEdit. (You're just going to copy a resource, so you don't need to work on a copy of the application.)

2. Open the 'ppt#' resource type, then copy the pattern list containing all the familiar pattern palette patterns. (The first several patterns are relative patterns, so they appear black and white.)

3. Close ResEdit then open the ResEdit Preferences file (it's in the Preferences Folder in your System Folder). Paste the 'ppt#' resource into the type picker.

4. Open the 'ppt#' resource you just pasted. Now you can add, subtract, and modify patterns as you please.

5. When you're through, close the Preferences file. Now ResEdit will use your custom patterns in its pattern palette.

Adding Color Desktop Patterns to the Control Panel

This is the color counterpart of the black-and-white case described at the end of Chapter 5. The desire to add desktop patterns is stronger with color, however, because the General Controls Control Panel includes so few color patterns—even though color patterns give you a zillion more options. You can permanently add a pattern by double-clicking the miniature desktop in the General Controls Control Panel, but ResEdit offers much better editing tools anyway.

The bad news is that the Control Panel can't accommodate all the possibilities the color pattern resources offer. It can only handle 8-by-8 patterns in no more than eight colors. To protect you from the frustrating outcome of giving the Control Panel larger patterns having too many colors, ResEdit scans 'ppt#' resources when you open them. If all the patterns are 8 by 8 with eight colors, ResEdit asks you some questions to make sure any patterns you add follow suit.

1. Open a copy of your System file with ResEdit, and open the 'ppt#' resource type.

2. Double-click anywhere on the patterns list (the bar of patterns) in the 'ppt#' picker to open the 'ppt#' editor. Click Yes in the two dialogs ResEdit presents. (Yes, you do want to edit and save uncompressed. Yes, it is a list of desktop patterns from your System file.)

3. Scroll to the end of the pattern list, click the last pattern, then choose Insert New Pattern from the Resource menu.

4. Now you're ready to create a new pattern by clicking fatpixels, or touching up a pattern copied from somewhere else. Remember that dragging a selection can create new patterns and visual effects. ResEdit won't let you use more than eight colors (and two of them must be black and white), and the Pattern Size command is dimmed so the pattern remains 8-by-8 pixels.

5. If you want to add more patterns, just repeat Steps 3 and 4.

6. Once you're satisfied with your results, save the file, quit ResEdit, and reinstall the copy of your System file.

After you restart, you'll be able to switch among your new desktop patterns in the General Controls Control Panel. If you still feel hampered and want to spread bigger patterns over your desktop, check out the next tip.

Adding a Bigger Color Desktop Pattern

You *can* use a color desktop pattern larger than 8-by-8 pixels, but you'll have to bypass—and effectively disable—the desktop pattern part of your General Controls Control Panel. Here's the deal: The System stores your current desktop pattern selection in a 'ppat', so you can just edit it directly. But when you install a desktop pattern that breaks the eight-color, 8-by-8 pixel rule, the Control Panel can no longer cope. You lose the ability to edit color desktop patterns from the Control Panel—even ones that follow the rules. The disability isn't permanent, you can put everything back the way it was.

1. Open a copy of your System file with ResEdit, and open the 'ppat' resource type. Select 'ppat' ID 16 (it's probably the only resource there) and choose Duplicate (Command-D) from the Edit menu. This duplicate resource that obeys the rules is your ticket back to a working Control Panel later if you change your mind.

2. Now open 'ppat' ID 16. Color and enlarge it to suit yourself. Remember, you can see the pattern spread over your desktop by choosing Try Pattern on the 'ppat' menu.

3. Once you're satisfied with your results, save the file, quit ResEdit, reinstall the copy of your System file, and restart.

If you tire of your new large desktop pattern and decide you want to go back to using the General Controls Control Panel, here's what to do.

1. Open a copy of your System file with ResEdit, and open the 'ppat' resource type.

2. Select 'ppat' ID 16, then choose Get Resource Info (Command-I) from the Resource menu. Change the ID to 130 or to some ID not already present.

3. Select the desktop 'ppat' you duplicated in Step 1 (it's probably ID 128), then choose Get Resource Info (Command-I) from the Resource menu. Change the ID to 16.

4. Save the file, quit ResEdit, reinstall the copy of your System file, and restart.

Your Control Panel will work again, just as it always did.

Color Pointers

Another resource type added when the Mac II was introduced is the 'crsr' resource used to store color pointers (or cursors). Since there was no editor available to create these resources until ResEdit 2.1 was released, few applications use color pointers. Unfortunately, it's not possible to simply substitute a color pointer for a black-and-white pointer as you can with color icons. For these reasons, you won't find many color pointers to customize, and we can't pass on any fun tips.

The color pointer editor shown in Figure 18-3 should seem familiar to you. It works almost the same as the black-and-white 'CURS' editor described in Chapter 6. The only additions are the foreground and background color swatches and the eyedropper tool. The color aspects of this editor work just as they do in other fatpixels editors.

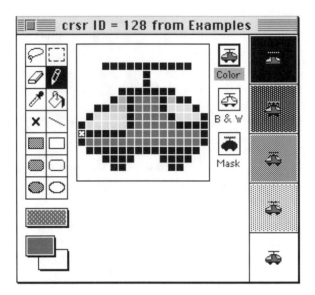

Figure 18-3. The 'crsr' editor lets you edit color pointers.

Customizing Menus with Color

ResEdit gives you a variety of ways to add color to menus, which can make them more effective and easier to use. Of course, if you take advantage of *every* option on any one menu, you risk creating something jarringly garish. To avoid gaudy menus, try to have a plan or design in mind. Try not to splash everything with color just because you can. This section assumes you're familiar with the 'MENU' editor, which we describe in Chapter 8. Here we discuss only the editor's color fields.

When the 'MENU' editor opens, the title is automatically selected, and you see the first three color options, two of which apply to the entire menu. The first field allows you to set the color for that menu's title. The second field lets you set the default color for all the menu item text. The last field lets you set the menu's background color. In each case, simply press the mouse button with the pointer in the field of your choice and a standard palette pops down. (You get the standard palette that corresponds to your screen depth.) Release the mouse button to select the color of your choice. Figure 18-4 shows this palette displayed for the last field. As you make your selections, the 'MENU' editor applies the colors appropriately in the editor window and the test menu so you can see how the menu will look.

Once you select one of the menu's items, you see the next three color options. The first field lets you set the color for the selected item's text, thus overriding the default color. The next field lets you set the color for the Command key, which doesn't have to match the item text. The last field lets you set the color for any marks (such as checkmarks or diamonds) a menu item might have.

The first time you click one of the color fields, ResEdit alerts you that it's about to create an 'mctb' (Menu Color TaBle). That's where the color information is stored, and when you edit your menu's colors, you're editing the 'mctb'. (A 'MENU' and its 'mctb' have the same resource ID. If you try to open an 'mctb', ResEdit opens the 'MENU' editor and the 'MENU' resource having the same ID.) If you copy or delete the 'MENU' resource, remember that you have to do the same for the associated 'mctb'. If you'd like all the menus in an application to have the same overall appearance, you don't have to set the colors for each one, which clutters up the file with duplicate 'mctb's. You can make one default 'mctb' do the job for all the menus in the file. We talk about that next.

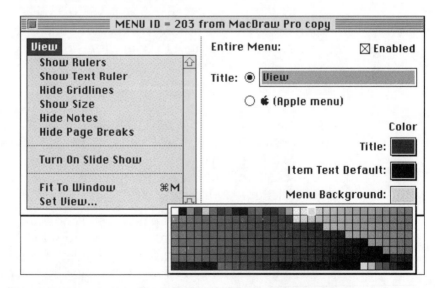

Figure 18-4. To pick a color for any of the fields, simply click the field and drag the mouse pointer onto the pop-up color palette that appears.

Giving an Application's Menus a Uniform Color Scheme

You can set the default colors for the title, background, and item text for one menu in an application, then make those color selections apply to every other menu in the file. (You can't set default Command Key or Mark colors, however. They use the item text color unless you specify colors for them on individual menus.)

1. Use ResEdit to open a copy of the file. Open the 'MENU' type, choose a menu to color, and double-click it. (It doesn't matter which menu you pick.)

2. When the menu opens in the 'MENU' editor, the title is selected and the color fields apply to the whole menu—that's just what you want. Make your color selections for the title, menu background, and default item text.

3. Close the 'MENU' editor and 'MENU' picker and go back to the type picker. Double-click the 'mctb' type. In the 'mctb' picker, you should see an 'mctb' with the same ID and name as the 'MENU' resource you just edited. (ResEdit uses the menu's title to give the 'mctb' a name.) Click it, then choose Get Resource Info from the Resource menu. In the dialog that appears, change the ID to 0. Because the name is no longer accurate, you should change that, too. "Default" might be a good name. Close the Resource Info window.

4. Now open the 'mctb'. (When the resource ID of an 'mctb' doesn't match the ID of a 'MENU' resource in the file, the 'mctb' is opened in a template. If you need information about using templates, see Chapter 14.) You should see a template that looks something like the one in Figure 18-5. Change the first two fields (Menu ID and Item No.) to 0.

5. Next you have to swap the second and fourth set of RGB values, which are expressed in hexadecimal. Copy the value in Red 2 to Red 4, and vice versa. (You may need to jot down some notes.) Do the same for Green 2 and Green 4, and Blue 2 and Blue 4. The example in the figure shows values for grays, so the RGB values in each set are the same. Yours may be different. (Hint: $0000 is black and $FFFF is white.)

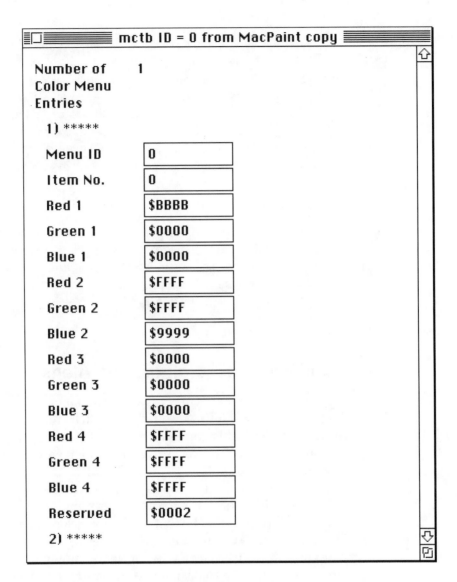

Figure 18-5. An 'mctb' template.

6. Close all the windows, save the file, and quit ResEdit. When you start up your application, all the menus should have the same colors.

By The Way You may be wondering why you had to swap values in the 'mctb'. It's because you created the 'mctb' for one situation (for use with a single menu), but you're using it in a different situation (for use with many menus). Your Mac looks at 'mctb's differently in these two situations—the second and fourth sets of RGB values are swapped—so you have to put your color values where the Mac expects to see them. (Otherwise, the color you chose for your menu background shows up in your menu bar!)

Hint If you want your menu color scheme to apply systemwide instead of just application-wide, copy the 'mctb' you just modified into your System file, leaving the ID set to 0. After you restart, many applications will use your menu color scheme. It won't work with any application that has its own 'mctb'.

Colorizing Windows, Dialogs, and Alerts

If you read Chapter 10, you probably remember that window ('WIND'), dialog ('DLOG'), and alert ('ALRT') resources are closely related. So it probably comes as no surprise that adding color works similarly for these three resources. (If you haven't read Chapter 10, now might be a good time to do so. This section assumes you're already familiar with the editors described in that chapter.)

You can add color to two parts of alerts, and to five parts of windows and dialogs. The first step is to click the Custom radio button beside the Color label in the upper-right corner of these editors, which causes the five color fields shown in Figure 18-6 to appear. Clicking the color fields causes a standard color palette to appear, just as in the 'MENU' editor discussed previously. As you make your selections, the editors apply the colors appropriately to the sample resource in the MiniScreen so you can see what they'll look like.

In the Content field, you set the background color for the area defined by the resource's rectangle. You can make title text a vibrant hue by setting the Title text field. Of course, dialogs and windows

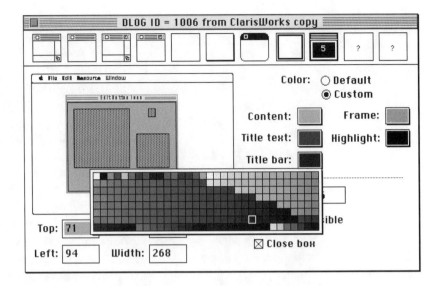

Figure 18-6. You can choose different colors for five areas of windows and dialogs and two areas of alerts.

don't always have title text, and alerts never do. The Title bar field lets you set the background color for the title bar. In the Frame field, you can choose a color for the frame, which is the borderline that runs around the content area and title bar. Finally, the Highlight field lets you set the color of the horizontal lines in the title bar. Because alerts have no title bars, you can colorize only their content areas and their frames.

The first time you click one of the color fields, ResEdit alerts you that it's about to create an associated color table resource. (The resource types are 'actb', 'dctb', or 'wctb' for alert, dialog, or window color table, respectively.) That's where the colors you choose are stored; for example, when you edit an alert's colors, you're editing the 'actb'. If you copy or delete one of these resources, remember that you have to do the same for the associated color table resource.

Now, after having said all of this, please note that applying colors may not be quite as easy as it sounds—or as straightforward as it used to be under System 6. Apparently, only some colors work together under System 7, so you may have to experiment a little to get the results you want. Depending on the color scheme you choose, you may not be able to color all the possible parts of dialogs.

By The Way The Mac doesn't provide you with an easy way to make all the dialogs or alerts in an application have the same color scheme. It's possible to create a default 'wctb' that contains a set of colors you'd like to see, and the Mac can refer to this color table resource for *all* windows—which means document windows as well as dialogs and alerts. Unfortunately, the Mac can't faithfully apply all those "default" colors unless each dialog and alert has its own associated color table resource that lets the Mac know it's supposed to use color. (The frame and title bar text, highlight, and background colors come through OK, but the content, or background, color gets overridden.)

If you're an experienced ResEdit user and want to give it a try, here's a brief set of instructions. Your results may vary greatly with the application you try it on, so be sure to work on a copy. Create a 'WIND' resource; choose your default color scheme in the 'WIND' editor; delete the 'WIND'; and change the resource ID of the 'wctb' to 0. Now note the resource ID of each dialog or alert in which you'd like to see this color scheme. From the type picker, create an 'actb' or 'dctb' (this automatically opens the 'ALRT' or 'DLOG' editor, which you can just close), and make its resource ID match that of the dialog or alert. (You don't have to change anything in the color table template—in fact, doing so would override the 'wctb'.)

Just for the record, if you really, really like the colors you chose when you made your 'wctb', you can make them apply system-wide, rather than just applicationwide, by copying the 'wctb' you created to your System file. Leave the ID set to 0. Your System file already contains a 'wctb' with ID 0, so you might want to renumber it first, rather than override it. That way you can easily switch back to black and white just by switching resource IDs. Remember, you probably won't see your background color because you can't possibly create color look-up tables for every dialog and alert.

As you sit back and gaze at your colorful dialog or alert, you may think, "Wait. The text inside remains boring old black." Yup. Remember, the items inside dialogs and alerts are stored in dialog item lists, or 'DITL' resources. Unfortunately, ResEdit's 'DITL' editor can't help you with colorizing dialog items.

Summary

You can add color to your Macintosh work environment in several ways. This chapter begins by describing color pattern resources and their editors. The color pattern resource types ('ppat' and 'ppt#') are analogous to the black-and-white pattern resource types ('PAT ' and 'PAT#'), but you can make color patterns in sizes larger than 8 by 8. You can add color desktop patterns by editing the System file's 'ppt#' resource. Menus can also appear in color. The title, background, item text, and Command keys can all appear in different colors. You can choose default colors for a whole menu, or color items individually. You can also make all the menus in an application use the same set of colors by making a few simple modifications to an 'mctb' (Menu Color TaBle) resource. Finally, you can add color to windows, dialogs, and alerts by altering their frame and content colors. For windows and dialogs, you can also color three aspects of the title bar: the title text, the background color, and the highlight or horizontal lines.

Part Five

Programming
with ResEdit

Chapter 19

 Creating Windows,
Dialogs, and Alerts

When you're prototyping or implementing an application, one of your primary uses for ResEdit will be laying out the windows, dialogs, and alerts that you'll use. Although not every application uses resources to store its window information, it's hard to imagine how an application could get by without dialog and alert resources. Dialogs and alerts are especially important because they provide the means by which you communicate with your users. If you need to inform them of a problem, you use an alert. If you need some information from them, only a dialog makes sense. Since dialogs and alerts are so crucial to an application, it's important to make them easy to use and understand. ResEdit provides the tools you need to lay out your windows, dialogs, and alerts and see what they'll look like on different size screens.

Table 19-1 shows the eight resources that define windows, dialogs, and alerts and their four associated editors. In this chapter we assume you have a basic understanding of how the editors work. If you need a refresher, refer to Chapter 10 for information about the editors and Chapter 18 for information about using them with color.

Since 'WIND' resources are very similar to 'DLOG' resources, we won't discuss the 'WIND' editor in this chapter. If you want to create a 'WIND', just look at the discussion of the 'DLOG' editor and ignore the parts about the associated 'DITL' resource.

Table 19-1. Window, Dialog, and Alert Resource Types

Resource Type	Editor	Description
'WIND'	'WIND'	Window resource
'wctb'	'WIND'	Window color table for 'WIND' resource
'DLOG'	'DLOG'	Dialog resource
'dctb'	'DLOG'	Dialog color table for 'DLOG' resource
'ALRT'	'ALRT'	Alert resource
'actb'	'ALRT'	Alert color table for 'ALRT' resource
'DITL'	'DITL'	Dialog item list for 'DLOG's and 'ALRT's
'ictb'	None	Item color table used for 'DITL' resource

The Dialog Editor

The dialog editor lets you create and edit 'DLOG' and 'dctb' resources. Its basic use was described in Chapter 10 so we focus here on the parts of interest to someone writing an application. Figure 19-1 shows a typical 'DLOG' editor window.

In the lower-right side of the window shown in the figure, you'll notice two check boxes labeled Initially visible and Close box. These two check boxes correspond to the *visible* and *goAwayFlag* boolean fields in the *DialogTemplate* data structure. If the Initially visible check

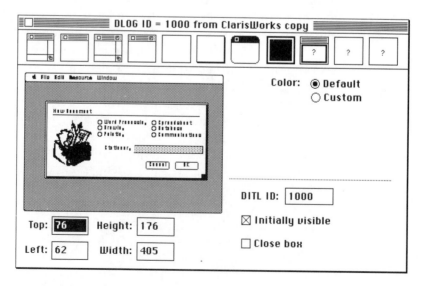

Figure 19-1. A typical dialog editor window showing a 'DLOG' from ClarisWorks.

box isn't checked, the dialog won't be drawn when it's initialized (it can be drawn later by calling the **ShowWindow** Toolbox procedure). If the Close box check box isn't checked, modeless dialog boxes are drawn with no close box. "What," you might ask, "is a modeless dialog box with no close box?" It's probably a dialog that lets you switch to other windows, but that requires you to click a button when you're done. (Of course, the application could treat it in a variety of different ways. For example, MacWrite II uses this method to implement moveable modal dialogs.)

Picking a Window Definition ID

Across the top of the 'DLOG' editor window you see pictures of different kinds of windows. Just click the picture of the type of window you want to create. Table 19-2 shows each picture and the window definition ID it represents. The movable modal window type is only available with System 7 unless you add a custom window definition procedure.

Table 19-2. Window Pictures and Their Corresponding Window Definition IDs

Picture	ID	Description
	0	Standard document window
	4	Document window without a size box
	8	Document window with both zoom and size boxes
	12	Document window with zoom box but no size box
	2	Plain box
	3	Plain box with a drop shadow
	16	Rounded corner window with black title bar
	1	Standard alert or modal dialog box
	5	Movable modal (also available for custom window definition ID)
	–	Available for custom window definition ID

Using Your Own 'WDEF'

If you have your own window definition procedure ('WDEF') that you like to use for dialogs, you'll want to add it to the list of pictures at the top of the window. You can do this by double-clicking one of the last two pictures (the ones containing a "?" character). You can also change the one showing the movable modal dialog picture since this type of dialog is available only on System 7. Figure 19-2 shows the dialog that appears. You should enter the window definition ID, not the 'WDEF' ID, into the dialog. You can calculate the window definition ID by multiplying the 'WDEF' ID by 16 and adding the variation code. (Variation codes are explained in *Inside Macintosh*.) Using this method of calculation, you'll notice that all the window definition IDs in Table 19-2 are just variations that use the same basic 'WDEF' ID (with a resource ID of 0) except the rounded corner window.

Once you've defined your own window definition IDs, why not add a mini-picture of the window? All you have to do is add a 'PICT' resource to the ResEdit Preferences file, and ResEdit will use that 'PICT' instead of just showing an empty rectangle with a number in the middle. Follow these steps to add your own 'PICT'.

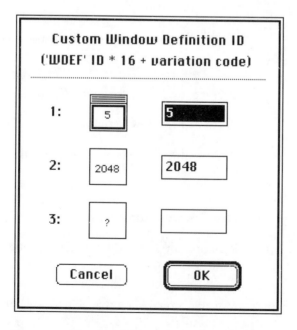

Figure 19-2. This dialog lets you define custom window definition IDs.

1. Use ResEdit to open ResEdit (or a copy).

2. Open the 'PICT' picker and type 1810. (You can also use 1808 or 1809. These three 'PICT' resources correspond to the last three choices in the 'DLOG' editor window.) This moves you to the 'PICT' resource with ID 1810, which should be an empty rectangle.

3. Copy this 'PICT' resource.

4. Close the file (ResEdit or a copy) but don't quit.

5. Open your favorite paint or draw program and paste the 'PICT' you copied. Make whatever changes you want inside the rectangle to make it look like a miniature version of a window that your 'WDEF' would draw.

6. Select just the rectangle containing your mini-window and copy it.

7. Go back to ResEdit and open the ResEdit Preferences file (it's in the Preferences Folder in the System Folder).

8. Paste the 'PICT' you copied from your paint or draw program.

9. Open the 'PICT' picker and select your new 'PICT'.

10. Choose the Get Resource Info command from the Resource menu. Change the resource ID to 1810, (or 1808 or 1809, depending on which of the three available window definition mini-pictures you're using). Also set the Purgeable attribute for the resource.

11. Close and save the Preferences file.

Drawing with Your 'WDEF'

If you have a simple 'WDEF' that doesn't depend on any other part of your application's data when it draws the window, you're probably pretty happy with the way ResEdit handles custom 'WDEF's. If, on the other hand, you have a 'WDEF' that needs information provided by your application to correctly draw the window, you're probably not quite so happy. For 'WDEF's like these, having ResEdit use them to draw the miniature window may cause the system to crash since ResEdit isn't providing the environment they were written to expect (normally provided by the application). Fortunately, it's easy to get around this problem. Just choose the Never Use Custom 'WDEF' for

Drawing command from the 'DLOG' menu. Once this menu item is checked, ResEdit always uses one of the standard system 'WDEF's to draw the miniature picture of the window.

Dialog Characteristics

The Set 'DLOG' Characteristics command on the 'DLOG' menu displays the dialog shown in Figure 19-3. The Window title field simply contains the title that will be used in the title bar when the dialog is displayed (assuming there is a title bar). You probably won't want to store anything in the refCon field. It's typically filled in with a handle to an important data structure when the dialog is about to be used. This field can, however, contain anything you like, so if you have 4 bytes of information you'd like to store there, go right ahead.

The ProcID field contains the window definition ID (or window PROCedure ID). This is the same value that's specified by selecting one of the mini-windows at the top of the main 'DLOG' window. This field can, however, contain a value that's not available from the main window. In this case, none of the mini-window pictures is highlighted. Since this is a little confusing, it's best to add any special window definition IDs you'll be using to the main window. Of course, if you use more than three custom 'WDEF's, you have to assign them here since you can add only three to the main window.

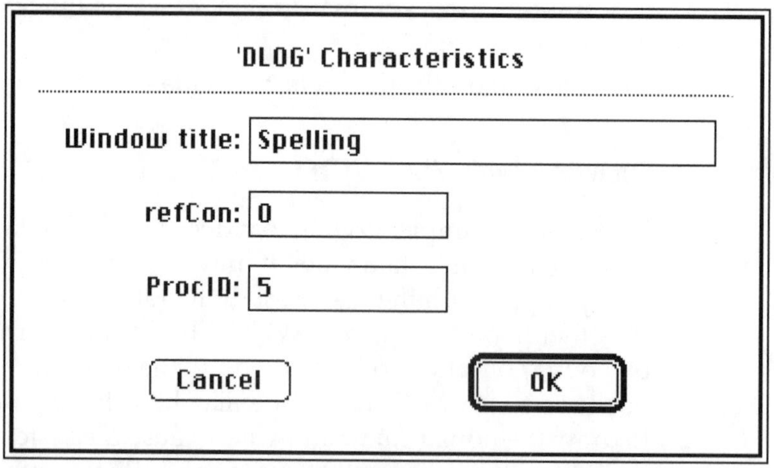

Figure 19-3. The 'DLOG' Characteristics window.

The Alert Editor

The 'ALRT' editor is similar to the dialog editor because alerts are similar to dialogs. In fact, alerts are really just special cases of dialogs that are used to give information to the user. As you can see in Figure 19-4, the alert editor doesn't include the list of window types across the top of the window since alerts are always modal. The Initially visible and Close box check boxes found in the dialog editor's window are also missing since they have no meaning for alerts.

Although alert resources use 'DITL' resources to specify their contents just as dialogs do, the 'DITL's for alerts shouldn't contain fields for entering data. In fact, alerts should only contain static text, 'ICON's, 'PICT's, and buttons. Alerts come in four varieties, which are explained in Table 19-3.

Hint You don't have to add the icons shown in Table 19-3 to your alerts. In fact, you shouldn't. All you need to do is leave room in an alert's 'DITL' resource so the System can add the icon for you. The type of icon added depends on the Toolbox procedure you call: **StopAlert**, **CautionAlert**, **NoteAlert**, or just **Alert**.

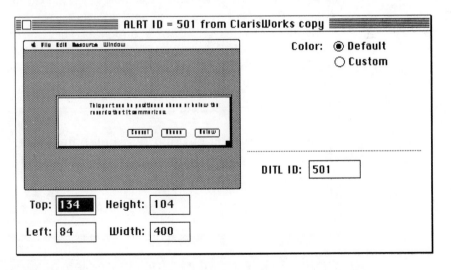

Figure 19-4. A typical alert editor window showing an 'ALRT' from ClarisWorks.

Table 19-3. The Four Kinds of Alerts

Icon	Description
	Stop alert. Used when a serious problem has occurred. Contains one button, labeled OK.
	Caution alert. Usually contains a warning about an operation that could have an undesirable side effect. Always provides a way for the user to cancel the operation (such as with a Cancel or No button).
	Note alert. Contains information the user needs to know but that isn't critical to the performance of the application. For example, the results of an operation could be displayed in a note alert. Contains one button, labeled OK.
none	Plain alert. These are usually equivalent to Note alerts.

Standard Layout

Since alerts should always have a similar layout, Apple has defined some standards to make them as consistent as possible. Figure 19-5 shows a typical "correct" alert. When deciding on the wording for your alerts, be sure to phrase them so users know which button to press. It's all too easy to phrase a question in a Caution alert so users have to guess which button does what they want. Make the question simple, and use words in the buttons that really answer the question.

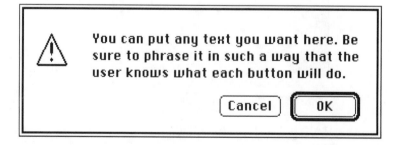

Figure 19-5. An alert that follows Apple's guidelines for item placement.

"Yes" and "No" are often better than "OK" and "Cancel." The book *Macintosh Human Interface Guidelines* can give you more hints for creating clear and effective alerts.

Alert Stages

The Set 'ALRT' Stage Info command on the 'ALRT' menu lets you set up the stages of your alert. Each stage of an alert represents an occurrence of the problem that triggers the alert. For example, if the user makes an invalid entry, a Stage 1 alert is triggered. If the user makes the same mistake again (without doing something else first), a Stage 2 alert occurs. Choosing the Set 'ALRT' Stage Info command displays the dialog shown in Figure 19-6. Most applications configure their alerts with all the stages the same—usually visible, with one sound, as shown in the figure. Set the Default button to OK if button number 1 should be the default (shown with a dark outline), and to Cancel if button number 2 should be the default. You can find more information about alert stages in the "Dialog Manager" chapters of *Inside Macintosh*.

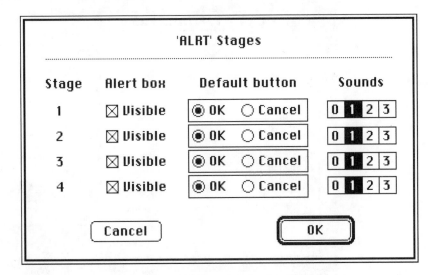

Figure 19-6. The 'ALRT' Stages dialog containing typical settings.

The 'DITL' Editor

When you're designing a dialog or alert, you'll spend most of your time in the 'DITL' editor. This is where you'll design the contents of your dialogs or alerts, adding and arranging fields as necessary. Chapter 10 described how to use the 'DITL' editor to customize dialogs and alerts; here we show you how to create your own 'DITL's.

You can create a new 'DITL' from the 'DLOG' or 'ALRT' editor by opening the 'DITL' using any of the methods described in Chapter 10 (press the Return key, for example). Of course, you can also create a 'DITL' from the 'DITL' picker. Either way, you'll end up with a new window like the one shown in Figure 19-7. On the right side of the figure, you see the floating item palette, which you can use to add items to your new 'DITL'—just drag the type of item you'd like to add to where you want it to appear in the 'DITL' window. Repeat this process until you have defined all the item fields you want.

The size of the 'DITL' editor window is determined by the size specified for the associated 'DLOG' or 'ALRT'. You don't have to go

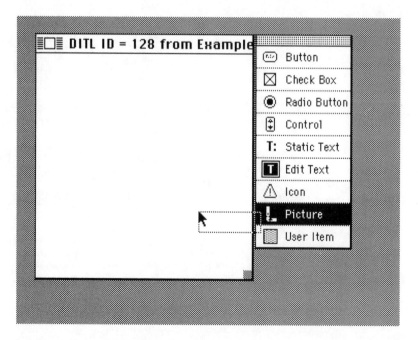

Figure 19-7. You can add items to a 'DITL' by dragging them from the floating palette.

back to the 'DLOG' or 'ALRT' editor to change the size, however. Just
grab the size box in the lower-right corner of the 'DITL' editor's
window and change the size to whatever you want. The size saved in
the 'DLOG' or 'ALRT' resource is changed to match the new size of
your 'DITL' window.

The Dialog Item Editor

You can arrange dialog items right in the 'DITL' editor window, but
sometimes you need to change characteristics of an individual item.
You can do this by double-clicking an item to open a Dialog Item
editor window like the one shown in Figure 19-8. Dialog Item editor
windows are modeless windows—you can have as many of them
open as you like. As you can see in the figure, there are four parts to
the Item editor window. You can use the pop-up menu to change an
item to any of the other item types. The Enabled check box determines whether the item will be active (whether the user can interact
with the item by clicking or typing) when the 'DITL' is used. Remember, though, a disabled control item can still be active—you must use
the **HiliteControl** Toolbox procedure to make a control inactive. The
editable field in the upper right of the window is used to specify the
title for buttons, check boxes, and radio buttons; the text for static text
and edit text items; and the resource ID for icons, controls, and pictures. Lastly, the four fields at the bottom right of the window set the
size and location of the item. The Item menu lets you choose between
showing the Bottom and Right or the Height and Width of the item.

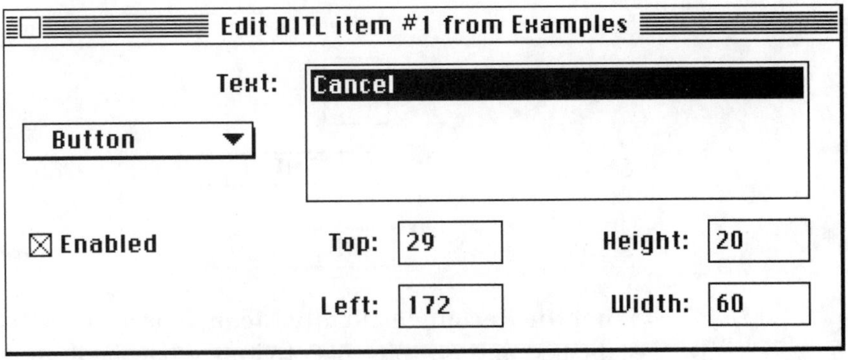

Figure 19-8. A typical Dialog Item editor window.

Any changes you make in the item editor window (such as changing the item's location or title) are reflected immediately in the 'DITL' editor window so you can see the effect of your change.

Dialog Item Tips

Most of the item types in the floating item palette are probably familiar to you, so we won't go into much detail about them. A few, though, can be a little tricky—we talk about them next. Complete details about dialog items can be found in the "Dialog Manager" chapters of *Inside Macintosh*.

Resource Items

As you no doubt know, you can include 'ICON', 'CNTL', and 'PICT' resources as items in a 'DITL'. When you first drag a resource item off the palette, it appears in the 'DITL' window looking like one of the default resources shown in Table 19-4. To make the item show up using the resources you want, you need to set the item's resource ID. You can do this by double-clicking the item to open the Dialog Item editor, where you can enter the resource ID. You should then see the resource in the 'DITL' editor window. If you still don't see your resource, that means ResEdit couldn't find it, and you should go to the 'ICON', 'CNTL', or 'PICT' picker to verify the ID of the resource you want to use.

Table 19-4. The 'DITL' Editor's Default Resource Items

Resource Type	Default Appearance	Name in Palette
'ICON'	ICON	Icon
'CNTL'	CNTL	Control
'PICT'	PICT	Picture

What the Rectangles Really Mean. For most item types, such as static text and buttons, it's obvious what the item rectangle is used for—it defines the size of the item. For the resource items, however, it's less clear since the resources also either contain their own rectangles ('CNTL's and 'PICT's) or are a fixed size ('ICON's are always

32 by 32). If the item rectangle for an 'ICON' or 'PICT' is different from the size of the resource, the resource is scaled to fit the item rectangle. 'CNTL' resources behave differently, however. The top and left coordinates of the control are determined by the item rectangle, but the height and width are determined by the rectangle stored in the 'CNTL' resource. Whatever the item type, you'll more than likely want to use the size associated with the resource you're displaying. You can easily make the item rectangle the same as the resource's rectangle by selecting the item and choosing Use Item's Rectangle from the 'DITL' menu. For controls, this command will set only the height and width and won't change the top and left coordinates.

Editing Resource Items.   As with any of the other item types, double-clicking a resource item opens an Item editor window. Many times, however, you'll want to edit the resource itself and not the dialog item using the resource. You can do this by using the two alternate Open commands on the Resource menu or their shortcuts. After selecting a resource item, the third item on the Resource menu changes to Open 'CNTL', Open 'ICON', or Open 'PICT', depending on the situation, and opens the appropriate editor. You can also choose Open Using Hex Editor to open the resource using the hexadecimal editor. You can use the Command-Option double-click shortcut to open the resource editor and the Option double-click shortcut to edit the resource using the hexadecimal editor.

By The Way You can substitute a color icon in a dialog by including in the file a 'cicn' with the same ID as that of the 'ICON'. If the 'cicn' is not 32-by-32 pixels, you can change the item rectangle to match. Note, however, that the 'DITL' editor doesn't show 'cicn's. Also, opening the editor for an 'ICON' item always opens the 'ICON' editor, even if a 'cicn' will be substituted when the dialog is displayed.

Adding System 7 Balloon Help Items

One of the features provided by System 7 is Balloon help. An application can specify text to appear in balloons as the user moves the mouse over a document or menu. Each part of the screen—such as windows, menus, menu items, and dialogs—can have its own set of balloon messages. Several new resource types were introduced to support these balloon messages ('hmnu', 'hdlg', 'hwin', and 'hrct'). ResEdit doesn't support these resources but BalloonWriter, an application available from Apple, does. One aspect of balloon help that ResEdit does support is the new balloon help dialog item that can be included in a 'DITL' resource. This new dialog item merely directs the Help Manager to the proper help resource. Figure 19-9 shows the dialog displayed when you choose the Balloon Help command from the 'DITL' menu. You can enter the resource IDs of the associated help resources. The pop-up menu lets you choose the type of the associated resource. You normally won't need to use this feature since BalloonWriter automatically adds the dialog items for you.

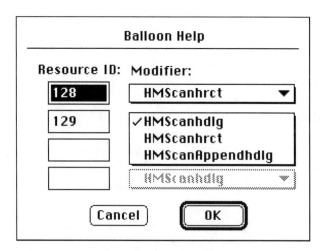

Figure 19-9. Adding help items to a 'DITL'.

What's On Top of What?

Usually each dialog item occupies its own area of the dialog, but sometimes it's useful or necessary to have items that overlap. For example, you might want to put a user item over a button so you can draw a dark frame to show that it's the default, or you may want a picture in the background of the entire 'DITL'. In any case, you need to know the order in which the dialog items are drawn so you can know which items appear on top. You might expect that the first item would be on the bottom and the last item would be on the top but, unfortunately, the Dialog Manager doesn't make it quite that easy. When drawing a 'DITL', the Dialog Manager first draws all buttons, check boxes, and radio buttons in *reverse* item number order. It then draws the rest of the items, this time in *ascending* order. You can never have a button, check box, or radio button on top of an item of one of the other types. User items are a little different since they're transparent—when they're on top of another item, you can still see through to the other item. You can tell that a user item is on top of another item if the entire user item is filled with gray (otherwise, you'll see the other item drawn across the user item). Because the 'DITL' editor uses the Dialog Manager to draw its window, the items are drawn in exactly the order they'll appear when you use the 'DITL'.

The 'DITL' Menu

The 'DITL' menu contains items to help you design your 'DITL' and set up the 'DITL' editor the way you like to work. Except for the first group of commands, which pertains to item numbering, this menu's commands are discussed in Chapter 10.

Renumber Items

When you choose the Renumber Items command, the editor temporarily turns on the Show Item Numbers command (described shortly) and every item in the 'DITL' is displayed with its current item number. Then, as the small floating dialog window that appears tells you, all you have to do is press the Shift key while you select the items in the order you want them renumbered. As you Shift-click, a white-on-black number appears for each item you've renumbered. Figure 19-10 shows how this looks. If you're satisfied with your new numbering scheme, click the Renumber button. (Shift-click also deselects an item already selected for renumbering. If you want to deselect all of the items and start over, just click once without pressing the Shift key.)

Set Item Number

The Set Item Number command lets you set the item number for a single item. (Other items are renumbered to avoid duplicate num-

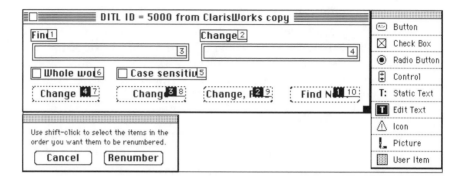

Figure 19-10. A 'DITL' in the process of being renumbered.

bers.) Using this command is simpler than using the renumber command if you only want to change one item or you want to change the number of an item that's hiding behind another item.

Select Item Number

The Select Item Number command lets you specify the number of an item to be selected. This is especially useful for items that aren't visible (because they're outside the dialog's rectangle) or are under another item. Once the item is selected, you can use the Open as Dialog Item command on the Resource menu to open an Item editor window (even if the item isn't visible).

Show Item Numbers

Choose Show Item Numbers when you want to see the item numbers of all the items. A black-on-white numeral appears in the upper-right corner of each item. This can be invaluable when you're designing a new dialog. Figure 19-10 shows a 'DITL' with the item numbers displayed.

> **Hint** Holding down the Option key is a shortcut for choosing the Show Item Numbers command. If Show Item Numbers is off, pressing the Option key displays the item numbers until you release the key. If Show Item Numbers is on, pressing the Option key turns the numbers off until you release the key.

The Alignment Menu

The Alignment menu contains commands that help you arrange the items in your dialog. The action performed by these commands is usually obvious from the name of the command. Chapter 10 has more details.

Summary

In this chapter we cover details of the 'DLOG', 'ALRT', and 'DITL' editors. We show you how to design dialogs and alerts from scratch, including using your own window definition procedures ('WDEF's). We also show you how to set up the various kinds of alerts and the alert stages. Finally, we show you how to use the 'DITL' editor to create the contents for both alerts and dialogs. More information about all these editors can be found in Chapter 10.

Chapter 20

Creating Menus

One of the editors you'll find most useful as you create an application is the 'MENU' editor. In Chapter 8 we showed you how to use the 'MENU' editor for updating an existing menu. This chapter fills in the remaining details about the 'MENU' editor by providing information that's useful only if you're writing the application that will use the menu. If you're not familiar with the 'MENU' editor, be sure to review Chapter 8 since we cover only new information here. Also remember that if you're using MacApp, you can use the same information to help you create 'CMNU' resources.

The Basics

When you create a new 'MENU' resource, you see a window similar to the one shown in Figure 20-1. The menu initially has no items, and its title is simply "Title." The first change you'll want to make is to enter the menu's title. Selecting the Apple radio button is equivalent to entering the character into the Title field. The Enabled check box in the upper-right corner of the window determines whether the entire menu is enabled or disabled when it's installed on the menu bar. ResEdit assumes the menu should be enabled and automatically checks the Enabled check box for you when you create a new menu.

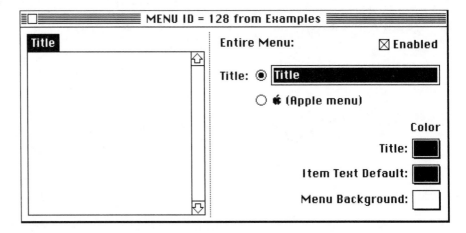

Figure 20-1. The 'MENU' editor showing a new resource.

Adding New Menu Items

Once you've entered the title, you're ready to start adding new menu items. As with many other operations in ResEdit, there's a menu command and a shortcut to add new items. You can choose Create New Item from the Resource menu or simply press the Return key. Either way, a new item is added at the end of the menu. In a menu that already has items, pressing the Return key moves to the next item. If the last item is selected, Return creates a new item. After you've added your first item, the window resembles the one shown in Figure 20-2. Notice that several new fields appear to let you set the characteristics of your new item. We'll talk more about the has Submenu and Mark fields later in this chapter. The Enabled check box in the upper-right corner of the window indicates whether the selected item is enabled. If you want the item to appear as a separator line, just click the separator line radio button (or type a hyphen into the Text field). You can continue pressing Return and entering item information until you've filled out your menu.

Rearranging Menu Items

Before you're finished with your menu, you'll probably want to move some items around, insert an item or two you forgot, or get rid of an item you don't really need. Most of these operations work just as

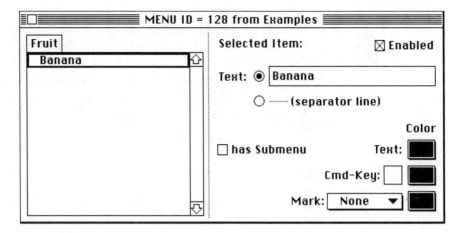

Figure 20-2. When you add a menu item, new fields appear in the 'MENU' editor window.

you'd expect. You can cut, copy, paste, clear, or duplicate a menu item simply by selecting it and choosing the appropriate command from the Edit menu (or typing the Command-key equivalent). Here are a few things to keep in mind when using the Edit menu with 'MENU' resources.

- If you want the Edit menu commands to affect an entire item, make sure the item is selected with a solid selection. A hollow selection in the list indicates that one of the text fields on the right side of the window is selected instead of the entire menu item.

- Because you can select only one item at a time, you can only copy and paste items one at a time.

- When you copy an item, all the information about that item (Command key, Mark, and so on), except the color information, is also copied. You'll have to reset any colors associated with the item you copied.

- Paste adds the new item after the currently selected item. If you want a new item to be at the top of the menu, you'll have to drag it there. (Dragging menu items is explained next.)

Hint If you need to create a menu that includes all the items in
another menu, here's a shortcut. In the 'MENU' picker, select and
cut or copy the menu whose items you want to include as part of
another menu. Now open the other menu, select the item after
which you want to add the new items, and paste. The entire menu
you copied (except the title) will be inserted into your menu.

Moving Items

You can move an item in a menu by selecting it and dragging it to a
new location. You don't actually drag the item when you're moving
it. Instead, the item remains in its original location (still selected)
and you drag a black line that indicates the place where the menu
item will end up when you release the mouse button, as shown in
Figure 20-3.

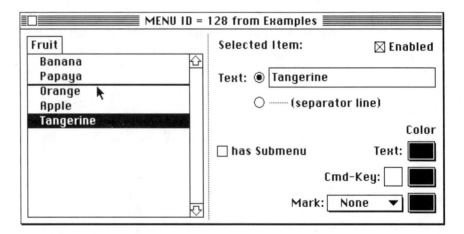

Figure 20-3. You can drag a menu item to a new location in the
menu.

Creating Hierarchical Menus

Creating hierarchical menus is as easy as clicking the has Submenu
check box. When you check the check box, the Cmd-Key and Mark
fields disappear and an ID field appears. You enter the resource ID of

the submenu in the ID field. Double-clicking an item with a submenu (or selecting Open Submenu from the Resource menu) opens the 'MENU' resource specified in the ID field. The 'MENU' resource is created for you if it doesn't exist. Submenus are not shown in the test menu to the right on the menu bar.

Using the Mark Menu

The Mark pop-up menu is easy enough to use if you like one of the marks on the menu—just select the mark. If the default set of marks doesn't fit your needs, however, you can add any character you want to the Mark menu. When you choose the Other item on the Mark menu, you see the dialog shown in Figure 20-4. Any character you enter in the dialog appears in the Mark menu. If you check the Remember in Preferences check box, the new mark is saved in ResEdit's Preferences file and appears on your Mark pop-up menu every time you use the 'MENU' editor.

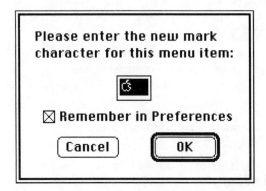

Figure 20-4. The 'MENU' editor's New Mark dialog.

Removing Marks from the Mark Menu

You've added a few marks to your Mark menu that you don't need anymore—how do you get rid of them? Just follow these steps.

1. Use ResEdit to open the ResEdit Preferences file in the Preferences Folder in your System Folder.

2. Open the 'MENU' picker.

3. Find the 'MENU' resource with ID 1652 (it's probably the only 'MENU' in the file).

4. If you want to go back to the default Mark menu, just delete this resource.

5. If you want to remove one or more marks, open the resource in the 'MENU' editor and delete the items you no longer need.

6. Close and save the Preferences file.

Changing the 'MENU' and 'MDEF' IDs

If your application includes a tool palette or tear-off menu, you'll need to write your own menu definition procedure ('MDEF'), and then set up a menu that uses your 'MDEF' instead of the normal System 'MDEF'. You can set up a menu to use any 'MDEF' by choosing Edit Menu & 'MDEF' ID from the 'MENU' menu. The dialog that appears is shown in Figure 20-5. Put the resource ID of your 'MDEF' into the MDEF ID field.

In the same dialog shown in the figure, you'll see a field labeled Menu ID. This field is a little confusing since it doesn't necessarily contain the resource ID of the 'MENU' resource being edited. Instead,

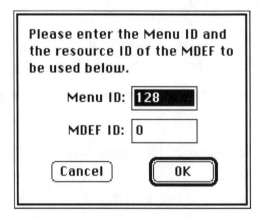

Figure 20-5. You can change the internal 'MENU' ID and the 'MDEF' ID with this dialog.

it contains the number the Menu Manager returns to your application when you call the **MenuSelect** or **MenuKey** Toolbox procedures. By convention, this number should always be the same as the resource ID of the 'MENU' resource (although you can set it to any number you want). When you change the ID of the 'MENU' (with the Get Resource Info command on the Resource menu), ResEdit asks if you want to update this other, hidden 'MENU' ID as well.

Summary

In this chapter we show you how to create and update menus for your applications. We show you how to add items to menus, as well as how to move existing items. We also give you some tips on how to use marks and a custom 'MDEF'. Many other important parts of the 'MENU' editor are described in Chapter 8.

Chapter 21

Editing 'BNDL', 'vers', and 'TEXT' Resources

This chapter describes several different resource types. These resources aren't related, but they aren't complex enough to warrant chapters of their own.

Every application has a 'BNDL' resource that tells the Finder what icons to use for the application and its document files. Most applications also have 'vers' resources, which provide the version information the Finder displays in its Get Info window. We also discuss the 'TEXT' resource and its associated 'styl' resource. These resources let you store styled text for use in your application.

Editing 'BNDL' Resources

You may have heard (or experienced) horror stories involving 'BNDL' resources, but ResEdit's 'BNDL' editor should quickly change the 'BNDL' resource's reputation. Every application needs a 'BNDL' resource if it's to display a custom icon for itself and its document files. The 'BNDL' resource describes a bundle of other resources. It associates a signature resource with file reference resources ('FREF's) and Finder icons ('ICN#', 'ics#', etc.) by using something called *local IDs*. With ResEdit's 'BNDL' editor you don't have to worry about any of these peripheral resources or the local IDs—they're all created for you. Figure 21-1 shows a typical 'BNDL' editor window.

The right side of the 'BNDL' editor window shows the icons the Finder uses for the application's files. The associated file Types are

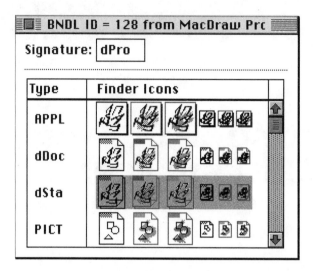

Figure 21-1. A typical 'BNDL' from MacDraw Pro.

listed on the left side of the window. The APPL Type associates an
icon with the application itself. (If you need to refresh your memory,
file Types and Creators are discussed in Chapter 7.) The other file
Types can be anything you like. At the top of the window is a field for
you to enter the application's signature resource. The signature is the
same as the Creator for the application and its documents, and the
Finder uses it to find a document's Creator. You can use the Create
New File Type command on the Resource menu to add new file
Types to the end of the list.

As you move the pointer across the window, you'll notice that it
can assume three shapes: the normal arrow, the I-beam, and the plus
symbol. This changing pointer indicates that clicking the mouse
selects different parts of the 'BNDL'. You see the arrow when the
pointer is over the icons or when it's in those parts of the window
where there's nothing to select. You can double-click the icons to edit
them. You see the I-beam when the pointer is over the Signature field
or one of the Type fields. When you see the plus symbol, clicking
selects an entire row. Once a row is selected, you can cut, copy, clear,
or duplicate it.

Bundles of Icons

You may be wondering why you see so many icons associated with each Type in the 'BNDL' editor window. The first icon is the familiar 'ICN#' resource the Finder has always used to represent documents and applications. The other five icons are used by System 7 to give you more flexibility when creating your icons. These five icon types are (in order from left to right): 'icl4', 'icl8', 'ics#', 'ics4', and 'ics8'. The Finder uses the appropriate icon based on the number of colors available on the screen and the size of icon it needs. If one of the icons hasn't been defined, it's shown as a gray square. If a Type already has associated icons, you can edit them simply by double-clicking any of the icons. You can edit all of them in one editor—the Icon Family editor, shown in Figure 21-2. This editor is described in Chapter 17.

If no icons are associated with a file Type, double-clicking the gray squares displays the Choose Icon dialog, shown in Figure 21-3. If you already have an icon but you'd like to pick a different one, you can choose Choose Icon from the 'BNDL' menu to see the same dialog. This dialog shows you all the 'ICN#' resources in the file being edited. You can select one of these icons or you can click the New button to create a new icon from scratch. If you like one of the icons but want to

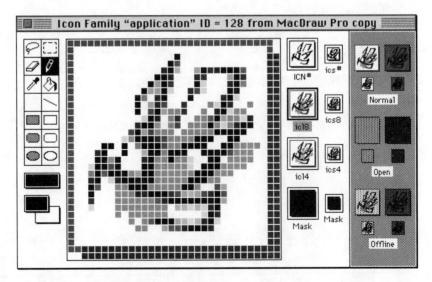

Figure 21-2. The Icon Family editor lets you create all the icons the Finder needs.

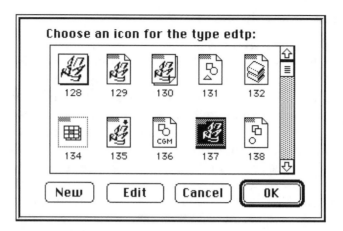

Figure 21-3. You can use the Choose Icon dialog to choose an icon to add to your 'BNDL'.

change it a little before you add it to your 'BNDL', you can select the icon and click the Edit button. (Editing an icon changes its appearance every place it's used, not just in the 'BNDL'.)

Hint Once you've changed the icon for an application, you'll probably want the Finder to use the new icon when it displays the application or document files. Unfortunately, the Finder stores the icons in its Desktop database and there's no easy way to tell the Finder that it should look for a new icon. The most straightforward way to force it to use your new icon is to rebuild the Desktop database from scratch. You can do this by holding down the Command and Option keys when you restart your Mac. Remember that you'll lose any comments you've entered into the Finder's Get Info window when you rebuild your desktop database.

Hint If you've just created a 'BNDL' in a new application, don't forget to set the *bundle* attribute to let the Finder know it should look in the file for a 'BNDL' resource. Just check the Bundle check box in the file's File Info window (choose Get File/Folder Info from the File menu).

> **By The Way** Five of the six icons are used only with System 7
> and you should think about including at least some of these icons.
> At the least, you should include an 'ics#' resource so the Finder
> won't have to shrink your 'ICN#' to use for the icon in the upper-
> right corner of the screen. Of course, your application will still
> work with System 7 even if you include only an 'ICN#'.

The Extended View

If you miss the days when you had to figure out your own local IDs
and set up your own 'BNDL' resource, the Extended View command
on the 'BNDL' menu is for you. Selecting this command changes the
display to look like Figure 21-4. If you really need to use this view of
the 'BNDL', you can find details about the extra fields in *Inside
Macintosh*.

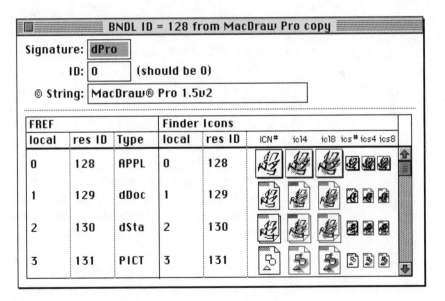

Figure 21-4. **The extended view of a 'BNDL' resource.**

> **Hint** In versions of the Finder before version 6.1, the text shown in the extended view's String field was displayed in the Finder's Get Info window. More recent versions of the Finder use a file's 'vers' resource (described next) instead, if one is present. If your application might be used with very old versions of the system software, you might want to include a copyright string in the String field of the 'BNDL' resource.

Editing 'vers' Resources

In version 6.1 of the Finder, the 'vers' resource type was introduced to hold an application's version information. The Finder uses this version information in its Get Info window. The 'vers' resource has several advantages over the older method of storing a version string inside the 'BNDL' resource.

- It stores more information, including a numeric form of the version number, rather than just a string of unformatted text.
- The 'vers' resource type can be used in any file, not just applications containing 'BNDL' resources.
- Applications can include two 'vers' resources: one to indicate the version number of the file itself, and one for the version number of a set of files that work together (for example, system files can have their own version number yet still indicate the system release they belong to).
- The structure of the 'vers' resource type helps standardize the release numbering scheme that applications use. This helps users understand how different versions of the same application are related.

The 'vers' resource editor is shown in Figure 21-5. Most of the information in the window is pretty standard and doesn't need much explanation. The Long version string field contains the most important information in this window because that text is displayed in the Finder's Get Info window, as shown in Figure 21-6. As you can see in the figures, The Get Info window contains room for only one line of text from resource ID 2, and two lines from ID 1.

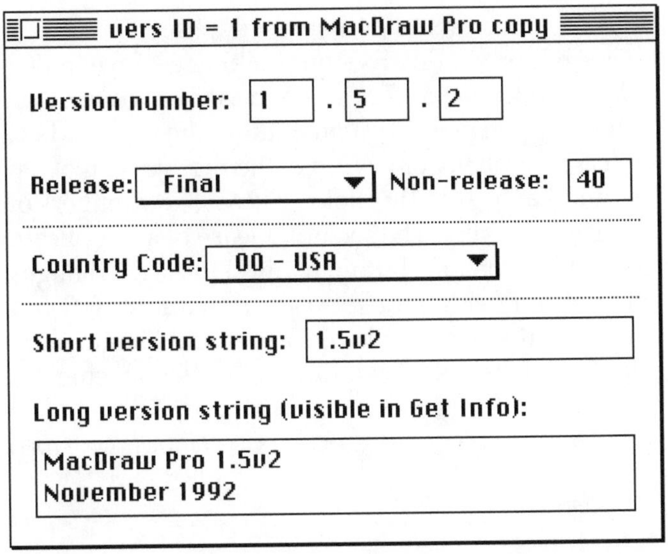

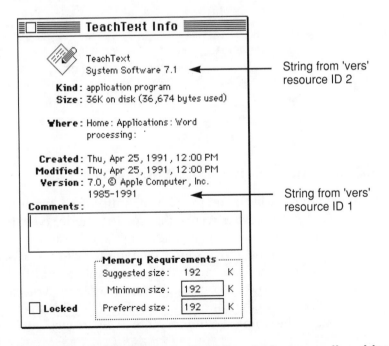

Figure 21-5. The 'vers' editor lets you set the information displayed in the Finder's Get Info window.

String from 'vers' resource ID 2

String from 'vers' resource ID 1

Figure 21-6. The Finder's Get Info window uses the strings from two 'vers' resources.

The version number displayed in three fields across the top of the 'vers' editor window is stored in the resource in BCD (Binary Coded Decimal) format and can be accessed for comparison purposes by utility applications. By convention, the first field contains the major release number. For example, the first version of a product to ship would have a 1 in this field. The second number contains the minor revision number. The second release of an application that contains a few enhancements but no really significant changes might have a 1 in the second field. If the release was made strictly to fix a few bugs but had no other feature changes, it would increment the third field. Table 21-1 shows a few examples of this scheme.

Table 21-1. Recommended Use of Version Number Fields

Version	Meaning
1.0.0	The first release
1.0.1	The first bug fix release of the file
1.1.0	The first minor update of the file
2.0.0	The second release

Hint Remember, you can put a 'vers' resource in any file. This is a better way to add comments to a file than by adding a Get Info comment since it won't be lost if you need to rebuild your Desktop database. See Chapter 13 for more details.

Editing 'TEXT' and 'styl' Resources

When the Mac II and the SE were introduced, the Mac's built-in text editing capabilities were enhanced to include styled text. This styled text is stored in two resources. The 'TEXT' resource contains the characters, and the 'styl' resource contains the associated style information. Few applications have taken advantage of styled text because there was no way to create the resources. Now you can edit this styled text in the editor shown in Figure 21-7. As you can see, this is one of the simplest editors you're likely to encounter. You can use it

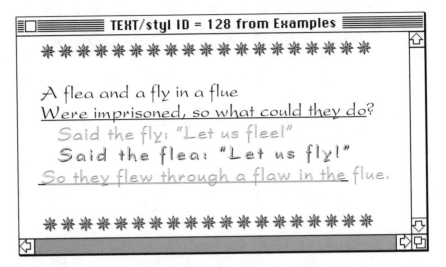

Figure 21-7. The 'TEXT' and 'styl' editor is a simple text editor.

like any other simple word processing application, although its capabilities are limited. You can enter up to 32,000 characters and change the font, size, or style as often as you like.

Summary

In this chapter we summarize the use of three editors that you'll find useful when you're programming with the Mac. The 'BNDL' editor lets you associate icons with your application and its documents. The 'vers' editor lets you enter the version information the Finder displays in its Get Info window. Finally, the 'TEXT' and 'styl' editor lets you save styled text for your application to use.

Chapter 22

 ## File, Folder, and Resource Info Windows

Files, folders, and resources all have various characteristics that control their use by the System and the Finder. You can change these characteristics (or in some cases just observe them) in ResEdit's info windows. For example, by changing these characteristics you can modify a folder's Finder label, the last modified date of a file, or the ID of a resource. You can make a file or folder invisible, or change the Type and Creator of a file or the name of a resource. In this chapter we show you what each of the characteristics is used for and how to change them.

The File Info Window

The File Info window lets you change file characteristics important to both the Finder and the operating system. When you choose Get File/Folder Info from the File menu, the dialog shown in Figure 22-1 is displayed. This dialog is slightly different from most other standard file directory dialogs because it allows you to select either a file or a folder. The only way to see the contents of a folder is to double-click the folder. Pressing the Return or Enter key when a folder is selected displays the Folder Info window (rather than showing the contents of the folder). Just remember: Double-click to open a folder and show its contents in the standard file directory dialog; click the Get Info button to show a file's or folder's info window. Of course, double-clicking a file is equivalent to clicking the Get Info button

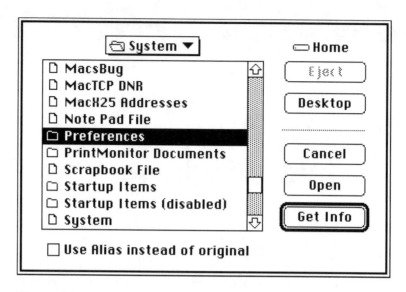

Figure 22-1. The standard file directory dialog for the Get File/Folder Info command lets you select either a file or a folder.

with the file selected. If you've selected an alias, clicking the Use Alias instead of the original check box at the bottom of the window causes ResEdit to show you the file info for the alias file (otherwise, you'll see the file info for the original file).

After you've selected a file and clicked the Get Info button, you see a window similar to the one shown in Figure 22-2. The top half of the window contains the file name, Type, and Creator, as well as some file system characteristics, the creation date, and last modified date of the file, and the size of its data fork and resource fork. The bottom half of the window contains a set of check boxes that let you change flags the Finder uses. Table 22-1 lists the use for each field in the File Info window. A few of the fields are too complex (or interesting) to capsulize in the table, so they're described in more detail after the table. These fields are marked with an asterisk in the table. As you can see in Figure 22-2, you can see either the System 7 or System 6 Finder flags. Only the System 7 flags are described here.

```
┌─────────────────────────────────────────────────────────┐
│ ▤□═══════════ Info for System copy ═══════════           │
│                                                           │
│    File: │System copy                    │    ☐ Locked    │
│                                                           │
│    Type: │zsys   │   Creator: │MACS │                      │
│    ☐ File Locked      ☐ Resources Locked    File In Use: No │
│    ☐ Printer Driver MultiFinder Compatible  File Protected: No │
│                                                           │
│    Created: │Thu, Aug 27, 1992 │   Time: │1:00:00 AM │    │
│                                                           │
│    Modified: │Wed, Sep 1, 1993 │   Time: │3:37:08 PM │    │
│       Size: 1352980 bytes in resource fork               │
│             924 bytes in data fork                        │
│    ─────────────────────────────────────────────────     │
│    Finder Flags: ⦿ 7.x  ○ 6.0.x                           │
│       ☒ Has BNDL    ☐ No INITs    Label: │ None      ▼ │  │
│       ☐ Shared      ☒ Inited      ☐ Invisible            │
│       ☐ Stationery  ☐ Alias       ☐ Use Custom Icon      │
└─────────────────────────────────────────────────────────┘
```

Figure 22-2. A File Info window.

> **Hint** Sometimes after you change a file's characteristics, you won't see the change take effect right away. Usually closing and reopening the folder containing the file makes the change take effect. For example, if you make a file into stationery by setting the stationery characteristic, you need to close and reopen the folder containing the file before its icon changes to a stationery icon.

Table 22-1. Fields of a File Info Window

Field Name	Description
File	The name of the file. You can enter any name up to 31 characters long.
Locked*	Checked if the file's name can't be changed from the Finder.
Type*	A file's Type (APPL for applications, for example).
Creator*	A file's Creator. An application and its associated documents all have the same Creator.

Table 22-1. Fields of a File Info Window (continued)

Field Name	Description
File Locked	Checked if the file is locked and can't be thrown into the Trash. File Locked is the same as the locked check box in the Finder's Get Info window.
Resources Locked*	Checked if changes can't be made to the file's resources.
File In Use	Yes, if the file is open (either the resource fork or data fork is open by ResEdit or another application).
Printer Driver	Checked if the file is a printer driver that can be used
MultiFinder compatible	when MultiFinder is in use (in other words, if the printer driver can be shared by several applications at once).
File Protected	Yes, if the Finder can't copy the file.
Created*	The time and date the file was created.
Modified*	The time and date the file was most recently modified.
Finder Flags	System 7 or System 6 Finder flags can be displayed. System 7 flags are described here.
Has BNDL	Checked if the file contains a 'BNDL' resource. Any application that has its own desktop icon or opens document files must contain a 'BNDL' resource. Chapter 21 explains the use of 'BNDL' resources.
No INITs	Checked if the file doesn't contain any 'INIT' resources. (Actually, the file can still contain 'INIT's, but they're ignored.)
Label	A pop-up menu containing the label the Finder uses when it displays the file's icon. This is the same label selected from the Finder's Label menu.
Shared*	Checked if a file can be opened more than once simultaneously.
Inited	The Finder checks this the first time it notices a file. The Finder saves certain information (such as the file's icon) when the file is inited.
Invisible*	Checked if the file's icon is invisible in the Finder. You can always see invisible files in ResEdit's standard file directory dialogs.

Table 22-1. Fields of a File Info Window (continued)

Field Name	*Description*
Stationery	Checked if the file is a stationery file. Stationery files are copied before they are opened, so the original is never changed. Stationery is the same as the Stationery Pad check box in the Finder's Get Info window.
Alias	Checked if the file is an alias to another file.
Use Custom Icon	Checked if the file contains a custom icon that the Finder should use in place of the default icon provided by the application that created the file.

* Indicates characteristics with more detailed explanations following this table.

Type and Creator

Every file has a Type field and a Creator field, which the Finder uses to establish the relationship between documents and applications. The Type and Creator are both four characters long (just like a resource type). The Creator field of a document file is the same as the Creator of the application that created it. Applications must have unique Creators so the Finder will know which document files belong to which application. The Type field of a document file distinguishes between different document types of the same application. The Type field of an application is always set to 'APPL' so the Finder will know it's an application. Types and Creators are explained in more detail in Chapter 7.

Locked and Invisible

If other people use your computer and you want to protect yourself from their careless mistakes, you can turn on the Locked or Invisible characteristics for important files. For files whose names you don't want changed, just check the Locked characteristic. If you're worried that someone might inadvertently delete one of your important files, just make it invisible. You can even make your applications invisible, as long as you have a document to double-click when you want to start the application. (See Chapter 13 if you want step-by-step instructions.)

Resources Locked

Clicking the Resources Locked check box makes the resource fork of the file read only. Resources Locked can only be checked if no changes have been made to the file.

Setting a File's Created and Last Modified Date

When you set a file's creation date or last modified date, you must enter the date and time in a format ResEdit can understand. The date format shown is the abbreviated long date format set in the 'itl1' resource (or the Date & Time control panel). When you make changes, any format shown in the Date & Time control panel will work.

Shared

If you have a site-licensed application and a network, you can let a group of people share one copy of the application by checking its Shared characteristic. For example, you could put a copy of HyperCard into a locked folder on a server (be sure to lock it so the Home stack won't be changed), and everyone connected to the server could use it.

The Shared characteristic should only be checked for applications that several people share. Don't check the Shared characteristic for a file that you write to, though. With Shared checked you could, for example, use ResEdit to edit an application while it's running. This would more than likely result in a system crash and could possibly destroy your application. If you want to share an application, it's best to contact the application's developers and get their assurance that the application works properly in a shared environment.

The Folder Info Window

The Folder Info window is used to set the characteristics for a folder; it is shown in Figure 22-3. Characteristics for a folder are just a subset of the characteristics for a file and are explained in Table 22-1.

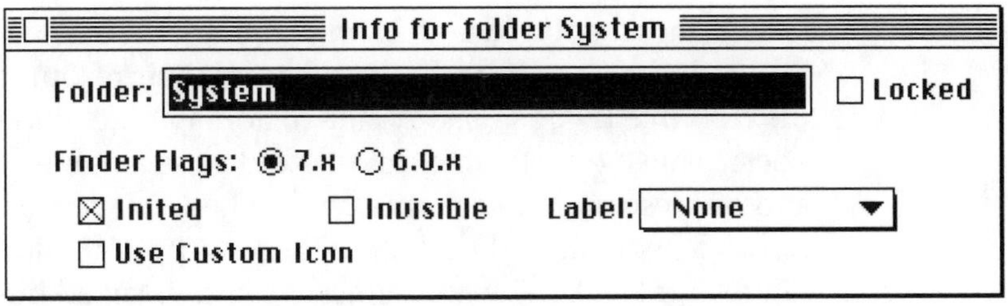

```
┌──────────────────────────────────────────────────────┐
│ ▤□▥▥▥▥▥▥▥▥ Info for folder System ▥▥▥▥▥▥▥▥▥▥▥ │
├──────────────────────────────────────────────────────┤
│  Folder: │System                          │   □ Locked │
│                                                         │
│  Finder Flags:  ◉ 7.x  ○ 6.0.x                          │
│     ⊠ Inited        □ Invisible   Label: │ None    ▼ │ │
│     □ Use Custom Icon                                   │
└──────────────────────────────────────────────────────┘
```

Figure 22-3. A Folder Info window.

The Resource Info Window

Selecting the Get Resource Info command from the Resource menu
(when a resource picker or editor is the frontmost window) opens a
Resource Info window like the one shown in Figure 22-4. The
Resource Info window lets you change characteristics that control
how the System treats the resource. Two fields at the top of the
window let you change the resource's ID and name. These two fields
control how an application finds the resource it's looking for. It's

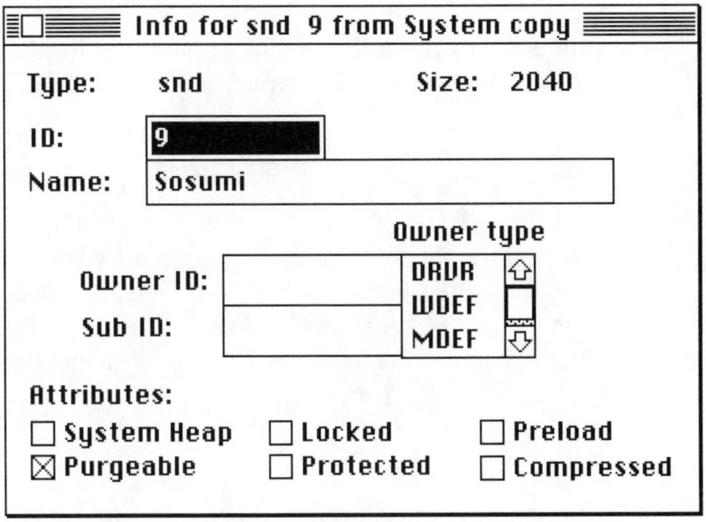

```
┌──────────────────────────────────────────────────────┐
│ ▤□▥▥▥▥ Info for snd  9 from System copy ▥▥▥▥▥ │
├──────────────────────────────────────────────────────┤
│  Type:     snd              Size:   2040               │
│                                                         │
│  ID:     │9                │                            │
│  Name:   │Sosumi                        │               │
│                                                         │
│                              Owner type                 │
│        Owner ID:  │          │ ┌──────┬─┐               │
│                   │          │ │ DRVR │⇧│               │
│          Sub ID:  │          │ │ WDEF │ │               │
│                   │          │ │ MDEF │⇩│               │
│                                └──────┴─┘               │
│  Attributes:                                            │
│  □ System Heap   □ Locked      □ Preload                │
│  ⊠ Purgeable     □ Protected   □ Compressed             │
└──────────────────────────────────────────────────────┘
```

Figure 22-4. A typical Resource Info window.

usually not a good idea to change the resource ID of an existing resource since most applications locate their resources by looking up the resource ID. It's usually safe to add a name to a resource that doesn't have one. Just be careful not to use a name already taken by another resource of the same type. When you're creating a new resource, you should be sure to follow Apple's guidelines for allocating resource IDs. The guidelines are summarized in Table 22-2. Other restrictions may apply for some resource types. For example, icons used in menus must have IDs between 257 and 511.

Table 22-2. Guidelines for Allocating Resource IDs

Resource ID Range	Use
–32,768 to –16,385	Reserved by Apple
–16,384 to –1	Reserved for owned resources (explained shortly)
0 to 127	Used for System resources
128 to 32,767	Available for applications to use

Resource Attributes

A resource's attributes control where it's loaded into memory and what happens to it after it's loaded. Whenever you create a new resource, it's important to make sure you set its attributes properly. The resource attributes are explained in Table 22-3.

Hint Whenever possible, be sure to check the Purgeable attribute. This helps avoid memory shortages by allowing the Memory Manager to remove the resource when memory starts getting full. However, don't set the Purgeable attribute unless you're sure the application can recover if the resource is purged from memory. For example, the Menu Manager doesn't recover purged 'MENU' resources.

Table 22-3. Resource Attributes

Resource Attribute	Description
System Heap	Checked if the resource should always be loaded into the System heap. Use this only for resources that need to be shared by multiple applications. This should generally not be checked for an application's resources.
Purgeable	Checked if it's OK for the Memory Manager to remove the resource from memory if more space is needed.
Locked	Checked if the resource can't be moved in memory. The Locked attribute overrides the Purgeable attribute.
Protected	Checked if the resource and its ID and name can't be modified or deleted by an application.
Preload	Checked if the resource should be loaded when the file is opened.
Compressed	Checked if the resource is compressed. You'll probably only find this checked in ResEdit itself and in some System 7 files. You can't change this attribute.

Hint Be very cautious about checking the Locked attribute. A locked resource can't be moved when the Memory Manager needs to make room for new information. You can end up with plenty of unused memory but no way to make use of it because you have a locked resource right in the middle of the memory you need. If you need to use a locked resource, it's a good idea to also check the Preload attribute. This ensures that the resource is loaded into memory before any other memory is allocated, and keeps the resource out of the Memory Manager's way.

Owned Resources

Since the System file is a collection of lots of resources (drivers and controls, for instance) from many different places, there needs to be a way to determine which groups of resources belong together. So, how does this work? It works by convention. Apple has reserved certain ranges of ID numbers for resource types that are likely to "own" other resource types. The System file can contain 64 resources of each of these special owner types before it runs out of unique resource IDs. Each owner can own up to 32 resources of any other type. Table 22-4 lists each possible owner type and the range of resource IDs it can own. The resource ID of the owning resource must be between 0 and 63 or it won't be recognized as a possible owner of other resources. Note that, because only certain resource IDs are valid for owned resources, some resource types having restricted ID ranges (such as 'FONT' and 'WDEF') can't be owned.

Table 22-4. Owned Resource ID Ranges

Owner Type	ID Range of Owned Resources
'DRVR'	−16,384 to −14,337
'WDEF'	−14,336 to −12,289
'MDEF'	−12,288 to −10,241
'CDEF'	−10,240 to −8193
'PDEF'	−8192 to −6145
'PACK'	−6144 to −4097
Reserved 1 (RSV1)	−4096 to −2049
Reserved 2 (RSV2)	−2048 to −1

In the middle of the Resource Info window are two fields and a list to help you figure out the correct resource ID for an owned resource. As you fill these in, ResEdit automatically calculates the proper resource ID for you. Figure 22-5 shows a Resource Info window for an owned 'DLOG' resource. The Owner ID field contains the resource ID of the owning resource. The Sub ID field contains a number to uniquely identify each resource of the same type owned by a given resource. For example, if a resource owns two 'DLOG' resources, the first one could have a Sub ID of 0 and the second one could have a Sub ID of 1. You can follow these steps to set up the resource ID of an owned resource.

1. In the Owner type list, click the type of resource that will own your new resource.

2. Enter the resource ID of the owning resource in the Owner ID field (remember, it must be between 0 and 63).

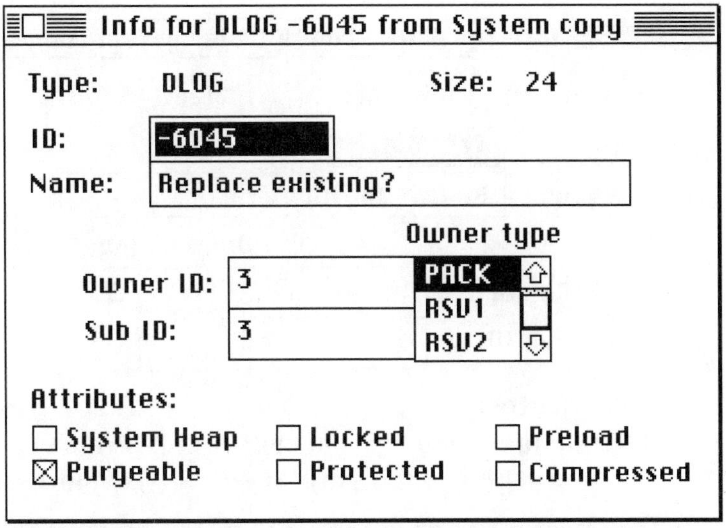

```
┌──────────────────────────────────────────────────────┐
│ ▤□≡  Info for DLOG -6045 from System copy ≡           │
├──────────────────────────────────────────────────────┤
│  Type:     DLOG              Size:   24                │
│                                                        │
│  ID:      ┌──────────────┐                             │
│           │ -6045        │                             │
│           └──────────────┘                             │
│  Name:    ┌──────────────────────────────┐            │
│           │ Replace existing?            │            │
│           └──────────────────────────────┘            │
│                                Owner type              │
│                          ┌─────────────┬──┐            │
│     Owner ID:  │ 3     │ │ PACK        │⬆│            │
│                          ├─────────────┤  │            │
│                          │ RSU1        │  │            │
│     Sub ID:    │ 3     │ ├─────────────┤  │            │
│                          │ RSU2        │⬇│            │
│                          └─────────────┴──┘            │
│  Attributes:                                           │
│  ☐ System Heap   ☐ Locked      ☐ Preload              │
│  ☒ Purgeable     ☐ Protected   ☐ Compressed           │
└──────────────────────────────────────────────────────┘
```

Figure 22-5. A Resource Info window using the Owner ID and Sub ID fields.

3. Enter the Sub ID number. If this is the first resource of this type to be owned by this owner, enter 0. Otherwise, enter the number equal to the count of all resources of the same type owned by the same owner. Sub ID numbers must be between 0 and 31, inclusive.

Desk Accessories and Drivers

You may be wondering why desk accessories aren't among the resource types that can own other resources. In fact, they are. 'DRVR' resources can include both drivers (such as printer and network drivers) and desk accessories. The resource ID for a 'DRVR' resource that contains a desk accessory must be between 12 and 31, inclusive. The System uses the first character of a 'DRVR' resource's name to determine whether it's a desk accessory or a driver. For drivers the first character must be a period (.), and for desk accessories it must be a null (0). ResEdit helps make sure that the name starts with the correct character by providing a pair of radio buttons in 'DRVR' Resource Info windows. A Resource Info window for a 'DRVR' is shown in Figure 22-6. When the resource info is saved, ResEdit sets

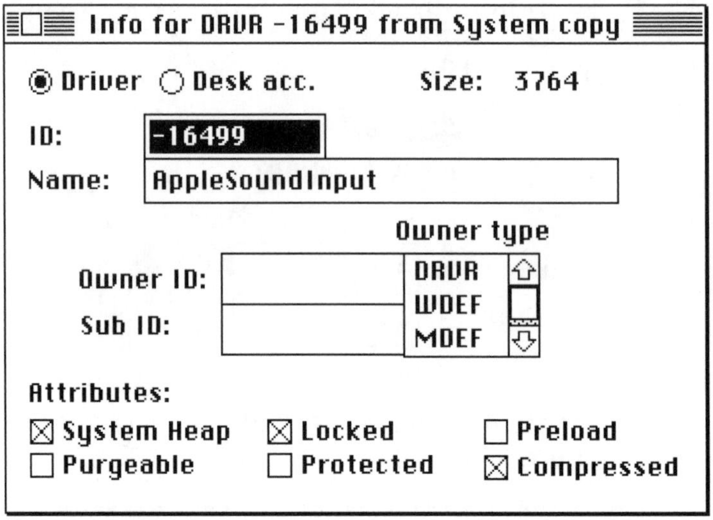

Figure 22-6. The Resource Info window for a 'DRVR' resource has two radio buttons at the top.

the first character to the proper value depending on the state of the radio buttons. With System 7 you'll no longer find desk accessories in the System file. However, the 'DRVR' resources must still follow these same conventions.

Summary

This chapter begins with an introduction to the File Info window and all the interesting information it tells you about a file. You see how to change various characteristics the Finder stores for each file. You also see how the Finder uses a file's Type and Creator. Next, we explore the Folder Info window and its smaller set of Finder characteristics. We finish the chapter with a discussion of the Resource Info window. You see how to change various attributes of a resource as well as how to set up a resource ID for an owned resource.

Chapter 23

 Creating Templates for Your Resources

In Chapter 14 you learned how to use templates to edit a variety of resource types. But wouldn't it be nice if you could create custom templates for resource types you've defined? ResEdit's template editor lets you do just that. This chapter gives you all the information and examples you need to create templates for your own resources.

A template enables you to display in a dialog a field for every field that occurs in your resource. Although templates can represent most types of data you're likely to have in your resource, a few constructs are just too complex. Understanding the limitations of templates before you design your resource's data structures helps assure that you can define your resource in such a way that you can create a suitable template.

ResEdit stores its templates in 'TMPL' resources. The name of the 'TMPL' resource determines which resource type it's used with. For example, the 'TMPL' resource named CNTL is used to define a window layout to edit 'CNTL' resources. One of the templates that comes with ResEdit is for the 'TMPL' resource, so you use the template editor itself to create your templates! If you're not familiar with the procedure for filling in templates (especially repeating lists), be sure to review Chapter 14.

The 'TMPL' resource contains a list of labels and field types that correspond to the data contained in your resource and to fields in a window when the template is used. Each field in the template tells ResEdit how to treat a certain part of your resource. One field may say to display the next two bytes as a decimal number, while the next field may say to skip 4 bytes.

Let's begin by taking a look at a simple template. The 'CNTL' template is shown in use in Figure 23-1.

The 'TMPL' resource named CNTL that defines the window layout used to edit 'CNTL' resources is shown in Figure 23-2. Each Label/Type pair shown in Figure 23-2 corresponds to a label and field in Figure 23-1.

As you can see in Figure 23-2, the template is made up of a long list of Labels and Types. The types tell ResEdit how to format the data for a field. For example, the first field contains a rectangle (RECT) called BoundsRect, while the second field contains a decimal word (DWRD). You can interpret the rest of the fields similarly.

ResEdit recognizes about 40 different field types. When you use these types, remember to enter them exactly as they're shown in the descriptions that follow. All the types must be entered in uppercase, and they're all four characters long. The types can be broken down into two groups: those that define single fields and those that define lists. We'll describe the single field types next, followed by a few examples; then we'll describe the list types. At the end of the chapter are some tables you can reference when you become more familiar with how the different types work.

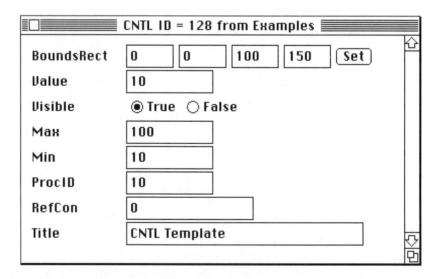

Figure 23-1. The 'CNTL' template is one of the simplest templates you'll see.

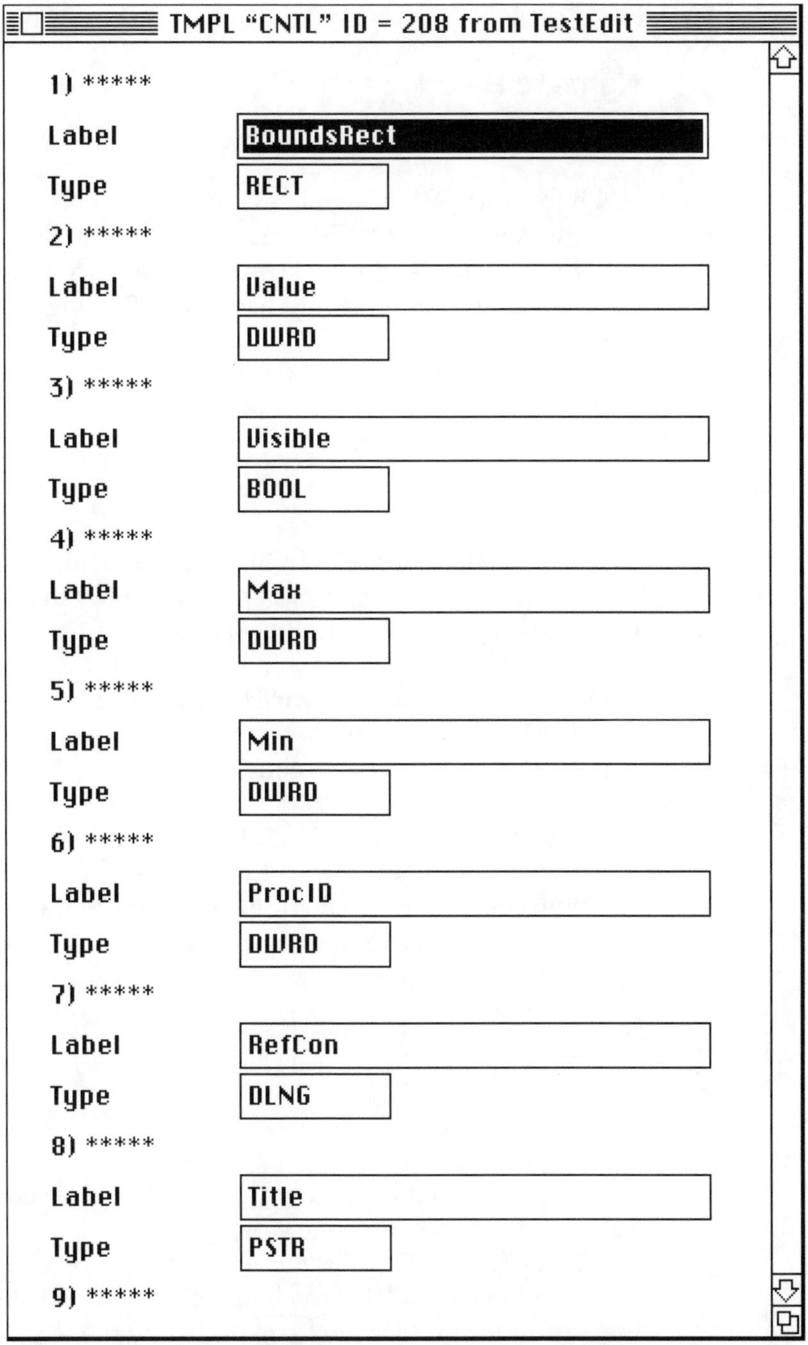

Figure 23-2. The definition of the 'CNTL' template.

Field Types

Numeric Field Types

AWRD, ALNG

Align to word (AWRD) and align to long (ALNG) act like spacers and don't show up when ResEdit displays the template—they just make sure the template editor looks in the right place in the resource for the data. For example, you could have the following data structure in a Pascal module:

```
animal:  RECORD
             isHuman: BOOLEAN;
             numberOfLegs: INTEGER;
         END;
```

The boolean occupies only 1 byte, but the integer must start on an even-word boundary, so Pascal puts an empty byte in between the two fields. The template for this data structure would contain:

DBYT	For the 1-byte boolean field
AWRD	To skip the next byte
DWRD	For the decimal word

You need to use an AWRD field any time you have a single byte followed by a multibyte field. Keep in mind, though, that compilers are smart enough to avoid adding spare bytes if you have two 1-byte fields in a row. For example, if you changed your data structure to

```
animal:  RECORD
             isHuman: BOOLEAN;
             hasHair: BOOLEAN;
             numberOfLegs: INTEGER;
         END;
```

you wouldn't need to include an AWRD field because the two booleans would occupy one word.

When you use an AWRD or ALNG field, you can leave the Label field blank or add a label that will help you understand the template the next time you look at it. Anyone using the template never sees the label.

DBYT, DWRD, DLNG

Decimal byte, decimal word (2 bytes) and decimal long (4 bytes) fields are shown in Figure 23-3. The numbers shown in the fields in the figure are the largest numbers you can enter.

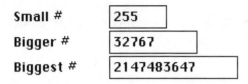

Small #   255

Bigger #   32767

Biggest #   2147483647

Figure 23-3. Decimal fields.

FBYT, FWRD, FLNG

Adding fill byte, fill word, or fill long to your template definition causes the byte, word, or long always to be filled with zero. The field acts like a spacer and does not appear when the template is used— the template user doesn't even know the field exists. These types are useful if you have unused or reserved fields you might want to use later. If you fill them with zero now, you can use them later and not worry that old versions of the resource might contain unknown values.

HBYT, HWRD, HLNG

HBYT, HWRD, and HLNG are hex versions of the decimal fields. The only real difference is that the numbers are formatted in hex ($1F02, for example) when the window opens.

Pascal String Field Types

PSTR

A Pascal string field contains 1 byte containing the length of the string, followed by the text of the string, as shown in Figure 23-4. For example, if you have a field of type *STR255* in your data structure, you could use this template type if you want to save only the number of characters that are actually used in your string. That is, this type represents a variable amount of data in the resource—from 1 byte (an empty string) to 256 bytes.

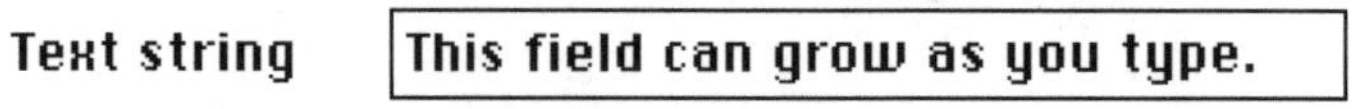

Text string | This field can grow as you type. |

Figure 23-4. All the string field types look like this.

WSTR

Word string. WSTR is similar to PSTR, except that the length occupies a word (2 bytes).

LSTR

Long string. LSTR is similar to PSTR, except that the length occupies a long word (4 bytes).

ESTR

Even string. ESTR is the same as PSTR, except that the total length (including the length byte) must always be even. If the user enters an even number of characters (which, with the length byte would give the string an odd length), ResEdit adds a byte filled with zero to the end. For example, if the string contained the character *a*, the resource would contain $01 (length byte), $61 (*a*). If the string contained *ab*, the resource would contain $02 (length byte), $61, $62 (*ab*), $00 (a null pad byte) to make the total length even (four).

OSTR

Odd string. OSTR is the same as ESTR except padded to an odd length. For example, *a* will be $01, $61, $00 (null pad byte) and *ab* will be $02, $61, $62.

P0nn

P0nn represents a Pascal fixed-length string. You should replace the nn with a hex number representing the maximum length of the string (not including the length byte). Since this is a Pascal string, it starts with a byte for the length and is limited to a maximum length of 255 characters (P0FF is the largest allowable string). The length byte indicates how much of the fixed-length string is actually being used. For example, P010 would represent a 16-byte string with a 1-byte length.

This is the most commonly used of the fixed-length string types. For example, if you have an *STR64* field in your Pascal data structure, you could include a P040 in your template. This way, you wouldn't have a variable-length field in your resource as you would if you used a PSTR field to save only the part of the *STR64* that was actually used.

C String Field Types

CSTR

CSTR is similar to PSTR, except that it's used for C strings, which have no length byte and end with a null ($00) byte.

ECST

Even C string. ECST is similar to ESTR, except that it's used for C strings. For example, *a* will be $61, $00 (null termination byte) and *ab* will be $61, $62, $00 (null termination byte), $00 (pad byte).

OCST

Odd C string. OCST is similar to OSTR, except it's used for C strings. For example, *a* will be $61, $00 (null termination byte), $00 (pad byte) and *ab* will be $61, $62, $00 (null termination byte).

Cnnn

Cnnn represents a C fixed-length string. You should replace the nnn with a hex number indicating the maximum size of the field. There's no length byte involved as there is for P0nn, so the length can be up to $FFF (4095 decimal). Since it's a C string, the characters are displayed up to the first null (0) byte. Unlike Pascal strings, no extra byte is added for C strings. For example, C010 would represent a 15-byte string plus a null byte. Don't forget to leave room for the extra byte used by the null terminator.

Hex Dump Field Types

Hnnn

Hnnn represents a fixed-length hex list. Unlike the Cnnn and P0nn fields all nnn bytes in an Hnnn field are always shown. The length can be up to $FFF (4095 decimal) bytes. This type is especially useful if you have some structured data that doesn't match any of the other template types. For example, if you have a black-and-white pattern (*Pattern = PACKED ARRAY [0..7] of 0..255*) in your data structure, you could use an H008 template field to display it.

HEXD

HEXD represents a hexadecimal dump field. This type may be specified only as the last type in a template and displays the rest of the resource in a hex field. Many resources contain formatted information at the beginning that can be modified, and constant or complex information at the end that won't be modified. This situation is perfect for a HEXD field.

Miscellaneous Field Types

BOOL

BOOL represents a 2-byte boolean value as shown in Figure 23-5. It's displayed as a pair of radio buttons. A 0 value is interpreted as false and a 1 is true. Note the warning with the BBIT definition below.

> **By The Way** This field type is not nearly as useful as you might think. You can't use this type for C or Pascal booleans since they take up only 1 byte.

This is fun   ⦿ True   ◯ False

Figure 23-5. True is 1 and false is 0 for boolean fields.

BBIT

A binary bit field represents 1 bit of a byte as a pair of radio buttons. BBIT fields must come in sets of eight. If you're only using 1 bit of a byte, you must still include the other 7 bits (you can label them as "Unused"). The first BBIT field represents the high-order bit of a byte. A few BBIT fields are shown in Figure 23-6.

Warning Be cautious in your use of these fields. If you have a lot of BBIT or BOOL fields (for example, if you use them in a repeating list), scrolling can become painfully slow.

First bit:	○ 0	⦿ 1
Second bit:	⦿ 0	○ 1
Third bit:	○ 0	⦿ 1
Unused bit:	⦿ 0	○ 1

Figure 23-6. Each pair of radio buttons represents 1 bit of a byte.

CHAR

CHAR fields are used for a single character (1 byte).

RECT

RECT represents a rectangle made up of four words. As shown in Figure 23-7, it also includes a Set button used to set the values in the RECT fields. See Chapter 14 for more information about the Set button.

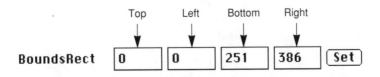

Figure 23-7. RECT fields can be filled in using the Set button.

TNAM

Type name. A TNAM field, like the one in Figure 23-8, contains a four-character type name. For example, the 'BNDL' template uses a TNAM field for the application's signature resource, and the installer script templates use it to tell the installer which resources to install.

Type name   [ICON   ]

Figure 23-8. TNAM fields can contain resource types.

A Few Examples

That's all the different types of fields, so let's take a look at a few examples.

Defining a 'CNTL' Template

Table 23-1 shows the definition of a 'CNTL' resource and the template types that would be used to make a 'CNTL' template (the template was shown in use in Figure 23-1). As you can see, for a simple data structure like this there's an easy one-to-one mapping between the Pascal data type and the template field type. This is a case where the BOOL type can be used because the visible field is not really saved as a Pascal boolean.

Table 23-1. Template Types for a 'CNTL' Resource

'CNTL' Field	Pascal Data Type	Template Field Type
boundsRect	Rectangle	RECT
value	Integer	DWRD
visible	Integer	BOOL
max	Integer	DWRD
min	Integer	DWRD
procId	Integer	DWRD
refCon	LongInt	DLNG
title	Str255	PSTR

Defining a 'ppat' Template

Now let's look at a slightly more complex example. The 'ppat' resource contains a pixel pattern that can vary in size and can contain up to 256 colors. As you can imagine, this is a complex data structure. The first part of the resource directly corresponds to the memory-resident data types PixPat and PixMap. This part of the resource contains lots of useful information, such as the size of the pattern and the bits per pixel (number of colors). The last part of the resource contains the pixel data itself and the table of colors that goes along with it. This last part of the resource would be much too difficult to edit in an unstructured way. (People have done it, but few survived unscathed.) Table 23-2 shows a way that a 'ppat' template could be designed.

Table 23-2. Designing a Template for a 'ppat' Resource

'ppat' Field	Pascal Data Type	Template Field Type	Description
PixPat			
patType	Integer	DWRD	Type of pattern
patMap	PixMapHandle	DLNG	Offset to PixMap
patData	Handle	DLNG	Offset to pixel data
patXData	Handle	FLNG	0
patXValid	Integer	FWRD	–1
patXMap	Handle	FLNG	0
pat1Data	Pattern	H008	Old-style pattern
PixMap			
baseAddr	Ptr	FLNG	0
rowBytes	Integer	HWRD	Offset to next line
bounds	Rect	RECT	Boundary of image
pmVersion	Integer	DWRD	Version number
packType	Integer	DWRD	Packing format
packSize	LongInt	DLNG	Length of pixel data
hRes	Fixed	HLNG	Horizontal resolution
vRes	Fixed	HLNG	Vertical resolution
pixelType	Integer	DWRD	Pixel type
pixelSize	Integer	DWRD	Number of bits in pixel
cmpCount	Integer	DWRD	Number of components in pixel
cmpSize	Integer	DWRD	Number of bits per component

Table 23-2. Designing a Template for a 'ppat' Resource
(continued)

'ppat' Field	Pascal Data Type	Template Field Type	Description
planeBytes	LongInt	DLNG	Offset to next plane
pmTable	CTabHandle	DLNG	Offset to color table
pmReserved	LongInt	FLNG	0
pixel data	—	HEXD	Data for pattern
color data	—	—	Data for color table

There are several things to note in this table.

- Since the resource's format is the same as the data structure in RAM, several fields in the resource are not used (they're mostly reserved for handles used when the pattern is loaded into RAM). These fields are represented by one of the fill types, so the user doesn't have to worry about them at all.

- The old-style pattern is represented by an 8-byte hex field since it's 8 bytes of unformatted data.

- The last part of the resource is structured data that can't be edited using a template, so it's just listed in hex with the hex dump type.

Using Lists in Templates

Now let's move on to some more complex resource types. Many resources contain a standard element repeated a variable number of times. For example, the 'FOND' resource contains a bunch of fixed information about a 'FONT' followed by the style and 'FONT' resource ID for every available size of the font. Since the resource has a variable number of fields, you can't use the field types described previously without some additional constructs. For this situation, ResEdit lets you define several kinds of repeating sequences. Any of the normal field types can appear within a repeating list (including other repeating lists).

By convention, the label for list-start and list-end fields is five asterisk (*) characters. Always using the same label makes it easy for users to know when they're editing a repeating list. Whenever you create a list, remember to include an LSTE field to mark the end of the list.

LSTZ, LSTE

List zero, list end. These lists repeat until the first byte of the list entry contains zero. You probably won't find much use for this kind of list, but ResEdit uses it for both 'MENU' and 'cmnu' templates. The menu template definition is shown in Table 23-3. The fields between the ***** labels are repeated until the first byte of the MenuItem string contains a zero. This is especially convenient for 'MENU' resources since the zero would also indicate that the MenuItem was a zero-length string.

Table 23-3. The 'MENU' Template

Label	Template Field Type
MenuID	DWRD
Width	FWRD
Height	FWRD
ProcID	DWRD
Filler	FWRD
EnableFlgs	HLNG
Title	PSTR
*****	LSTZ
MenuItem	PSTR
Icon#	DBYT
Key equiv	CHAR
Mark Char	CHAR
Style	HBYT
*****	LSTE

ZCNT, LSTC, LSTE

Zero count, list count, list end. A list of this kind is preceded by a zero-based count of the number of entries in the list. A ZCNT field must always be followed immediately by an LSTC field. This count occupies 2 bytes and contains –1 if there are no items in the list. The user can't modify the count field but sees it as a constant number maintained by ResEdit. For example, part of a 'clut' template is shown in Figure 23-9. The CtSize field shows how many colors (minus one, since the count is zero-based) are in the table, and it can only be changed by adding or removing colors.

The 'clut' template definition is shown in Table 23-4. The fields between the ***** labels are repeated the number of times indicated by the ZCNT field, plus one. Note that the ZCNT field has a label and appears in the template but is not part of the list, as shown in Figure 23-9.

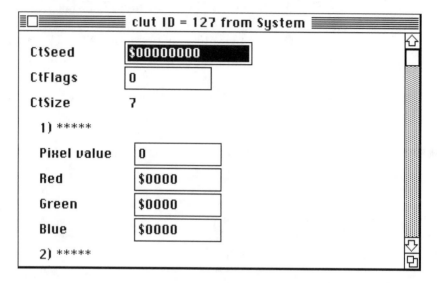

Figure 23-9. Part of a 'clut' resource that contains eight colors.

Table 23-4. The 'clut' Template Definition

Label	Template Field Type
CtSeed	HLNG
CtFlags	DWRD
CtSize	ZCNT
*****	LSTC
Pixel Value	DWRD
Red	HWRD
Green	HWRD
Blue	HWRD
*****	LSTE

OCNT, LSTC, LSTE

One count, list count, list end. This type of list is identical to the ZCNT, LSTC, LSTE lists just described, except that the count that precedes the list is 1-based rather than zero-based.

LSTB, LSTE

List begin, list end. This list repeats until it reaches the end of the resource. For example, the 'pltt' template defined in Table 23-5 contains some information about the palette followed by a list of the colors making up the palette. Notice in this template that although there's a count of the number of palette entries, it's not immediately preceding the list, so an OCNT, LSTC, LSTE type of list can't be used. Using a template to edit 'pltt' resources would have been much more convenient if an OCNT, LSTC, LSTE list could have been used because the count would have been automatically updated when a color was added or removed. Try to avoid this kind of mistake when you design your data structures.

Table 23-5. The 'pltt' Template Definition

Label	Template Field Type
Color table count	DWRD
Reserved	FLNG
Reserved	FWRD
Reserved	FLNG
Reserved	FLNG
*****	LSTB
Red	HWRD
Green	HWRD
Blue	HWRD
Color usage	DWRD
Tolerance value	DWRD
Private flags	HWRD
Private	FLNG
*****	LSTB

Creating Complex Templates

Now let's look at an example of creating a template for a more complex resource. This example illustrates techniques you can use to create templates for your own resource types.

When you add files to ResEdit's Open Special menu, your selections are stored in a resource of type 'FILE' in the ResEdit Preferences file. The data structure it uses contains some general information followed by a list of files.

```
FileListItem = RECORD
                  volName:    STR64;
                  dirID:      LONGINT;
                  cmdKey:     CHAR;
                  dupName:    BOOLEAN;
                  name:       STR64;
               END;
FileListRec =  RECORD
                  count:      INTEGER;
                  unused:     INTEGER;
                  version:    INTEGER;
                  theFiles:   ARRAY [1..5] OF FileListItem;
               END;
```

Here's an outline of what you could do to convert this data structure into a template so you could look at the Open Special menu data stored in the Preferences file.

- The first and third fields of the FileListRec are simple integer fields that can be represented by DWRD fields in the template.

- You can use an FWRD field for the unused integer.

- The rest of the resource contains an array of file information that ends at the end of the resource. Since there's no count field, you can use an LSTB, LSTE list to represent the array.

- The first field in the array is a 64-character Pascal string. Since all 64 bytes, not just the number of characters used in the string, are saved in the resource, a P0nn field can be used in the template. The "nn" in P0nn is the number of characters in the string represented in hexadecimal. The number 64 decimal is 40 hexadecimal, so you can use a P040 field.

- The length of the string is odd (64 characters plus the length byte), so an AWRD field is needed to make sure the next field starts on a word boundary.

- The dirID field is a long integer and can be represented by a DLNG template field.

- Since this is not a packed data structure, the Command key occupies 2 bytes. Characters always fit in a single byte, so the first byte has no meaning and can be represented by an FBYT field. The Command key itself can be a CHAR field.
- The dupName boolean only uses one byte, so you can't use a BOOL field type. Instead, use a DBYT field (a zero represents false and a one represents true).
- Since the boolean was only one byte, another AWRD field is needed to keep things lined up properly.
- The last field is another *STR64* and can once again be represented by a P040 field followed by another AWRD. The last AWRD is important to keep the next set of fields in the list in the right place.
- Finally, use an LSTE to mark the end of the list.

The finished template definition is shown in Table 23-6. If you want to give this a try, just create a template with the fields shown in the table. Use the Get Info Command on the Resource menu to give the template a name of "FILE". Now you can open the 'FILE' resource in the ResEdit Preferences file, and you'll see the contents of your Open Special menu, as shown in Figure 23-10.

Table 23-6. A Template for ResEdit's 'FILE' Resource Type

Label	Template Field Type
Count	DWRD
Unused	FWRD
Version	DWRD
*****	LSTB
Vol name	P040
(none)	AWRD
Dir ID	DLNG
(none)	FBYT
CMD Key	CHAR
Duplicate?	DBYT
(none)	AWRD
Name	P040
(none)	AWRD
*****	LSTE

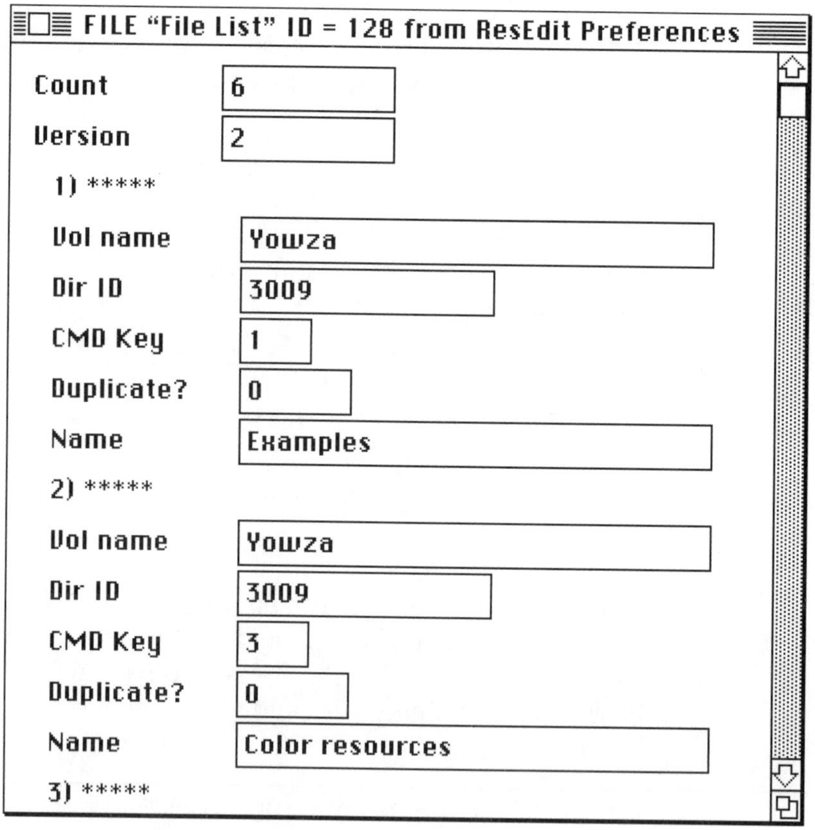

```
▤□▤  FILE "File List" ID = 128 from ResEdit Preferences ▤▤
```

Count   6

Version   2

   1) *****

Vol name   Yowza

Dir ID   3009

CMD Key   1

Duplicate?   0

Name   Examples

   2) *****

Vol name   Yowza

Dir ID   3009

CMD Key   3

Duplicate?   0

Name   Color resources

   3) *****

Figure 23-10. The 'FILE' template in use.

What You Can't Do with Templates

As you have seen, you can create templates for most data structures you're likely to use in your resources. However, you could easily create a data structure that couldn't be edited with a template. The 'ictb' resource type (dialog item color table) is a good example of a resource type that can't be edited using a template. This resource type is used to set colors and styles for items in dialogs and alerts. Unfortunately, to make sense of the 'ictb', you have to simultaneously look in the corresponding 'DITL' (dialog item list) resource. For example, the 'ictb' resource starts with an array that contains two words for each item in the dialog, but there's no way of knowing how many items are in the dialog without looking in the 'DITL' resource.

Another technique that strikes terror into the hearts of template designers is the inclusion of pointers or offsets within a resource. The 'ppat' resource contains several offsets, including one to the color table, which is stored at the end of the resource. It would be useful to edit the color table, but there's no way to let the template know where the colors start. If the color table data had been stored before the pixel data at the end of the resource, and a count of the number of colors had been added, the table could have been edited.

The third bane of template designers is variable-length blocks of data. The 'cicn' resource contains several variable-length fields for things like the mask data and the color table. Since there's no way to know the size of these in advance (the size of these fields must be computed from other fields in the resource), there's no way to create a template to edit them.

The 'snd ' resource provides an example of another technique that's sure to ruin your template-designing dreams. Depending on the value in the first word of the resource, the structure of the rest of the resource changes! Making a template to deal with this situation is impossible.

Template Size Limitations

Templates have a few limitations, but you shouldn't have to worry about running into them. If you even get close to these limits, your resource probably isn't suited for editing in a template. For example, the 'pltt' template works only for very small palettes. Since the typical palette contains 256 entries and each entry contains 6 fields, a template would contain over 1500 data fields! You wouldn't want to wade through 1500 data fields to find the color you want to change.

Each field of a template can contain no more than 32,000 characters (this is a limit of the TextEdit routines in the Macintosh Toolbox). For fields containing just text, this limitation is straightforward. However, for fields that display the information in hex (such as HEXD), one character in the resource can translate into several characters in the field. For hex fields, you can display about 8770 bytes before you hit the 32,000-character limit.

There can be no more than 2048 total fields in a template. Needless to say, templates this big get a bit unwieldy. This field limitation is imposed by the Macintosh's Dialog Manager, so it includes all fields—not just data fields, as you might expect. Calculating the number of fields you're using can be tricky, but here is a formula that should work.

1. Count the number of fields outside of repeating lists and multiply by 2 (one for the data and one for the label). We'll call this number "Constant" in our formula.

2. Count the number of times your lists repeat. We'll call this "ListCount."

3. Count the number of fields inside one instance of your list. Call this "Fields."

Now, using these names, our formula would be:

TotalFields = Constant + (ListCount + 1) + (ListCount * Fields * 2)

In the formula, the (ListCount + 1) item accounts for the ***** labels and the (ListCount * Fields * 2) accounts for the labels and data fields inside the lists.

Here's an example. A 'pltt' resource has one visible field of constant information and six fields for each palette entry. If we have a 'pltt' resource with 157 palette entries, we can use the formula to figure out that

2 + (157 + 1) + (157 * 6 * 2) = 2044 fields.

So, this resource could just barely be displayed. Adding one more palette entry would put it over the limit.

Caring for Your Templates

Name Your Templates

Be sure to give your template a name that's exactly the same as the resource type you designed it to edit. For example, if you want to edit an 'ABCD' resource, you need a 'TMPL' resource named "ABCD".

Where to Keep Your Templates

ResEdit looks in all open files when it needs to find a template. If you'll only need to use your template with one file, you could put it into that file. This would guarantee that it would always be available when you edit that file.

If you want to use your template on several files, the best place to put it is in the ResEdit Preferences file. ResEdit automatically opens this file, which is in the Preferences Folder in your System Folder.

Make Them Purgeable

Don't forget to make your 'TMPL' resources purgeable. If you don't, memory will be wasted on resources you're no longer using. Here's how to do it.

1. Open your 'TMPL' resource.

2. Choose Get Resource Info from the Resource menu.

3. Check the Purgeable check box.

4. Close the info window and save the file.

Adding an Icon for Your Resource Type to ResEdit

When you select View by Icon from a type picker's View menu, you see a custom icon for each resource type that ResEdit can edit—except yours. This problem is easy to fix, however. All you have to do is add an 'ICON' resource and an 'icl4' resource (if you want to have a color icon) to your ResEdit Preferences file. The resource ID you use doesn't matter, just make sure the name of each resource is the same as the resource type it represents. For example, if you want to add an icon for the 'FOOB' resource type, just add an 'ICON' and an 'icl4' named "FOOB." On a color screen, ResEdit first looks for an 'icl4', but if it doesn't find one, it uses the 'ICON'.

Data Type Reference

This section contains a partial list of Pascal and C data types and their corresponding template field types. Table 23-7 lists common Pascal types, and Table 23-8 lists C types. If you need to use a data type not in the list, just find out how many bytes it occupies and look for a template type that's the same size.

Remember, you need to use the AWRD type after a boolean or even-length string field (unless the data structure was not declared as *PACKED* in Pascal).

Table 23-7. Pascal Data Types and Their Corresponding Template Field Types

Data Type	Size	Template Field Type
boolean	1 byte	DBYT
SignedByte	1 byte	DBYT
Byte	2 bytes	FBYT + DBYT, FBYT + HBYT
Char	2 bytes	FBYT + CHAR
Integer	2 bytes	DWRD
Longint	4 bytes	DLNG
Ptr	4 bytes	HLNG
Handle	4 bytes	HLNG
Real, Single	4 bytes	HLNG, H004
Double	8 bytes	H008
Comp	8 bytes	H008
Extended	10 bytes	H00A
ResType	4 bytes	TNAM
Rect	8 bytes	RECT
String[nn]	n+1 bytes	P0nn
STR255	256 bytes	P0FF

Table 23-8. C Data Types and Their Corresponding Template Types

Data Type	Size	Template Field Type
boolean	1 byte	DBYT
unsigned char	1 byte	DBYT, HBYT
char	1 byte	DBYT, CHAR
short	2 bytes	DWRD
unsigned short	2 bytes	DWRD, HWRD
int	4 bytes	DLNG
unsigned int	4 bytes	DLNG, HLNG
long	4 bytes	DLNG
enum	1-4 bytes	DBYT, DWRD, DLNG
Ptr	4 bytes	HLNG
Handle	4 bytes	HLNG
float, single	4 bytes	HLNG, H004
double	8 bytes	H008
comp	8 bytes	H008
extended	10 bytes	H00A
long double	10 bytes	H00A
ResType	4 bytes	TNAM
Rect	8 bytes	RECT
STR255	256 bytes	P0FF

Template Field Type Summary

Numeric Field Types

AWRD, ALNG	Align to word, align to long
DBYT, DWRD, DLNG	Decimal byte, decimal word, decimal long
FBYT, FWRD, FLNG	Fill byte, fill word, fill long with zero
HBYT, HWRD, HLNG	Hex byte, hex word, hex long

String Field Types

Pascal String Types

PSTR   Pascal string starting with length byte
WSTR   Pascal string starting with length word
LSTR   Pascal string starting with length long word
ESTR   Even-padded PSTR
OSTR   Odd-padded PSTR
P0nn   Fixed-length Pascal string nn characters long

C String Types

CSTR   C string terminated by a null (0) byte
ECST   Even-padded CSTR
OCST   Odd-padded CSTR
Cnnn   Fixed-length C string nnn characters long

Hex Dump Field Types

Hnnn   Hex dump of nnn bytes
HEXD   Hex dump of the rest of the resource

Miscellaneous Field Types

BOOL   2-byte boolean
BBIT   Binary bit—must use in sets of eight
CHAR   1-byte character
RECT   Rectangle made up of four words
TNAM   4-character type name

List Field Types

LSTB, LSTE   Repeat list to end of resource
LSTZ, LSTE   Repeat list until first byte of list is zero
OCNT, LSTC, LSTE   List starts with a one-based count
ZCNT, LSTC, LSTE   List starts with a zero-based count

Summary

This chapter contains all the information you need to create your own templates. The detailed description of each field type will help you decide which types to use. We include several real-life examples of creating templates from scratch. A set of tips and suggestions finishes off the how-to part of the chapter. The chapter concludes with some reference tables that will be indispensable when you start creating your own templates. Now that you have all the information you need, the next step is up to you—go forth and create templates!

Chapter 24

 Mapping Resources

Occasionally you'll find that a resource type you've defined looks exactly like one that already has a template or editor in ResEdit (though it may serve a very different purpose). There's a special type of resource you can create to tell ResEdit to pretend that a resource of one type is really a different type. This 'RMAP' resource must be located either in ResEdit itself or in the ResEdit Preferences file (located in the Preferences Folder in your System Folder). For example, ResEdit uses an 'RMAP' resource to make sure the 'MENU' editor is started when an 'mctb' (menu color table) resource is opened. When you create a new 'RMAP', you fill out a template that tells ResEdit which two resource types to consider equivalent.

 Warning Be very careful when you create 'RMAP' resources. Most editors simply won't work if you ask them to edit a resource containing data that's different from what they expect. Make sure the structure of the two resource types really is the same before you create an 'RMAP'.

Creating an 'RMAP' Resource

Suppose you've defined a new resource type, 'ABCD', that has a structure just like the standard 'STR#' resource type. Instead of

397

creating a new template, you can follow these steps to add an 'RMAP' to ResEdit's Preferences file.

1. Open the ResEdit Preferences file found in the Preferences Folder in your System Folder.

2. Open the 'RMAP' resource type and create a new resource.

3. Type 'STR#' in the MapTo field of the window that appears.

4. Put a 0 in the Editor only field.

5. Choose Get Resource Info from the Resource menu.

6. Change the name of the resource to "ABCD," and click the Purgeable check box.

7. Close the Resource Info window. The window should now look like Figure 24-1.

8. Close and save the Preferences file.

Now when you open an 'ABCD' resource, you'll see it displayed using the normal ResEdit 'STR#' template.

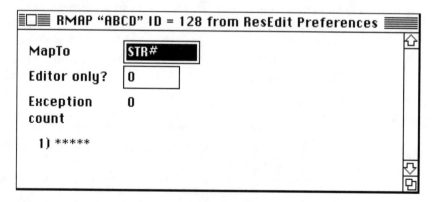

Figure 24-1. An 'RMAP' for 'ABCD' resources.

Mapping by Resource ID

Sometimes it's convenient or desirable to have resources with different resource IDs, but the same resource type, contain different types of data. For example, the old 'INTL' international resource type always contained two resources. The 'INTL' resource with ID 0 contained the format for numbers, short dates, and times, while the 'INTL' resource with ID 1 contained the long date format. Because of the limitations of the template editor, it would be impossible to create an 'INTL' template that would satisfy the needs of both these data structures.

Creating an 'RMAP' resource to map individual resource IDs to different editors or templates solves this problem. For example, the 'RMAP' for the 'INTL' resource maps resources with ID 0 to the 'itl0' editor, and those with ID 1 to the 'itl1' editor, as you can see in Figure 24-2.

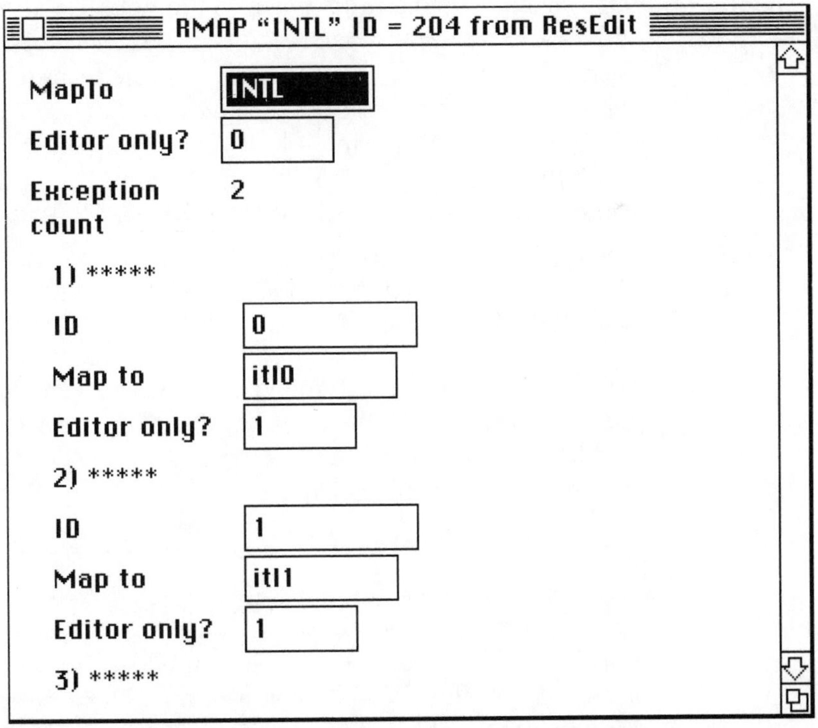

Figure 24-2. An 'RMAP' can map each resource ID to a different editor or template.

All resource IDs that aren't specified in the exception list will be mapped to the resource type specified in the MapTo field at the top of the 'RMAP' template. For example, in Figure 24-2, an 'INTL' resource with ID 6 would be edited as an 'INTL' resource—in other words, not mapped at all.

What Does "Editor Only" Mean?

Set the Editor only field to true (1) if you're mapping a resource to an editor, and false (0) if you're mapping it to a template. For example, in Figure 24-2, the 'INTL' resource is being mapped to the 'itl0' and 'itl1' editors, so Editor only is true. However, when the 'FCMT' (Finder comment) resource is mapped to the 'STR#' resource, Editor only is false because the resource is being mapped to a template.

Here are the sordid details behind this obscure mechanism. One of the most important jobs of the 'RMAP' resource is to map resources (such as 'mctb's) to editors (such as the 'MENU' editor) that can understand more than one resource type. The problem arises when an editor decides that it can't really edit the resource for some reason (for example, the 'mctb' doesn't have an associated 'MENU' resource, so the 'MENU' editor can't edit it). When an editor detects this situation, it tells ResEdit to start up the template editor for the resource (for example, launch the template editor with the 'mctb' resource). The template editor looks through the 'RMAP' resources and sees that the resource should be mapped ('mctb' is mapped to 'MENU'). It then uses the template for the *mapped to* resource to open the *mapped* resource (for example, it opens the 'mctb' resource using the 'MENU' template), giving you really screwy results since the resource won't match the template. So, to prevent such a mess, if the template editor is looking for a template, it will not use the 'RMAP' resource if Editor only is true.

Summary

This chapter shows you how to set up an 'RMAP' resource to allow more than one resource type to be edited by the same editor. This can be useful if ResEdit already contains an editor or template for a resource type that's just like the one you're creating. Use this feature with caution, however—make sure the resource types really are identical before you proceed.

Appendix A

 Shortcuts and Hints

General Macintosh

- You can copy a file by dragging it to a folder or to the desktop while holding down the Option key.
- You can force the Finder to quit and restart by typing Command-Option-Esc and clicking the Force Quit button in the dialog that appears.
- You can rebuild your Desktop database by holding down the Command and Option keys when you restart your Mac (or after forcing the Finder to quit and restart).
- Within an application you can move a window without making it the active window by holding down the Command key while you drag the window by its title bar.
- To open a file (an application or a document) with ResEdit, just drag its icon onto ResEdit's icon.

General ResEdit

- When the splash screen is displayed, any event causes the splash screen to go away, and ResEdit also acts upon the event. For example, clicking the menu bar removes the splash screen and pulls down the selected menu. Similarly, typing a Command key removes the splash screen, and ResEdit acts on the command.

- If you press the Option key while you click the close box of a window, all that file's windows will close except the type picker.
- Pressing the Option key while opening a resource picker causes the resource picker to appear in view by ID.
- If you're having trouble editing a file (if you get bombs when you try to edit it, for example), try using the Verify command on the File menu to make sure the file is OK.
- To be on the safe side, check the "Verify files when they are opened" check box in the Preferences dialog. This makes opening a file take longer, but you'll know the file is OK.
- If you press the Option key when you open a file (if "Verify files when they are opened" is checked in the Preferences dialog) or when you verify a file, you see a diagnostic window that lists details of any damage.
- If you have a few files that you use frequently with ResEdit, add them to the Open Special menu so you can assign Command-key shortcuts. That way, you can open them from the splash-screen, or any time you want to get to them quickly.
- You can customize or override any resource in ResEdit by placing your own version of the resource in ResEdit's Preferences file. That way, you only have to remove the Preferences file from the Preferences Folder in your System Folder to put ResEdit back in its original, default state. Plus, you won't lose your changes when you update to a new version of ResEdit.

Resource Pickers

- Pressing the Option key when you copy or cut one or more resources adds them to any resources already on ResEdit's clipboard. Normally, when you cut or copy, you replace the contents of the clipboard.
- Pressing the Option key while double-clicking a resource opens the resource in the hexadecimal editor. This is the same as choosing Open Using Hex Editor from the Resource menu.
- Pressing the Option and Command keys while double-clicking a resource opens the template editor instead of the normal custom editor. You see a dialog asking you to select the template you want to use. This is the same as selecting Open Using Template from the Resource menu.

Fatbits Editors (Except the 'FONT' Editor)

- Double-clicking the eraser clears the fatbits editing area.

- Double-clicking the rectangular selection tool selects the whole fatbits editing area. Select All on the Edit menu gives the same result.

- Double clicking the lasso tool lassos the entire image. It's like dragging the lasso around the whole fatbits editing area.

- If you hold down the Option key while you drag out a selection with the rectangular selection tool, the selection will collapse to fit the image as if you had used the lasso selection tool.

- If you hold down the Option key while you drag a selection, you'll duplicate the selection.

- You can use the arrow keys to move a selection one bit in the desired direction as a shortcut for selecting the nudge commands from the Transform menu.

- Pressing the Shift key constrains several of the drawing tools:

    The line tool draws lines only at 45- and 90-degree angles;
    The empty and filled rectangle tools draw only squares;
    The empty and filled rounded rectangle tools draw only
        rounded squares;
    The empty and filled oval tools draw only circles;
    The pencil and eraser are constrained to horizontal or vertical
        lines.

- You can tear off the pattern and color pop-up palettes.

- In editors with multiple views (icon and mask in the 'ICN#' editor, for example), you can fill in any of the views by dragging the image from one view to another.

- In the list editors ('SICN', 'PAT#', and 'ppt#'), you can reorder elements in the list by dragging. (This is most useful during software development. Be careful about reordering existing list resources.)

- You can add your own patterns to ResEdit's pop-up pattern palettes. Open ResEdit and find the 'ppt#' (for color patterns) or 'PAT#' resource named Fill Pattern. Copy the resource and paste it into the ResEdit Preferences file. Add, remove, or update the patterns until you have the set you want to use. For consistency, it's a good idea to keep the black-and-white patterns (both in the 'PAT#' resource and in each pattern of the 'ppt#' resource) the same as the color patterns.

- In the color fatpixels editors, pressing the Command key when picking a color from the foreground color palette changes all pixels of the current foreground color to the selected color.

- In the color fatpixels editors, pressing the Option key temporarily changes any of the drawing tools (not the selection tools, eraser, or hot spot tool) into the eyedropper tool.

- In the color editors, you can add your own sets of colors to the Color menu by putting a 'clut' resource in the ResEdit Preferences file. (You won't see them in the Icon Family editor, however, because these resources use fixed color tables.)

- Pressing the Option key when you create a color pattern (from the 'ppat' picker or the 'ppt#' editor) creates a relative pattern.

'MENU' Editor

- Pressing the Return key moves the selection to the next menu item in the list. If the selection is already at the end of the list, a new item is added.

- When you're designing a menu, you can reorder items by simply dragging an item to its new location. (Don't do this when customizing an existing menu!)

'DLOG', 'ALRT', and 'WIND' Editors

- You can use the arrow keys to move the window on the MiniScreen one bit in the specified direction.

- When you create a new 'WIND', 'ALRT', or 'DLOG', the default values are taken from a resource in ResEdit named "Default." You can override these with your own defaults by placing a resource of the appropriate type in your ResEdit Preferences file in the System Folder. Make sure your resource has the name "Default."

- You can double-click the mini-dialog or mini-alert, or press the Return or Enter key to open the associated 'DITL' resource.

'DITL' Editor

- Holding down the Option key temporarily toggles the Show Item Numbers command. If Show Item Numbers is off, pressing the Option key will show the item numbers. If Show Item Numbers is on, pressing the Option key will hide the item numbers.

- Pressing the Return or Enter key opens item editor windows for all selected items.

Appendix B

 Resource Types

This appendix lists some standard resource types and a brief description of each. The Editor column tells you whether ResEdit has a special editor (E) or a template (T) for that resource type.

Type	Editor	Description
'actb'	E,T	Alert color look-up table. Edited by 'ALRT' editor.
'acur'	T	Animated cursor resource
'ADBS'		ADB (Apple Desktop Bus) driver code
'alis'		System 7 file alias information
'ALRT'	E,T	Location and size of an alert window
'APPL'	T	Application list from the Desktop file
'bmap'		BitMap used by old versions of the Control Panel
'boot'		Boot blocks in System file
'BNDL'	E,T	Bundle resource used to attach icons to applications and their documents
'CACH'		RAM cache control code
'card'		Contains the name of a video card
'cctb'	T	Control color look-up table
'CDEF'		Code for drawing controls (Control DEFinition)
'cdev'		Code for a Control Panel device
'cicn'	E	Color icon
'clst'		Cached icon lists used by the Chooser and Control Panel

Type	Editor	Description
'clut'	E,T	Color look-up table
'CMDK'	T	List of Command keys used in ResEdit
'CMDO'		Used for MPW Commando interface
'cmnu'	E,T	MacApp temporary menu resource
'CMNU'	E,T	Command menu. MacApp menu resource.
'CNTL'	T	Definition data for controls such as scroll bars
'CODE'		Application code
'crsr'	E	Color mouse pointer
'CTY#'	T	City list from MAP Control Panel device
'CURS'	E	Mouse pointer
'dast'		In a desk accessory, contains an "about" string
'dctb'	E,T	Dialog color look-up table. Edited by 'DLOG' editor.
'DITL'	E,T	Dialog Item List. Defines the contents of dialogs and alerts.
'DLOG'	E,T	Defines the location and size of a dialog window
'dpsr'		System 7 Edition Manager section information
'DRVR'	T	Driver (printer, network, etc.) or desk accessory
'DSAT'		Startup and bomb alerts and code to display them
'eadr'		Slot number of an Ethernet card
'errs'	T	Error number to reason string mapping used by MacApp
'FBTN'	T	MiniFinder button
'fctb'	T	Font color look-up table
'FCMT'	T	Finder's GetInfo comments stored in the Desktop file
'FDIR'	T	MiniFinder button directory ID
'FILE'		Contents of ResEdit's Open Special menu (found in the ResEdit Preferences file)
'finf'	T	Font information
'FKEY'		Function key code usually found in the System file
'fld#'	T	List of folder names
'FMTR'		Format record for 3½ inch disks
'fmts'		System 7 Edition Manager available formats
'FOBJ'		Information about folders
'FOND'	T	Font family description
'FONT'	E,T	Font description
'FREF'	E,T	File reference

Type	Editor	Description
'fval'	T	System 7 Finder's data (similar to the 'LAYO' resource used by earlier Finders)
'FRSV'	T	Resource IDs of ROM font resources
'FWID'	T	Font width table
'gama'		Gamma table—color correction for monitors
'GNRL'	T	ResEdit's preference information (stored in the ResEdit Preferences file)
'hdlg'		System 7 help for dialogs
'hfdr'		Application's help balloon information
'hmnu'		System 7 help for menus
'hovr'		System 7 application balloon overrides
'hwin'	T	System 7 help for windows
'hrct'		System 7 help rectangles
'icl4'	E	System 7, 4-bit large (32 x 32) Finder icon
'icl8'	E	System 7, 8-bit large (32 x 32) Finder icon
'icmt'	T	Comment for Installer 3.0 and later
'ICN#'	E	Black-and-white Finder icon with mask
'ICON'	E	Icon used in dialogs, menus, etc.
'ics#'	E	System 7, black-and-white small (16 x 16) Finder icon with mask
'ics4'	E	System 7, 4-bit small (16 x 16) Finder icon
'ics8'	E	System 7, 8-bit small (16 x 16) Finder icon
'ictb'		Color dialog item list
'inbb'	T	Installer scripts for Installer 3.0 and later
'indm'	T	Installer scripts for Installer 3.0 and later
'infa'	T	Installer scripts for Installer 3.0 and later
'infs'	T	Installer scripts for Installer 3.0 and later
'INIT'		Code run at System startup time
'inpk'	T	Installer scripts for Installer 3.0 and later
'inra'	T	Installer scripts for Installer 3.0 and later
'insc'	T	Installer script
'INT#'		Integer list used by Find File DA
'INTL'	E	Old style 'itl0' and 'itl1'
'itl0'	E	Date, time, and number formats
'ITL1'	T	ResEdit international date sorting control
'itl1'	E	International date/time information
'itl2'		International string comparision code
'itl4'		Tables needed for international number formatting and conversion
'itl5'		Character set encoding and rendering information

Type	Editor	Description
'itlb'	T	International script bundle that determines which keyboard and which international formats to use
'itlc'	T	International script configuration
'itlk'	T	International exception dictionary for 'KCHR' resource
'itlm'		Preferred international sorting order
'KBDN'	T	Resources used to name keyboards in ResEdit's 'KCHR' editor
'KCAP'		Physical layout of the keyboard
'KCHR'	E	Mapping of virtual key codes to character codes
'kcs#'		Small black-and-white keyboard icon
'kcs4'		Small 16-color keyboard icon
'kcs8'		Small 256-color keyboard icon
'KEYC'		Old keyboard layout
'KMAP'		Keyboard mapping from raw keycode (generated by the keyboard) to virtual keycode
'kscn'		Small icons that correspond to 'KCHR' resources
'KSWP'		Key-plus-modifier combinations that can be used to toggle international keyboard scripts
'LAYO'	T	Finder layout resource
'LDEF'		Code used by the List Manager to draw lists
'lmem'		Globals to be switched by MultiFinder
'mach'		'cdev' filtering
'MACS'	T	Version number in System file
'MBAR'	T	Set of 'MENU's to be displayed together on the menu bar
'MBDF'		Menu bar definition code
'mcky'	T	Speed associated with the different choices in the mouse Control Panel
'mctb'	E,T	Menu color look-up table. Edited by 'MENU' editor.
'mcod'		MacroMaker information
'mdct'		MacroMaker information
'MDEF'		Code for drawing menus
'mem!'		MacApp memory utilization
'MENU'	E,T	Definition for a standard menu
'minf'	T	MacroMaker macro information
'mitq'		Default queue sizes for the MakeITable procedure
'MMAP'		Mouse tracking code

Type	Editor	Description
'mntb'		Relates a command number to a menu in MacApp
'mntr'		Monitor extension code—adds items to the Options dialog displayed by the Monitors Control Panel device
'mppc'		MPP configuration resource
'mst#'		MultiFinder string list used to identify menu and item used for Quit and Open commands
'mstr'		MultiFinder string used to identify menu and item used for Quit and Open commands
'NFNT'		New font description; similar to 'FONT' resource
'nrct'	T	Rectangle position list
'PACK'		Packages of code used as ROM extensions
'PAPA'	T	Printer access protocol address used for AppleTalk
'PAT '	E	8-by-8-bit black-and-white pattern
'PAT#'	E	A list of 'PAT ' resources
'PDEF'		Printer driver code
'PICK'	T	ResEdit's picker definitions
'PICT'	E,T	Picture used by many drawing programs
'pltt'	E,T	Palette of colors
'POST'	T	PostScript code
'ppat'	E,T	Pixel pattern, color patterns of variable size
'ppcc'	T	ppc toolbox configuration information found in the System file
'ppt#'	E	List of 'ppat' resources
'PREC'	T	Printer driver's private data storage. ID 0 contains the default page setup info
'PREF'		ResEdit editors'' preference information
'PRER'		Nonserial printer Chooser code
'PRES'		Serial printer Chooser code
'prvw'		System 7 Edition manager—similar to a 'PICT'
'PTCH'		Code to patch the ROM
'ptch'		Code to patch the ROM
'qrsc'	T	System 7 Database Access Manager query record
'RDEV'		Network Chooser code
'RECT'		Coordinates of a single rectangle
'resf'	T	System 7 reserved fonts
'RMAP'	T	ResEdit resource map
'ROv#'	T	List of ROM resources to override

Type	Editor	Description
'ROvr'		ROM override code
'RSSC'		ResEdit editors and pickers
'RVEW'	T	ResEdit picker view information
'scrn'	T	Screen configuration
'sect'	T	Section record definition used by the Edition Manager
'seg!'		MacApp segmentation control
'SERD'		RAM serial driver code
'sfnt'		True Type outline font description
'SICN'	E	List of small (16-by-16) icons
'SIZE'	T	MultiFinder size information
'snd '		Sound used for the System beep, HyperCard, and other applications
'snth'		Sound synthesizer code
'STR '	T	String of characters
'STR#'	T	List of strings
'styl'	E	Style information for characters in 'TEXT' resource
'TEXT'	E,T	Unformatted text—formatting can be provided in a 'styl' resource
'tlst'		Title list
'TMPL'	T	ResEdit template
'TOOL'	T	ResEdit fatbits editors tool layout
'vers'	E,T	Version information used in the Finder's GetInfo window
'wctb'	E,T	Window color look-up table. Edited by 'WIND' editor.
'WDEF'		Window definition code for drawing the structure part (title bar, frame, etc.) of windows
'WIND'	E,T	Size, location, and type of a window
'wstr'	T	Query string used by 'qrsc' resource

Appendix C

 Editing Resources in Hexadecimal

Sometimes you'll have to dip down into the hexadecimal editor to change a resource that doesn't have an associated editor or a template. There's really nothing scary about it if you understand a little about the editor and how the hexadecimal number system works.

The Hexadecimal Number System

Hexadecimal is a base-16 number system, which is a convenient system for computers because two hex digits can represent one byte. The numbers 1 through 9 are the same in decimal as they are in hexadecimal. The numbers 10 through 15 are represented as shown in Table C-1.

Table C-1. Hexadecimal Equivalents of Decimal Numbers

Decimal	Hexadecimal
10	A
11	B
12	C
13	D
14	E
15	F

Table C-2 shows some examples that should help you get the hang of converting from decimal to hexadecimal and back.

Table C-2. Hexadecimal to Decimal Conversions

Hexadecimal	Conversion	Decimal
10	1 × 16	16
23	2 × 16 + 3	35
2A	2 × 16 + 10	42
56	5 × 16 + 6	86
C5	12 × 16 + 5	197
FF	15 × 16 + 15	255

The Hexadecimal Editor

When you open a resource with the hexadecimal editor, you see a window like the one shown in Figure C-1. The left side of the window shows the offset (the number of bytes from the beginning of the resource) in hexadecimal, of course; the middle of the window shows hexadecimal numbers; and the right side shows their text equivalents. Each row displays 8 bytes of the resource. Since many numbers don't have understandable text equivalents, the right side of the window is often unintelligible, as you can see in the figure.

You can edit either the numbers or the text—just click the part of the window you want to edit. Entering text in the text side of the window works just like you'd expect—simply type the characters you want to add. Adding or changing numbers in the middle of the window is not quite as straightforward. Digits in the hex editor always come in pairs, so if you want to change a number, you have to change two digits. ResEdit trys to help you keep the digits in pairs by adding a 0 whenever you enter just one digit. For example, if you type a 3, 03 appears in the window. If you then type a 4, you'll have 34 (the added 0 will be removed). Likewise, since digits always come in pairs, you can't select just one digit—you always have to select pairs of digits.

You can use all the standard editing commands on either the numbers or the text. If you want to copy between two resources, just select the numbers you want, copy them, and paste them into the other resource. If you paste when numbers or text are selected, the

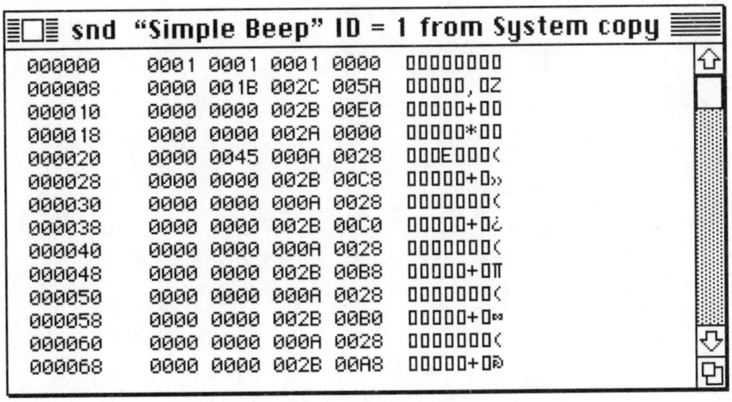

```
▤▢▤ snd  "Simple Beep" ID = 1 from System copy ▤▤▤
  000000     0001 0001 0001 0000    □□□□□□□□              ⬆
  000008     0000 001B 002C 005A    □□□□□,□Z
  000010     0000 0000 002B 00E0    □□□□□+□□
  000018     0000 0000 002A 0000    □□□□□*□□
  000020     0000 0045 000A 0028    □□□E□□□⟨
  000028     0000 0000 002B 00C8    □□□□□+□››
  000030     0000 0000 000A 0028    □□□□□□□⟨
  000038     0000 0000 002B 00C0    □□□□□+□¿
  000040     0000 0000 000A 0028    □□□□□□□⟨
  000048     0000 0000 002B 00B8    □□□□□+□π
  000050     0000 0000 000A 0028    □□□□□□□⟨
  000058     0000 0000 002B 00B0    □□□□□+□∞
  000060     0000 0000 000A 0028    □□□□□□□⟨      ⬇
  000068     0000 0000 002B 00A8    □□□□□+□®      ⬒
```

Figure C-1. The hexadecimal editor shows offsets on the left, numbers in the middle, and text on the right.

selection is replaced. If you paste when there's no selection, the Clipboard contents are inserted at the insertion point.

The hexadecimal editor has a Find menu to help you find your way around the resource. The Find Hex command lets you find and change hexadecimal numbers. The Find Hex window doesn't help you make sure you enter only pairs of digits, so you have to check that for yourself. The Find ASCII command lets you search for and change a string in the text part of the window. The Find Offset command just moves the insertion point to the specified offset within the resource. All these dialogs are nonmodal windows, so you can leave them open while you're working on the resource.

Index